STECK-VAUGHN

# HISTORY *of Our*
# WORLD

## People, Places, and Ideas™

---

### Volume 1
## The Ancient World

Henry Billings

Rigby · Saxon · Steck-Vaughn

www.HarcourtAchieve.com
1.800.531.5015

## About the Author

Henry Billings received his B.A. from the University of Massachusetts and his M.A.T. in World History from Salem State College. He has more than 16 years experience as a classroom teacher. He is the author of several Social Studies textbooks on topics ranging from Economics to History to Geography.

## Content Reviewer

Jonathan Lee, Ph.D.
Assistant Professor of History
San Antonio College

## Educational Reviewer

Roberta L. Frenkel
Director of English Language Arts and
   Social Studies, District 3
Scarsdale, New York

## Acknowledgments

Editorial Director: Diane Schnell
Editor: Terra G. Tarango
Associate Editor: Victoria Davis
Associate Director of Design: Joyce Spicer
Senior Designer: Joan Cunningham
Project Assistant: April Litz
Production Manager: Mychael Ferris-Pacheco
Production Coordinator: Susan Tyson Fogarasi

Image Services Coordinator: Ted Krause
Senior Technical Advisor: Alan Klemp
Electronic Production Specialists: David Hanshaw,
   John-Paxton Gremillion, Scott Melcer, Marc Watson
Electronic Production Artist: Perla Arce
Senior Photo Researcher: Alyx Kellington
Director of New Media: Sammi Frye
Website Producer: Linda LeFan

## Credits

*Illustrations:* Leslie Evans p. 11 (icon), 14 (globe icon), 22, 43 (icon), 82 (icon), 106, 118, 125, 147 (icon), 152, 180, 194, 202 (icon), 242, 243 (icon), 265 (icon); David Chapman p. 19 (Egyptian children), p. 137 (Great Wall detail), p. 148 (Feudalism in Western Europe), p. 236 (Feudalism in Japan)

*Cartography:* Maps.com / MAGELLAN Geographix

*Voices in History Excerpts:* p. 28 Adapted from "Tutankhamun: Anatomy of an Excavation. Howard Carter's Personal Diaries, November 26, 1922." Copyright Griffith Institute, Oxford. Reprinted by permission; p. 200 From "The Creation," www.jaguar-sun.com/popolvuh.html by Jeeni Criscenzo. ©1999 by Jeeni Criscenzo. Reprinted by permission.

*Web Site Development:* Maximize Learning

**Photo Credits:** Cv-c ©Lee & Lee Communications/Art Resource, NY; cv-d ©Werner Forman/Art Resource, NY; cv-e©Adelman/Cohen/Getty Images; page iii(a) ©Douglas Mazonowicz/Art Resource, NY; iii(b) ©Araldo de Luca/CORBIS; iii(c) ©SuperStock; iii(d) ©Stock Montage; iii(e) ©Asian Art & Archaeology, Inc./CORBIS; iv(a) ©The British Museum; iv(b) ©Holton Collection/SuperStock; iv(c) The Metropolitan Museum of Art, The Harry G.C. Packard Collection of Asian Art, Gift of Harry G.C. Packard and Purchase, Fletcher, Rogers, Harris Brisbane Dick and Louis V. Bell Funds, Joseph Pulitzer Bequest and The Annenberg Fund, Inc. Gift, 1975 (1975.268.414) Photograph©1987 The Metropolitan Museum of Art; iv(d) ©Werner Forman/Art Resource, NY; iv(e) ©Danny Lehman/CORBIS; v(a) ©Archivo Iconografico, S.A. /CORBIS; v(b) ©Burstein Collection/CORBIS; v(c) ©Werner Forman/Art Resource, NY; v(d) ©Sandro Vannini/CORBIS; v(e) ©Kevin Schafer/CORBIS; p.2c ©Mireille Vautier/The Art Archive; p.2d ©Erich Lessing/Art Resource, NY; p.3a ©Giovanni Dagli Orti/CORBIS; p.3b ©CORBIS; p.3c ©Werner Forman/Art Resource, NY; p.7b ©SuperStock; p.8 ©Gianni Tortoli/Photo Researchers; p.9a ©Archivo Iconografico, S.A./CORBIS; p.9b ©Bettmann/CORBIS; p.11a ©Jonathan Blair/CORBIS; p.11 ©Jack Unruh/National Geographic Image Collection; p.12a ©Douglas Mazonowicz/Art Resource, NY; p.12b ©Jim Mann Taylor; p.12c ©Mireille Vautier/The Art Archive; p.13 ©Robert Frerck/Odyssey/Chicago; p.16a ©Christie's Images/SuperStock; p.16b ©Michele Burgess/ SuperStock; p.18a ©Musee De Grenoble/SuperStock; p.19b ©Erich Lessing/Art Resource, NY; p.20 ©Jonathan Blair/CORBIS; p.21a ©Egyptian National Museum, Cairo, Egypt/SuperStock; p.21b ©The British Museum; p.23a ©Staffan Widstrand/CORBIS; p.23b ©Gian Berto Vanni/CORBIS; p.24a ©Archivo Iconografico, S.A./CORBIS; p.24b ©Sandro Vannini/CORBIS; p.24c ©Roger Wood/CORBIS; p.25 ©Araldo de Luca/CORBIS; p.29a ©The Granger Collection; p.30a ©Werner Forman/Art Resource, NY; p.30b ©David Lees/CORBIS; p.31a ©British Museum, London/The Bridgeman Art Library; p.31b,c ©Gianni Dagli Orti/CORBIS; p.33 ©Brown Brothers; p.34a ©United Design; p.34b ©Archivo Iconografico, S.A./CORBIS; p.35b ©Stock Montage; p.37 ©The Granger Collection; p.40a ©Asian Art & Archaeology, Inc./CORBIS; p.41a ©Eye Ubiquitous/CORBIS; p.41b ©Christie's Images/CORBIS; p.42a ©Craig Lovell/CORBIS; p.42b ©Royal Ontario Museum/CORBIS; p.43 ©Giraudon/Art Resource, NY; p.44 ©Asian Art & Archaeology, Inc./CORBIS; p.45a ©Boltin Picture Library; p.46b ©©CORBIS; p.47a ©Diego Lezama Orezzoli/CORBIS; p.47b ©Archivo Iconografico, S.A./CORBIS; p.48a ©Arvind Garg/CORBIS; p.49 ©Archivo Iconografico, S.A./CORBIS; p.53a

*continued on page 288*

**ISBN 0-7398-7948-0**

# Contents

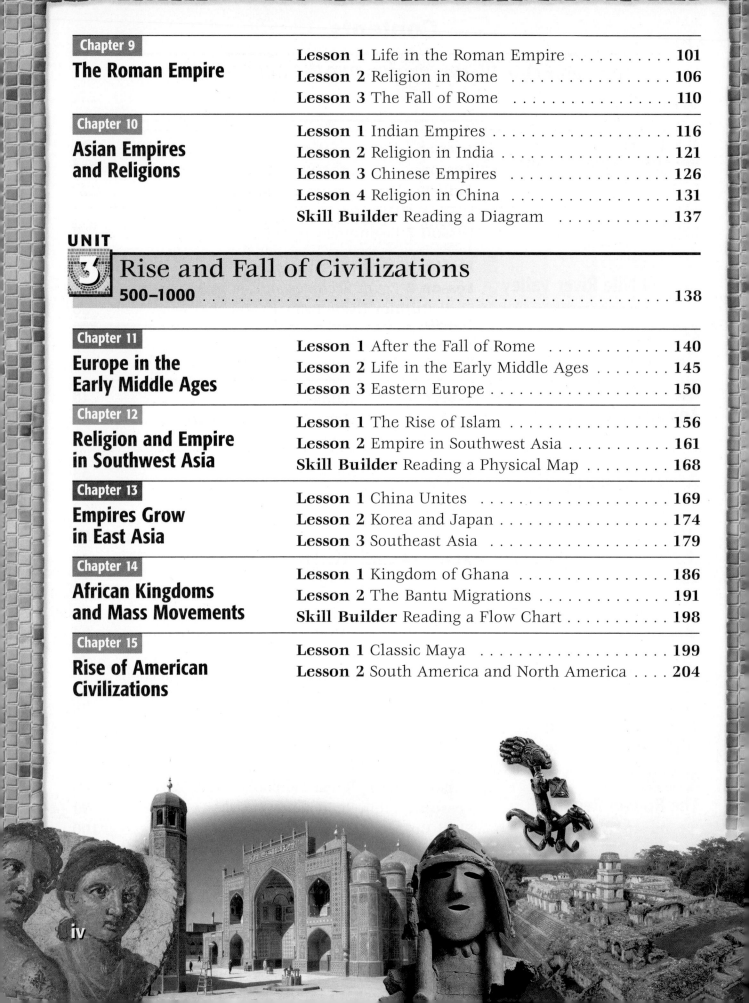

# UNIT 4

## Change and Growth Around the World

### 1000–1500 . . . . . . . . . . . . . . . . . . . . . . . . . . . . . . . . **210**

# Voices
## In History

# People
## In History

# Did You Know?

# Charts, Graphs, and Diagrams

## Maps

# Using *History of Our World: People, Places, and Ideas*

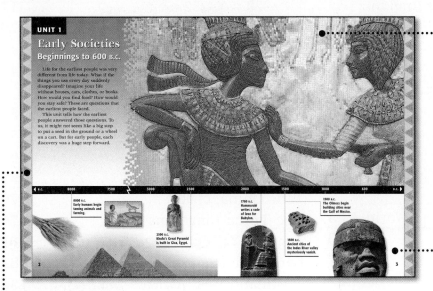

## Unit Opener

Each unit opens with a text introduction and a large image. Read the text and look at the image. See if they tell you anything about world history.

## Unit Timeline

The timeline shows the years discussed in the unit. Read the entries and study the images to see what you'd like to learn more about.

## Unit Borders

Each unit has a different border on the edge of the page. Use the borders to quickly identify what unit you're in.

## Before You Read

Read these questions before beginning a lesson. Use what you've learned from earlier lessons or past experiences to answer them.

## New Words

These are the new words that appear in each lesson. These words are defined in the Glossary. Be sure you know their meanings before you begin reading.

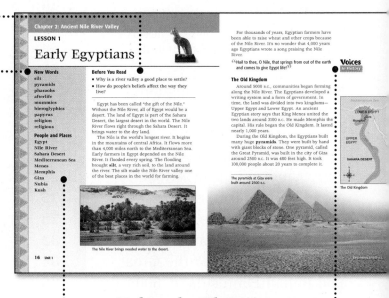

## People and Places

People and places are listed here the first time they are discussed. As you read, look for these people and places.

## Voices in History

These primary sources appear throughout the text. Read these to learn about history in the words of those who lived it.

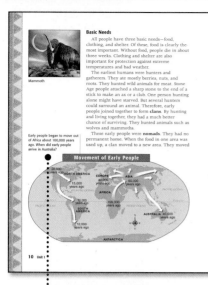

## Did You Know?

This special feature occurs two times in each unit. Read these to learn fun and interesting information related to the lesson.

## Map Questions

Map questions appear next to some maps. Study the map to answer each question.

## Using What You've Learned

After each chapter, you'll have a chance to show what you've learned. Read the questions and answer them carefully.

## People in History

Read these biographies to better understand some interesting people in world history.

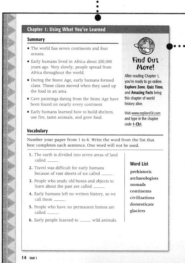

## Find Out More!

After reading a chapter, you can visit that chapter online to find out more.

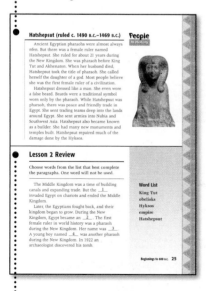

## Lesson Review

Each lesson ends with a summary. Choose words from the Word List to complete the Lesson Review.

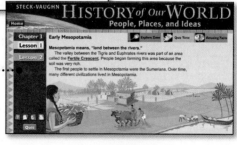

## Steck-Vaughn Online

The Steck-Vaughn *History of Our World: People, Places, and Ideas* website brings the chapters of your textbook to life.

# UNIT 1

# Early Societies
## Beginnings to 600 B.C.

Life for the earliest people was very different from life today. What if the things you use every day suddenly disappeared? Imagine your life without houses, cars, clothes, or books. How would you find food? How would you stay safe? These are questions that the earliest people faced.

This unit tells how the earliest people answered those questions. To us, it might not seem like a big step to put a seed in the ground or a wheel on a cart. But for early people, each discovery was a huge step forward.

| B.C. | 8000 | 7500 | 3000 | 2500 |
|------|------|------|------|------|

**8000 B.C.**
**Early humans begin taming animals and farming.**

**2500 B.C.**
**Khufu's Great Pyramid is built in Giza, Egypt.**

| 2000 | 1500 | 1000 | 600 | B.C. ▶ |

**1780 B.C.**
**Hammurabi writes a code of laws for Babylon.**

**1500 B.C.**
**Ancient cities of the Indus River valley mysteriously vanish.**

**1500 B.C.**
**The Olmecs begin building cities near the Gulf of Mexico.**

3

## LESSON 1

# History's Stage

### New Words

continents
glaciers
climate
archaeologists

### People and Places

Earth
Pacific Ocean
Atlantic Ocean
Indian Ocean
Arctic Ocean
Asia
Africa
North America
South America
Antarctica
Europe
Australia
United States

This photo of Earth was taken from space.

### Before You Read

- Do you think of the world as big or little?
- What could make a place difficult to live in?

People sometimes say the world gets smaller every day. In one sense, that is true. Planes fly halfway around the world in less than a day. You can see live sports or news on television from places thousands of miles away. You can send e-mail messages in an instant to someone across an ocean. So these days the world can indeed seem to be a pretty small place.

### A Big Place, Too

On the other hand, the world really is a big place. It is almost 25,000 miles around. If you rode a bike at ten miles per hour for eight hours a day, it would take you nearly a year to go that distance. But you couldn't ride that far in a straight line without running into water.

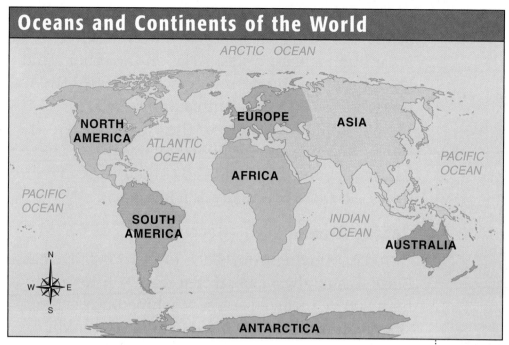

## Oceans and Continents of the World

ARCTIC OCEAN

NORTH AMERICA

EUROPE

ASIA

ATLANTIC OCEAN

PACIFIC OCEAN

AFRICA

PACIFIC OCEAN

SOUTH AMERICA

INDIAN OCEAN

AUSTRALIA

ANTARCTICA

Earth has seven continents and four oceans. On which continent do you live?

About two thirds of Earth is covered by water. The world has many seas, bays, lakes, and rivers. But most of Earth's water is in its four great oceans. The biggest—by far—is the Pacific Ocean. It is nearly twice the size of the second largest, the Atlantic Ocean. The Indian Ocean is the third largest. The mostly ice-covered Arctic Ocean is the smallest.

Look at the world map above. There are no boundary lines between oceans. That is because the oceans are all connected. It is possible to sail through all four oceans and never see land.

## The Land

The earth is divided into seven great areas of land, or **continents**. The largest continent is Asia. The second largest is Africa. North America is the third largest. The other four continents in order of size are South America, Antarctica, Europe, and Australia. Look again at the world map. Notice that some continents are joined together. Asia, Europe, and Africa are linked together. North America and South America are joined, too. Only Australia and Antarctica are separate from all the others.

PACIFIC OCEAN
64 million square miles

ASIA
17.4 million
square miles

UNITED STATES
3.7 million
square miles

**Relative Sizes of the Pacific Ocean, Asia, and the United States**

How big are these continents? The United States, including Alaska and Hawaii, is about 3.7 million square miles. Asia, on the other hand, is 17.4 million square miles. Asia is nearly five times bigger than the United States.

Now think once more of the Pacific Ocean. It covers more than 64 million square miles. The Pacific Ocean could hold the United States 17 times. So the earth really is a big place.

## Getting Around

Today, moving from place to place is fairly easy. But it hasn't always been that way. A little more than 200 years ago, George Washington was the first president of the United States. He couldn't get on a plane or e-mail his wife, Martha. For him, nothing moved faster than a running horse or a sailing ship.

But it was even harder hundreds of thousands of years before George Washington. Most scientists believe that modern humans began to live in Africa about 200,000 years ago. If these early humans wanted to go somewhere, they had to walk. However, they had no world maps showing them where they were or where they were going.

At least George Washington had maps. He knew about Asia and Africa and the Indian Ocean. Washington had some idea of the size of the world. As these early humans traveled, they couldn't know whether they were one mile or one thousand miles away from an ocean.

## Geography and History

The early humans didn't divide the earth into seven continents and four oceans. But they did use the land and water every day. They got everything they needed from the earth. But it wasn't always easy. Huge lakes, seas, and oceans were problems. Early humans had to travel around large bodies of water because they had no ships. Mountains were another problem. The huge Himalayas in Asia and the Alps in Europe could not be crossed easily.

There were other travel problems. The lack of water and the heat made it dangerous to cross a desert. Spring floods made many rivers impossible to cross. **Glaciers**, or vast sheets of ice, also blocked travel.

In addition, the **climate** of the earth affected the lives of the early humans. Different places on the earth have different kinds of climates. People living in cold climates had to dress differently from those living in warm climates. Also, climates have changed over time. For example, most of the northern part of Africa is now the largest desert in the world. But 10,000 years ago, the same region had many large lakes and plenty of rain.

Humans also used the land to help them. The land provided early people with stones for tools and caves for shelter. Rivers gave them drinking water. Over time, people learned to live in many kinds of climates. Humans began to find ways to travel over mountains and across oceans.

Snow-covered mountains

Northern Africa today

Northern Africa might have looked like this 10,000 years ago.

## The Story Begins

The geography of Earth provides a stage for people to live their lives. The story of the people living on Earth over time is what we call world history. This story begins about 200,000 years ago. That is when most scientists believe modern humans were living on the earth.

Archaeologists carefully dig objects out of the earth.

There are many parts of the story that are still a mystery. **Archaeologists** are people who study the past by digging up old bones and objects. Archaeologists can tell us a lot about how people lived long ago. But there will always be questions. We know that the early humans learned to live on the land. They passed their knowledge to their children. And humans have been learning ever since.

# Lesson 1 Review

Choose words from the list that best complete the paragraphs. One word will not be used.

**Word List**

glaciers

maps

continents

archaeologists

oceans

Today we can be in touch with the rest of the world by just turning on a television or sending an e-mail. In one way, the world is small. But it is also a large place, with four huge __1__ and seven large __2__ .

The earliest humans had to move from place to place to find food. Mountains and __3__ were two things that made it hard for these people to travel. Today we learn about the past from __4__ who study old bones and objects.

**LESSON 2**

# Beginnings to 6000 B.C.

## Before You Read

- What do people need in order to live?
- Why do people live in groups?

The early humans lived in a time that we call the **Stone Age**. The Stone Age lasted until around 5,500 years ago, or 3500 B.C. During this time, people made tools and weapons out of stone.

The Stone Age people didn't know how to write. They kept no diaries, exchanged no letters, and wrote no books. These early humans left no written history. That is why we call them **prehistoric**.

### New Words
Stone Age
prehistoric
clans
nomads
Ice Age
domesticate
civilizations

### People and Places
North Pole

This painting shows a prehistoric man making a stone tool.

Mammoth

## Basic Needs

All people have three basic needs—food, clothing, and shelter. Of these, food is clearly the most important. Without food, people die in about three weeks. Clothing and shelter are also important for protection against extreme temperatures and bad weather.

The earliest humans were hunters and gatherers. They ate mostly berries, nuts, and roots. They hunted wild animals for meat. Stone Age people attached a sharp stone to the end of a stick to make an ax or a club. One person hunting alone might have starved. But several hunters could surround an animal. Therefore, early people joined together to form **clans**. By hunting and living together, they had a much better chance of surviving. They hunted animals such as wolves and mammoths.

These early people were **nomads**. They had no permanent home. When the food in one area was used up, a clan moved to a new area. They moved

Early people began to move out of Africa about 100,000 years ago. When did early people arrive in Australia?

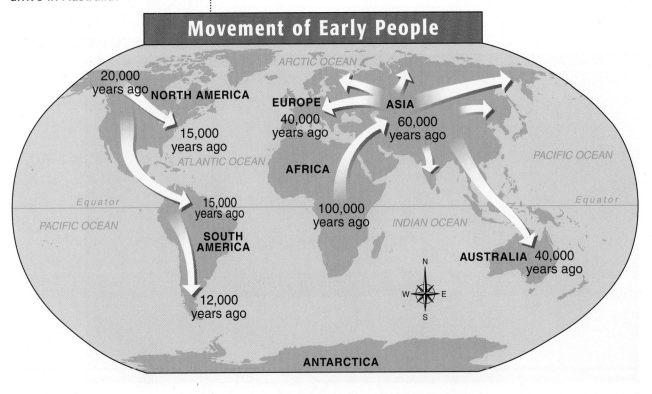

### Movement of Early People

20,000 years ago **NORTH AMERICA**

15,000 years ago

ATLANTIC OCEAN

**EUROPE** 40,000 years ago

**ASIA** 60,000 years ago

ARCTIC OCEAN

PACIFIC OCEAN

**AFRICA**

Equator

PACIFIC OCEAN

15,000 years ago

**SOUTH AMERICA**

100,000 years ago

INDIAN OCEAN

Equator

**AUSTRALIA** 40,000 years ago

12,000 years ago

N
W E
S

**ANTARCTICA**

two or three miles about every twenty years. Most scientists believed that humans slowly spread out from Africa to other parts of the world. By 60,000 years ago, humans were in Asia. By 40,000 years ago, they were moving into Australia and Europe. By about 20,000 years ago, they crossed from Asia into North America. From there they traveled down into South America.

Stone Age hunters used stone knives to remove the skin from animals. They made clothes from the hides. Many people needed warm clothes. Their world was often very cold. Sometimes huge glaciers moved south from the North Pole. This created an **Ice Age**. The last such Ice Age ended about 10,000 years ago.

In addition to food and clothing, Stone Age people needed shelter. Some made huts using mammoth bones, grass, and branches. Caves often were used as shelter, too. Stone Age people could stay in a favorite cave until the food in that area ran out. Then they were on the move again.

**Something to Chew On**

How old is gum chewing? For a long time, we thought it went back only a hundred years or so. But gum chewing is at least 9,000 years old. People back then chewed black lumps of tar from birch trees. Why did they do it? They might have chewed tar to clean their teeth. They might have been trying to help a hurting tooth. Or perhaps they just liked the taste. Most of the early people who chewed gum were between the ages of 6 and 15.

Stone Age people sometimes made huts using mammoth bones.

This horse was painted on the wall of a cave in France.

Cave painting in Africa

Some Stone Age people painted on the walls of caves. They used paintbrushes made with animal hair. For paint, they mixed animal fat with minerals. These Stone Age artists painted pictures of animals such as bison, deer, and horses. Some of the paintings are 30,000 years old. Cave paintings have been found in Africa, Europe, Asia, South America, and North America.

## A Few Good Ideas

Early in the Stone Age, people learned to make fire. At first they used fire only to keep warm. Later they learned to use it for cooking.

Much later, around 10,000 years ago, some of the hunters and gatherers began raising animals. They learned to **domesticate**, or tame, wild animals. They tamed dogs, sheep, pigs, goats, and cattle. With domesticated animals, they had meat whenever they needed it. But they still had to move when the animals ate all the grass in an area.

Dogs and other animals were tamed around 8000 B.C.

Early humans also found they could plant a seed in the earth and grow food. It took thousands of years to develop the skills of farming. But farming was one of the greatest discoveries ever. The new plants provided more seeds to plant.

## First Civilizations

After learning to farm, humans could settle in one place and stay there. They didn't have to hunt animals. They didn't have to gather wild roots, berries, and nuts. With more food available, communities began to grow.

Farmers needed a steady supply of water for their crops. So most early communities grew along the banks of rivers. By around 6000 B.C., some communities had grown into large **civilizations**. This means they had a language and a government. They had clear rules for living.

Several great civilizations developed in different parts of the world around the same time. You will learn about each of these in the following chapters.

The first civilizations might have had rooms like this.

# Lesson 2 Review

Choose words from the list that best complete the paragraphs. One word will not be used.

Life for early humans was hard. Finding food was difficult. These __1__ had to move many times just to find food. They wore animal hides to keep warm and lived in huts and __2__.

In time, Stone Age people learned how to __3__ wild animals. They also learned how to farm. With a steady supply of food, they could settle in one place. Their communities grew large. They developed languages and governments. The communities became __4__.

**Word List**

civilizations

prehistoric

caves

nomads

domesticate

### Summary

- The world has seven continents and four oceans.

- Early humans lived in Africa about 200,000 years ago. Very slowly, people spread from Africa throughout the world.

- During the Stone Age, early humans formed clans. These clans moved when they used up the food in an area.

- Cave paintings dating from the Stone Age have been found on nearly every continent.

- Early humans learned how to build shelters, use fire, tame animals, and grow food.

## Find Out More!

After reading Chapter 1, you're ready to go online. **Explore Zone**, **Quiz Time**, and **Amazing Facts** bring this chapter of world history alive.

Visit www.exploreSV.com and type in the chapter code **1-Ch1**.

### Vocabulary

Number your paper from 1 to 6. Write the word from the list that best completes each sentence. One word will not be used.

1. The earth is divided into seven areas of land called _____.

2. Travel was difficult for early humans because of vast sheets of ice called _____.

3. People who study old bones and objects to learn about the past are called _____.

4. Early humans left no written history, so we call them _____.

5. People who have no permanent homes are called _____.

6. Early people learned to _____ wild animals.

**Word List**

prehistoric

archaeologists

nomads

continents

civilizations

domesticate

glaciers

## Comprehension

Number your paper from 1 to 5. Write one or more sentences to answer each question below.

1. How are Earth's largest bodies of water and great areas of land divided?

2. What are two things that made travel difficult for early humans?

3. How did climate affect the lives of early humans?

4. How did early people get food?

5. What did early people use for clothing?

## Critical Thinking

**Categories**    Number your paper from 1 to 4. Read the words in each group below. Think about how they are alike. Write the best title for each group.

| Early Humans | Civilizations | Continents | Needs |
|---|---|---|---|

1. Africa
   North America
   Asia

2. food
   shelter
   clothing

3. hunters and gatherers
   nomads
   clans

4. language
   government
   rules for living

## Writing

Write a paragraph explaining how early people lived and why they lived in groups.

## LESSON 1

# Early Egyptians

## New Words

silt
pyramids
pharaohs
afterlife
mummies
hieroglyphics
papyrus
religion
religious

## People and Places

Egypt
Nile River
Sahara Desert
Mediterranean Sea
Menes
Memphis
Giza
Nubia
Kush

## Before You Read

- Why is a river valley a good place to settle?
- How do people's beliefs affect the way they live?

Egypt has been called "the gift of the Nile." Without the Nile River, all of Egypt would be a desert. The land of Egypt is part of the Sahara Desert, the largest desert in the world. The Nile River flows right through the Sahara Desert. It brings water to the dry land.

The Nile is the world's longest river. It begins in the mountains of central Africa. It flows more than 4,000 miles north to the Mediterranean Sea. Early farmers in Egypt depended on the Nile River. It flooded every spring. The flooding brought **silt**, a very rich soil, to the land around the river. The silt made the Nile River valley one of the best places in the world for farming.

The Nile River brings needed water to the desert.

For thousands of years, Egyptian farmers have been able to raise wheat and other crops because of the Nile River. It's no wonder that 4,000 years ago Egyptians wrote a song praising the Nile River.

"Hail to thee, O Nile, that springs from out of the earth and comes to give Egypt life!"

**Voices**
In History

## The Old Kingdom

Around 5000 B.C., communities began forming along the Nile River. The Egyptians developed a writing system and a form of government. In time, the land was divided into two kingdoms—Upper Egypt and Lower Egypt. An ancient Egyptian story says that King Menes united the two lands around 3100 B.C. He made Memphis the capital. His rule began the Old Kingdom. It lasted nearly 1,000 years.

During the Old Kingdom, the Egyptians built many huge **pyramids**. They were built by hand with giant blocks of stone. One pyramid, called the Great Pyramid, was built in the city of Giza around 2500 B.C. It was 480 feet high. It took 100,000 people about 20 years to complete it.

The pyramids at Giza were built around 2500 B.C.

Mediterranean Sea

LOWER EGYPT
Giza
Memphis

UPPER EGYPT

SAHARA DESERT

N
W E
S

The Old Kingdom

Egyptian mummy case

**Pharaohs**, or Egyptian rulers, were buried in the pyramids. Other wealthy people could also be buried in pyramids. The pyramids were important because Egyptians believed in an **afterlife**. They believed that after people died, they had another life. Clothing and jewelry often were placed inside the pyramids. The Egyptians believed the dead person would use these things in the afterlife.

Even the body itself was prepared for life after death. Egyptians who had enough money could have their bodies made into **mummies**. Their bodies would be preserved to last thousands of years. The process to turn a body into a mummy took about 70 days. Sometimes Egyptians even made animals into mummies.

Egyptians also improved their writing. They used a system of picture writing called **hieroglyphics**. Not every Egyptian knew how to use hieroglyphics. Only certain people were taught how to read and write. These same people also learned math. They collected taxes and kept important records for the Egyptian civilization.

Egyptians also found many uses for a plant called **papyrus**. The plant grew along the banks of the Nile River. Egyptians built boats with it. They used it to make baskets, shoes, and rope. They even made a special kind of paper using papyrus.

The Egyptians used a system of picture writing called hieroglyphics.

Ancient Egyptian children enjoyed playing games.

## Egyptian Way of Life

The Egyptian **religion** had many gods. One of the most important gods was the sun god. After the gods, the pharaoh was the head of Egyptian society. Egyptians believed that a pharaoh was the child of a god. As the child of a god, the pharaoh had total rule over Egypt. A pharaoh's power was not questioned.

There were many jobs in ancient Egypt. Some people worked in government. Others made crafts. Still others were farmers or slaves. Egyptians worked from sunrise to sunset. Many did not work on **religious** holidays.

Women were usually in charge of the house. Children enjoyed playing many games. Some Egyptian games, such as tug-of-war and leapfrog, are still played today.

## Nubia

Nubia formed around the same time as Egypt. Nubia was in an area south of Egypt where the land was very hot and dry. The Nubians, like the Egyptians, could not have survived without water from the Nile River.

The pharaoh Khufu was buried in the Great Pyramid at Giza.

The Nubians and the Egyptians traded with each other and shared ideas. For example, the Nubians built pyramids, but their pyramids were smaller and steeper than the Egyptian pyramids.

Nubian pyramids

The Nubians were well known for their beautiful pottery. They traded their pottery and other goods with Egyptians and other people. Nubia became an important trading area. It had trade routes connecting it with areas in Africa and Asia.

At times, Nubia and Egypt fought each other. Egyptians thought controlling the trade routes in Nubia would make them richer. Toward the end of the Old Kingdom, Egyptians took over northern Nubia. The Egyptians called the area Kush.

# Lesson 1 Review

Choose words from the list that best complete the paragraphs. One word will not be used.

**Word List**

papyrus 3
pottery
pyramids 2
hieroglyphics 4
Nile River 1

Two civilizations developed along the Nile River. One was Egypt. The other was Nubia. Without the __1__, neither of them would have existed.

The Egyptians of the Old Kingdom built giant __2__. Pharaohs were buried inside them. The ancient Egyptians developed a form of writing called __3__.

The Nubian civilization developed south of Egypt. The Nubians made beautiful __4__. In addition, Nubia had valuable trade routes.

**LESSON 2**

# Egypt Becomes an Empire

## Before You Read

- How do groups of people gain power over other groups?
- Why do people build temples and statues?

Around 2500 B.C., Egypt's Old Kingdom began to weaken. Pharaohs lost power. Government officials quarreled with one another. A war broke out. By 2100 B.C., the Old Kingdom had ended. There was no steady government because various kings were fighting for power. Each one wanted to rule Egypt.

Around 2050 B.C., the Middle Kingdom began. New rulers took over Egypt and moved the capital to Thebes.

## New Words
invaded
chariots
empire
obelisks
tomb

## People and Places
**Thebes**
**Red Sea**
**Hyksos**
**Akhenaton**
**Nefertiti**
**King Tut**
**Howard Carter**
**Hatshepsut**

During the Middle Kingdom, models of boats were sometimes buried with pharaohs.

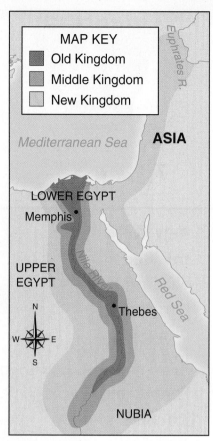

Mediterranean Sea

**ASIA**

Euphrates R.

LOWER EGYPT

Memphis

UPPER EGYPT

Nile River

Red Sea

Thebes

N
W E
S

NUBIA

Ancient Egypt

## The Middle Kingdom

Egyptians of the Middle Kingdom focused on art and writing. They didn't build as many pyramids as in the Old Kingdom. Instead, they built canals to drain swamps. This made even more land available for farming.

They also built a canal connecting the Nile River with trade routes near the Red Sea. This improved trade during the Middle Kingdom. Egyptians were able to get various kinds of wood from areas in Southwest Asia. This wood was used to build boats and furniture.

The Middle Kingdom lasted only a few hundred years. Around 1700 B.C., warriors called Hyksos **invaded**, or attacked, Egypt. They came from Asia on **chariots** pulled by horses. Each chariot carried two warriors. One man controlled the horse. The other carried a spear or a bow and arrow. The Egyptians were surprised by the chariots. They had always fought on foot.

The people of Kush joined with the Hyksos against the Egyptians. The Hyksos easily beat the Egyptians. For the first time, outsiders ruled the lands of Egypt.

The Hyksos used chariots to attack Egypt in 1700 B.C.

## The New Kingdom

The Hyksos ruled with great force. They burned cities and destroyed temples. The Hyksos were cruel to many Egyptians. But such force didn't work for long. The Egyptians fought back. They used chariots against the Hyksos. Around 1539 B.C., they drove out the Hyksos. The Egyptians set up a new government known as the New Kingdom. It lasted 500 years.

The New Kingdom was really an **empire**. An empire exists when one group of people rules over another. The Egyptians had an army for the first time. This army took control of lands far beyond the Nile River, including parts of Asia. Egypt became the strongest and richest nation in the world. Thebes, the capital, became one of the most powerful cities.

Egyptians of the New Kingdom built great temples and statues. The temples were both religious places and schools. Egyptians built **obelisks** that were carved from single stones. The obelisks were built to honor the gods.

Around 1372 B.C., Akhenaton became pharaoh. He and his wife, Nefertiti, believed that the sun god was the only god. They tried to get all Egyptians to stop believing in the other gods.

Egyptian obelisk

Egyptians of the New Kingdom built massive temples.

Akhenaton offers gifts to the sun god.

Akhenaton began building new temples for the sun god. They were open and let in sunlight. Art from the New Kingdom often shows the pharaoh and his family offering gifts to the sun.

After Akhenaton died, a nine-year-old boy became pharaoh. This boy was Tutankhamen, or King Tut. He only ruled for about nine years. He is remembered because of the treasures that were found in his **tomb**. Many tombs of pharaohs were robbed over the years. But King Tut's tomb was hidden beneath another tomb. No one knew about it until 1922. That is when Howard Carter, an archaeologist, found it. He wrote about going inside the tomb.

## Voices
### In History

"The scene grew clearer, and we could pick out individual objects. First . . . were three great . . . couches, their sides carved in the form of . . . animals . . . ."

Some New Kingdom pharaohs were wealthy. But they began losing power during the New Kingdom. By 1075 B.C., Egypt was weak. The people of Kush later took over Egypt for around 50 years. Then, invaders from the north and east took over all the lands of the Egyptian New Kingdom. These invaders were the Assyrians.

These objects were found in King Tut's tomb. The chest plate (above) is shaped like a beetle. The decorated box (right) was King Tut's war chest.

## Hatshepsut (ruled c. 1490 B.C.–1469 B.C.)

Ancient Egyptian pharaohs were almost always men. But there was a female ruler named Hatshepsut. She ruled for about 21 years during the New Kingdom. She was pharaoh before King Tut and Akhenaton. When her husband died, Hatshepsut took the title of pharaoh. She called herself the daughter of a god. Most people believe she was the first female ruler of a civilization.

Hatshepsut dressed like a man. She even wore a false beard. Beards were a traditional symbol worn only by the pharaoh. While Hatshepsut was pharaoh, there was peace and friendly trade in Egypt. She sent trading teams deep into the lands around Egypt. She sent armies into Nubia and Southwest Asia. Hatshepsut also became known as a builder. She had many new monuments and temples built. Hatshepsut repaired much of the damage done by the Hyksos.

## Lesson 2 Review

Choose words from the list that best complete the paragraphs. One word will not be used.

The Middle Kingdom was a time of building canals and expanding trade. But the __1__ invaded Egypt on chariots and ended the Middle Kingdom.

Later, the Egyptians fought back, and their kingdom began to grow. During the New Kingdom, Egypt became an __2__. The first female ruler in world history was a pharaoh during the New Kingdom. Her name was __3__. A young boy named __4__ was another pharaoh during the New Kingdom. In 1922 an archaeologist discovered his tomb.

**Word List**

King Tut

obelisks

Hyksos

empire

Hatshepsut

## Chapter 2: Using What You've Learned

### Summary

- The Egyptians and Nubians built civilizations along the Nile River around 5000 B.C.

- The Old Kingdom of Egypt began in 3100 B.C. when Menes united Upper and Lower Egypt.

- Nubia, also known as Kush, became an important trading center.

- Egypt's Middle Kingdom began around 2050 B.C. and ended when the Hyksos invaded around 1700 B.C.

- The New Kingdom began about 1539 B.C. when the Egyptians drove out the Hyksos.

- Hatshepsut, Akhenaton, and King Tut were some New Kingdom rulers.

### Find Out More!

After reading Chapter 2, you're ready to go online. **Explore Zone**, **Quiz Time**, and **Amazing Facts** bring this chapter of world history alive.

Visit www.exploreSV.com and type in the chapter code **1-Ch2**.

### Vocabulary

Number your paper from 1 to 6. Finish the sentences from Group A with words from Group B. Write the letter of the correct answer.

**Group A**

1. The __e/silt__ from the flooding of the Nile River was good for growing crops.

2. Rulers of Egypt were buried in __d/pyramids__

3. Egyptians used a system of picture writing called __a/hieroglyphics__

4. A belief in one or many gods is called a __f/religion__

5. The Hyksos used __chariots C__ to defeat the Egyptians.

6. The Egyptians built an __empire b__ by taking control of other lands.

**Group B**

a. hieroglyphics

b. empire

c. chariots

d. pyramids

e. silt

f. religion

## Comprehension

Number your paper from 1 to 5. Read each sentence below. Then write the name of the person or people who might have said each sentence. One name from the list will not be used.

1. "I united Upper Egypt and Lower Egypt."

2. "We made beautiful pottery and had trade routes in Africa and Asia."

3. "I am the pharaoh who built temples for the sun god."

4. "I am known for the treasures found in my tomb."

5. "I might have been the first female ruler of a civilization."

**Word List**

Akhenaton

Menes

Hyksos

Hatshepsut

Nubians

King Tut

## Critical Thinking

**Cause and Effect**   Number your paper from 1 to 4. Read the causes in the left column. Then choose the correct effect from the right column. Write the letter of the correct effect.

| Cause | Effect |
|---|---|
| 1. The Egyptians needed more land for farming, so | a. they left food and clothing in tombs. |
| 2. Ancient Egyptians believed in life after death, so | b. they built canals to drain swamps. |
| 3. Egyptians believed the pharaoh was a child of a god, so | c. they built temples and obelisks. |
| 4. Egyptians of the New Kingdom wanted to honor the gods, so | d. a pharaoh's power was not questioned. |

## Writing

Write a paragraph describing the many ways Egyptians used papyrus.

## Skill Builder: Using Primary Sources

**Primary sources** can tell us about the lives of people who lived at different times. Primary sources can be written, like letters, diaries, and newspapers. Primary sources can also be objects, like clothing, tools, and household items.

We know what life was like in ancient Egypt from objects that archaeologists have found. In 1922, archaeologist Howard Carter discovered the tomb of King Tut. You read a description of his discovery on page 24. Now read more of his description.

**accustomed**
used to

**interior**
inside

**gilded**
covered in gold

**ornamental caskets**
large decorated boxes

### Howard Carter's Diary

*"It was some time before [we] could see. The hot air escaping caused the candle to flicker, but as soon as [our] eyes became **accustomed** to the . . . light, the **interior** of the chamber gradually [appeared] before [us], with its strange and wonderful [group] of . . . beautiful objects heaped upon one another . . . . [There were] two strange . . . [statues] of a King, . . . **gilded** couches in strange forms, . . . **ornamental caskets**, . . . stools of all shapes and design, of both common and rare materials; and, lastly . . . overturned parts of chariots [shining] with gold . . . . We questioned one another as to the meaning of it all."*

Number your paper from 1 to 5. Write 1 to 2 sentences to answer each question.

1. What are many of the items Carter described made of?

2. What household items did Carter find in the tomb?

3. What object in the tomb shows how King Tut might have traveled?

4. How might Carter have known this was a pharaoh's tomb?

5. Why do you think Carter wrote about this experience?

## LESSON 1

# Early Mesopotamia

## Before You Read

- Why did early people settle in river valleys?
- How are laws important to a civilization?

In the last chapter, you read about the Nile River and how important it was to the people who settled near it. In Southwest Asia, two other rivers were important. They were the Tigris and Euphrates rivers. Together they formed a valley called Mesopotamia, or "land between the rivers."

Mesopotamia was part of the **Fertile Crescent**. Its soil was very good for farming. The Fertile Crescent extended from the Mediterranean Sea to the Persian Gulf.

Civilizations were developing in Mesopotamia around the same time they were forming in Egypt. Around 5000 B.C., settlers began building cities in a part of Mesopotamia called Sumer.

## New Words

Fertile Crescent
dikes
ziggurats
city-states
stylus
cuneiform
Code of Hammurabi

## People and Places

Tigris River
Euphrates River
Mesopotamia
Persian Gulf
Sumer
Sargon
Akkad
Hammurabi
Babylon
Hittites
Phoenicians
Assyrians

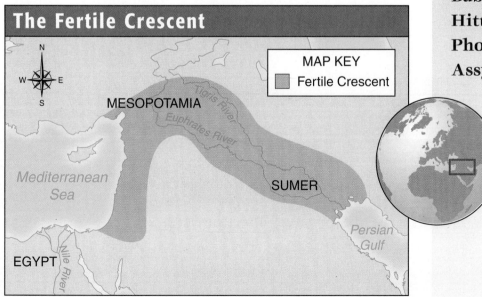

The Fertile Crescent

MAP KEY
Fertile Crescent

MESOPOTAMIA

Tigris River

Euphrates River

Mediterranean Sea

SUMER

Persian Gulf

EGYPT

Nile River

## The Sumerians

Unlike the Nile River, the Tigris and Euphrates rivers did not flood at the same time every year. When the rivers did flood, the Sumerians were surprised. The floods washed away their crops and their houses. The Sumerians built canals to control the flooding waters. They also built **dikes**, or mounds of dirt, to hold back flooding waters. Using the rich soil of the river valley, the Sumerians became excellent farmers.

Mesopotamia had few trees or stones for building. But there was plenty of clay. Sumerians made bricks from clay and let them dry in the sun. They used the bricks to build homes and temples. Their temples were called **ziggurats**. The ziggurats were built as special places for the gods. Sumerians believed they had to make the gods happy in order to have good crops.

Many Sumerian cities grew into **city-states**, independent cities surrounded by farming villages. A ziggurat was usually at the center of the city. A wall surrounded the city. There were farms and villages outside the wall. The wall protected the city from invaders. Each city-state had its own ruler. Sumerians believed that the ruler had the support of the local god. But unlike in Egypt, the ruler was not considered an actual child of a god.

Small Sumerian statue

The ziggurat was usually at the center of a Sumerian city-state.

## Sumerian Inventions

The Sumerians found a good way to use the wheel. They connected wheels to a cart. Then they used donkeys to pull the cart. This simple invention changed how people and things traveled from one place to another. The Sumerians also invented a sail for boats. The sail made water travel easier.

Like the Egyptians, the Sumerians created a form of writing. They did not have paper. Instead they used soft clay tablets. Writers used a pointed stick called a **stylus** to make their marks. The tablets were then dried in the sun to make them hard. The Sumerians used a type of writing called **cuneiform**.

By putting cuneiform symbols together, the Sumerians wrote stories, poems, and songs. They kept records of the goods they traded. They wrote down the names of cities and leaders. In this way, the Sumerians wrote their history.

## Akkadians and Babylonians

Around 2340 B.C., a man named Sargon attacked and defeated the lands of Sumer. He led his soldiers in battles until all of Mesopotamia was united under his rule. Sargon built a new capital city called Akkad. Sargon saw how much the Sumerians had done. He adopted many of their ways. For example, the Akkadians began to use cuneiform writing. Sargon and the kings who followed him stayed in power for about 200 years.

Next, the Babylonians gained control of Mesopotamia. Hammurabi became king of Babylon around 1792 B.C. He is remembered most for having all the Babylonian laws written down around 1780 B.C. Hammurabi knew the laws of the Sumerians and Akkadians. He changed them a little and made them a part of Babylonian laws. Hammurabi's collection of more than 250 laws is known as the **Code of Hammurabi**.

Sumerian cart

Sumerian clay tablet

This stone marker shows Hammurabi standing in front of the sun god. The Code of Hammurabi is carved below.

The code did not treat all people equally. Some had more rights than others. Still, the code told people what they could and could not do. Anyone who broke a law knew the punishment.

"If anyone steals the property of a temple or of the court, he shall be put to death, and also the one who receives the stolen thing from him shall be put to death."

## Other Fertile Crescent People

There were other people who lived in the Fertile Crescent. The Hittites ruled lands in the northern part of the Fertile Crescent. The Hittites knew how to make iron tools and weapons.

Another group, the Phoenicians, lived on the western edge of the Fertile Crescent. They set up colonies along the Mediterranean Sea around 1000 B.C. They built boats and sailed as traders. The Phoenicians spread their traditions to the people in the colonies. At first, the Phoenicians sailed only during the day. Later they learned to study the stars to find their way at night.

Several groups of people ruled lands in or near the Fertile Crescent. Which group ruled the largest area?

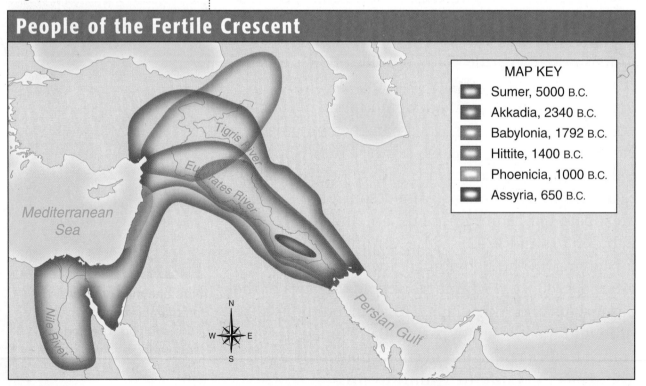

## People of the Fertile Crescent

MAP KEY

Sumer, 5000 B.C.

Akkadia, 2340 B.C.

Babylonia, 1792 B.C.

Hittite, 1400 B.C.

Phoenicia, 1000 B.C.

Assyria, 650 B.C.

Tigris River

Euphrates River

Mediterranean Sea

Nile River

Persian Gulf

The Phoenicians developed a simple alphabet. The Sumerians had used hundreds of letters. That made cuneiform hard to use. The Phoenicians used just 22 letters. Today many languages are based on the Phoenician alphabet.

Many groups ruled parts of the Fertile Crescent. The Assyrians came to power around 800 B.C. They expanded their control over the next 150 years. By 650 B.C., they ruled all the land of the Fertile Crescent and the Nile River.

The Assyrian Empire was a combination of all the groups of people who lived in the Fertile Crescent and Egypt. The people spoke many different languages. The Assyrian Empire controlled this large area by being cruel. The Assyrians often took people away from their homes and moved them to a different part of the empire. When the empire ended around 600 B.C., many people celebrated.

The Phoenicians traded with other groups.

# Lesson 1 Review

Choose words from the list that best complete the paragraphs. One word will not be used.

The land between the Tigris and Euphrates rivers was called Mesopotamia. It formed part of the Fertile Crescent. The __1__ developed the first civilization in this region. The Sumerians developed __2__. They wrote using cuneiform.

Other civilizations lived in the Fertile Crescent. Hammurabi is most remembered for his __3__ of laws. The Phoenicians learned to study the stars and sail at night. In time, the __4__ took over all the land of the Fertile Crescent and the Nile River.

**Word List**
Sumerians
Assyrians
Sargon
city-states
code

# LESSON 2

# The Hebrews

## New Words

Torah
covenant
Promised Land
Exodus
Ten Commandments
Judaism
contact

## People and Places

Hebrews
Abraham
Canaan
Moses
Sinai Desert
Mount Sinai
Israel
Philistines
David
Goliath
Jerusalem
Solomon
Judah

## Before You Read

- Did early people believe in one or many gods?
- Why are strong leaders important to a group of people?

Most of the early civilizations of the Fertile Crescent have disappeared. There are no longer any Sumerians or Akkadians. There are no Babylonians or Hittites today. The Phoenicians and Assyrians are gone, too.

The Hebrews are different. They survived. Jewish people today trace their history back to the Hebrews. Their laws are written in a group of five books called the **Torah**. The Torah is part of the Bible. Their story began in Mesopotamia around 4,000 years ago.

Abraham, the first leader of the Hebrews, traveled with his family to Canaan.

## Hebrew Beginnings

Like the Egyptians and the Sumerians, most early civilizations believed in many different gods. But the Torah tells of a man named Abraham who believed in only one God. He was the first leader of the Hebrews.

Jewish people believe that God spoke to Abraham and asked him to leave his home. Abraham and his family traveled west out of Mesopotamia. Around 2000 B.C., they came to a land called Canaan. There, Jewish people believe, God promised the Hebrews a home of their own. In return, the Hebrews promised to believe in God alone. This agreement was called a **covenant**. The Hebrews believed that Canaan was their **Promised Land**.

But Canaan was very dry. The Hebrews could not grow enough food. So, around 1800 B.C., they traveled south to Egypt. The Egyptians at first welcomed them, but later forced them to work as slaves. Centuries passed. Around 1290 B.C., the Torah says that Moses became the Hebrew leader. He led the Hebrews out of Egypt. This story is told in a part of the Torah called **Exodus**. The word *exodus* means "road out."

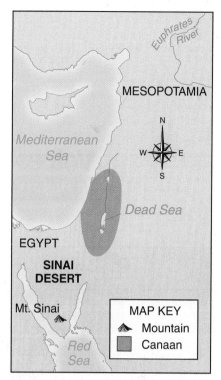

The Land of Canaan

Moses led the Hebrew people out of Egypt.

For years the Hebrews wandered in the Sinai Desert. They were going back to Canaan, the Promised Land. The Torah says that one day Moses went to the top of Mount Sinai. There, God gave him the **Ten Commandments**. These laws told the Hebrews how to behave.

**Voices**
**In History**

❝Respect your father and mother . . . . You shall have no gods other than me . . . . You shall not kill . . . . You shall not steal . . . .❞

## Return to Canaan

At last, the Hebrews reached Canaan. They set up a new kingdom called Israel. But there were many other people living in the area. The Hebrews had to fight to win back their Promised Land. One group, the Philistines, had a strong army. A famous Hebrew story tells of a boy named David who defeated a Philistine named Goliath. Goliath was a giant man. He challenged any Hebrew to fight him. Only David was brave enough to accept. David beat Goliath by hurling a stone from a slingshot. David became a Hebrew king. He made Jerusalem the capital of Israel.

When David died, his son Solomon became king. King Solomon built a beautiful temple in Jerusalem. When Solomon died, the kingdom was divided. Hebrew people in the north formed the Kingdom of Israel. Hebrew people in the south set up the Kingdom of Judah. **Judaism**, the name of the Jewish religion, comes from Judah.

This division weakened the Hebrews. They fought one another for many years. Then neighboring kingdoms invaded. These new forces were too strong for the divided Hebrews. One group of outsiders, the Assyrians, took over Israel and Judah. As you have read, the Assyrians controlled all the lands of the Fertile Crescent and the Nile River until around 600 B.C.

David and Goliath

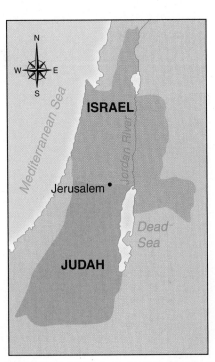

Kingdoms of Israel and Judah

## King Solomon (ruled c. 977 B.C.–937 B.C.)

King Solomon was known for being very wise. As king of Israel, he sometimes acted as a judge. When the people of Israel had questions, they often would seek his advice. King Solomon was also a poet. He wrote a book called the Song of Solomon. This book is in the Bible.

But Solomon is best known for his temple. It was made with beautiful white stone from Jerusalem. Jewish people today pray at the western wall of Solomon's temple.

During Solomon's rule, Israel had **contact** with many parts of the world. Solomon sent ships across the Mediterranean Sea to trade with people of other lands. He brought the traditions and religions of other people into the kingdom of Israel. Some people did not like the new traditions and religions. This weakened Solomon's rule. This was one reason why the kingdom became divided after Solomon's death.

## Lesson 2 Review

Choose words from the list that best complete the paragraphs. One word will not be used.

The Hebrews, now called the Jewish people, have survived 4,000 years. Their laws are written in the __1__. Unlike other early civilizations, the Hebrews believed in only one God. Abraham made a covenant with God.

While in Egypt, the Hebrews became slaves. __2__ led them out of Egypt. On Mount Sinai, he received the Ten __3__. The Hebrews had to fight to win back their Promised Land. One of the great Hebrew kings was David. Another king, __4__, built a beautiful temple in Jerusalem.

**Word List**

**Commandments**

**Goliath**

**Moses**

**Solomon**

**Torah**

## Chapter 3: Using What You've Learned

### Summary

- The Sumerians built the first civilization in the Fertile Crescent.

- The Akkadians, Babylonians, Hittites, Phoenicians, Hebrews, and Assyrians also lived in the Fertile Crescent.

- Hammurabi collected the Babylonian laws into the Code of Hammurabi.

- Abraham and Moses were Hebrew leaders. The Hebrews believed in one God.

- After Solomon died, the Hebrew kingdom split in two.

## Find Out More!

After reading Chapter 3, you're ready to go online. **Explore Zone**, **Quiz Time**, and **Amazing Facts** bring this chapter of world history alive.

Visit www.exploreSV.com and type in the chapter code **1-Ch3**.

### Vocabulary

Number your paper from 1 to 5. Write the letter of the correct answer.

1. Sumerians built **dikes** _____.
   - **a.** to protect cities from invaders
   - **b.** to hold back flooding waters
   - **c.** to live in
   - **d.** to honor their gods

2. Sumerians built **ziggurats** as special places for _____.
   - **a.** animals
   - **b.** farmers
   - **c.** gods
   - **d.** boats

3. The Hebrews believed that their **Promised Land** was _____.
   - **a.** Canaan
   - **b.** Thebes
   - **c.** Assyria
   - **d.** Mesopotamia

4. **Exodus** is the story of _____ leading the Hebrews out of Egypt.
   - **a.** Sargon
   - **b.** Moses
   - **c.** Goliath
   - **d.** David

5. The **Ten Commandments** were laws about how to _____.
   - **a.** trade goods
   - **b.** behave
   - **c.** dress
   - **d.** grow crops

## Comprehension

Number your paper from 1 to 4. Write **True** for each sentence that is true. Write **False** for each sentence that is false.

**1.** The Code of Hammurabi treated all people equally.

**2.** The Hittites only made tools and weapons out of stone.

**3.** Today many languages are based on the Phoenician alphabet.

**4.** The Torah contains Hebrew laws.

## Critical Thinking

**Conclusions**   Number your paper from 1 to 4. Read each pair of sentences below. Then look for a conclusion that follows from these sentences. Write the letter of the correct conclusion.

**1.** Mesopotamia had few trees or stones.
Mesopotamia had plenty of clay.

**2.** The Sumerians developed a cart with wheels.
The Sumerians invented a sail for boats.

**3.** Hammurabi wrote down the Babylonian laws.
These laws told people what they could and could not do.

**4.** After King Solomon died, the Hebrew kingdom divided in two.
The Hebrew kingdoms of Israel and Judah fought one another.

### Conclusions

**a.** The Sumerians changed how people and things traveled.

**b.** The people of Babylon knew whether they had broken the law.

**c.** The Sumerians made bricks from clay to build homes and temples.

**d.** The Hebrews were weakened.

## Writing

Write a paragraph describing what a Sumerian city-state might have looked like.

# LESSON 1

# Early China

## New Words

legends
historians
dynasty
bronze
millet
oracle bones
Mandate of Heaven

## People and Places

Huang He
Yangshao
Longshan
Shang
Yin
Zhou

## Before You Read

- What physical features might separate a place from the rest of the world?

- How do people try to tell the future?

The Chinese built their first civilization on a river, the Huang He, in northern China. The early Chinese knew nothing of the Egyptians or the Sumerians. They were separated from other people. The Pacific Ocean was to the east. Deserts and high mountains surrounded the rest of China. Like the Egyptians and the Sumerians, the Chinese learned to use the river to help them.

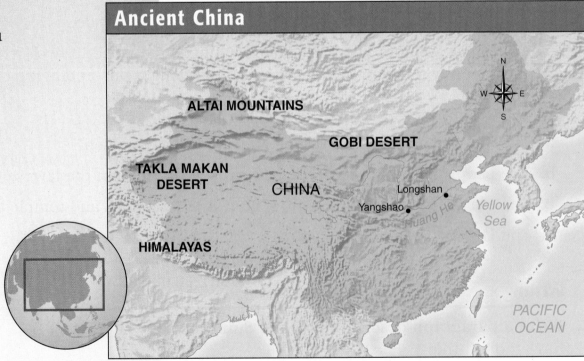

**Ancient China**

ALTAI MOUNTAINS

GOBI DESERT

TAKLA MAKAN
DESERT

CHINA

Longshan

Yangshao

Huang He

Yellow
Sea

HIMALAYAS

PACIFIC
OCEAN

The Huang He runs through northern China.

## First Cities

Chinese civilization probably began after civilizations in Egypt and Sumer. Still, Chinese civilization is very old. Early farming villages appeared in the area around 5000 B.C. The story of early China is mixed with **legends**. Until recently, many **historians** didn't believe the legends. But archaeologists have shown that many of the old stories are true. They have done this by digging up old cities, tools, and bones.

The earliest Chinese cities were Yangshao and Longshan. Most people in these cities were farmers along the Huang He. The Huang He is not deep, and the land around it is flat. So the river often flooded. The farmers needed the water, but they faced the same problem the Sumerians did. The floods often washed away whole villages. That is why the Huang He was called "China's Sorrow."

Yangshao pottery

Early Chinese people made pottery. The people of Yangshao used local clay. When they baked it, the clay turned red. The Longshan people lived farther down the river. They used a different kind of clay. They became famous for black pottery.

Farmers still plant large fields of millet.

Oracle bone

## The Shang

The Shang civilization was more advanced than the cities of Yangshao and Longshan. It was actually a **dynasty**, or family of kings. The Shang came to power around 1750 B.C. Tang was the first leader of this dynasty. He was a good ruler who treated people kindly.

Archeologists have dug up many objects from Yin, the capital city of the Shang Dynasty. They have discovered beautiful objects made from **bronze**. Bronze is a hard metal made by mixing copper and tin. The Shang made bronze cooking pots. They made bronze containers to hold wine. They also made tools and weapons from bronze. The Shang grew wheat and **millet** in the fields of the Huang He valley. They also raised pigs, sheep, and other animals.

The Shang created picture writing. It had thousands of symbols. One purpose of this writing was to tell the future. A person scratched the symbols on an animal bone or a turtle shell to ask a question. The question might have been, "Will the king have a son?" or, "Will I have a good day hunting?"

Then the bone or shell was heated in a fire. The answer to the question depended on how the bone or shell broke. That is why the bones were called **oracle bones**. An oracle is someone who tells the future.

Like the Egyptians, the Shang built places to bury their kings. The kings were buried with things they might need in the next life.

## The Zhou

The Shang lost power in 1027 B.C. The Zhou invaded from the west and set up a new dynasty. The Zhou Dynasty stayed in control for 200 years.

The Chinese believed their gods put the ruling family in power. Whoever held power had the right to do so. The Chinese called this special right the **Mandate of Heaven**. The people understood that a certain dynasty had the will, or mandate, of heaven. Just being in power proved it.

## Did You Know?

### All in the Family

In ancient China, the family was more important than the individual. That was true for both rich and poor families. If a boy or girl did something wrong, the whole family was punished. Parents chose husbands and wives for their children.

The family was almost holy. In fact, many ancient Chinese people prayed to their relatives who had died long ago.

Emperors of the Zhou Dynasty often traveled in chariots such as this.

This symbol represented the Mandate of Heaven.

But a dynasty could lose the Mandate of Heaven. If the kingdom experienced hard times, the people might think the gods no longer favored the ruling family. If the people thought a ruling family lost the Mandate of Heaven, they would no longer support the ruling family.

The Zhou rulers acted as if all the land and all the people belonged to them. They gave land and people to relatives and army leaders. In this way the Zhou created a lot of little kingdoms. These kingdoms had to obey the Zhou king. They also had to pay money to the king and supply him with soldiers in times of war. For more than 200 years, the Zhou kept the Mandate of Heaven.

Then, in 771 B.C., they lost this mandate. Many leaders of the little kingdoms didn't like the harsh rule of the Zhou. Also, the Zhou fought too many wars. That angered even more people. At last, an outside army invaded Zhou lands and killed their king. However, this was not the end of the Zhou. A new king moved further east and set up the Eastern Zhou Dynasty.

# Lesson 1 Review

Choose words from the list that best complete the paragraphs. One word will not be used.

**Word List**

Mandate of
 Heaven

legends

Sorrow

shallow

oracle bones

Chinese civilization began on the Huang He in northern China. Archeologists have helped us learn more about these early people. The Huang He often flooded because it was __1__. Because of these floods, the river was called "China's __2__."

The early Chinese civilizations made pottery. The Shang made bronze objects and used __3__ to tell the future. The Zhou replaced the Shang but later lost the __4__.

**LESSON 2**

# Indus River Civilizations

## Before You Read

- Why is it hard to know about early civilizations?

- How are most early civilizations alike?

Not long after the Egyptians and the Sumerians, the Harappa and Mohenjo-Daro civilizations began in the Indus River valley. The Indus River is located in the modern country of Pakistan, near India. It starts high in the mountains. In the spring, the snow melts in the mountains and floods the Indus River.

## New Words

subcontinent
monsoon
citadel
granary
Vedas
castes
Brahman
untouchables

## People and Places

Harappa
Mohenjo-Daro
Indus River
Himalayas
Hindu Kush
Aryans

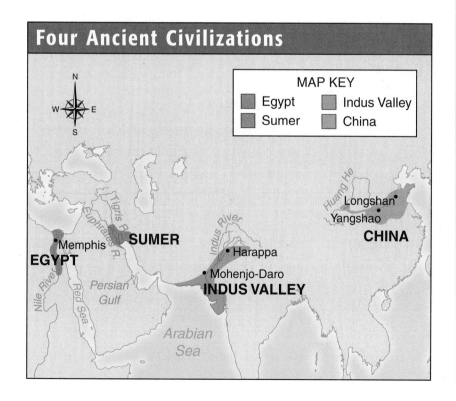

**Four Ancient Civilizations**

MAP KEY
- Egypt
- Sumer
- Indus Valley
- China

EGYPT
Memphis
SUMER
Tigris R.
Euphrates R.
Nile River
Red Sea
Persian Gulf
Indus River
Harappa
Mohenjo-Daro
**INDUS VALLEY**
Arabian Sea
Huang He
Longshan
Yangshao
**CHINA**

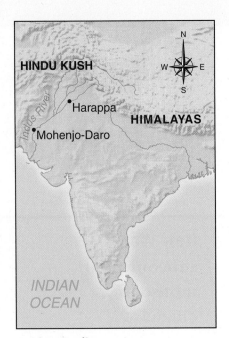

Ancient India

Ancient Indian game

The Harappa and Mohenjo-Daro civilizations started around 2500 B.C. and lasted more than 1,000 years. Then they vanished. Like some other early civilizations, they were lost to history for a very long time. But archaeologists continue to discover more and more about the early people of the Indus River valley.

## Geography and Climate

The modern country of India is sometimes called a **subcontinent**. India is a huge piece of land shaped like a triangle. The southern tip extends out into the Indian Ocean. To the north are two large mountain ranges. One is the Himalayas. The world's highest mountains are found there. The Himalayas separate India from China. The other mountain range is the Hindu Kush.

Except in the high mountains, the climate of India is mild. India has two seasons, dry and wet. From October to early June, the dry **monsoon** winds blow into India from Asia. From late June to September, the wet monsoon winds blow up from the Indian Ocean. These moist winds bring heavy rains. The word *monsoon* refers to both dry and wet winds.

## Harappa and Mohenjo-Daro

Two large cities formed along the Indus River. Today we call them Harappa and Mohenjo-Daro. We don't know what the people living there called them. Scientists have not yet learned to read the language of the people in these cities. Both cities were deserted around 1500 B.C. In 1922, archaeologists discovered the cities.

Harappa and Mohenjo-Daro were 400 miles apart. But they looked about the same. They did not, however, look like any other ancient city. For example, other ancient cities had twisting streets.

The ruins of Mohenjo-Daro are located in modern-day Pakistan.

In Harappa and Mohenjo-Daro the streets were straight and laid out in blocks. This shows that someone had a clear plan for how to build a city. The streets were wide and paved with bricks.

Most city people in Harappa and Mohenjo-Daro crafted goods. Shops inside the cities sold pottery and jewelry. Some sold cotton goods. Some crafts were traded with civilizations far away. Archaeologists have found crafts from the Indus River valley in the cities of Mesopotamia.

Most of the houses in the Indus River valley looked exactly alike. They were made with mud bricks, which were baked in ovens. Baking made the bricks harder and stronger than the sun-dried mud bricks of Sumer. The bricks in Harappa and Mohenjo-Daro were exactly the same size. The houses had no windows facing the street. The windows faced an open yard, which let sun and light into the house. Many homes had baths. Pipes along the streets drained the bath water out of the house.

Necklace from Mohenjo-Daro

These ruins are from Mohenjo-Daro.

Harappa and Mohenjo-Daro had no temples. They did, however, have a large **citadel**, or fort. The citadel at Mohenjo-Daro was five stories high and had many rooms. Next to the citadel was a **granary**. This was where extra grain was kept. When there was not enough food, the people took the extra grain out of the granary.

## Mysterious End and New Beginning

Around 1500 B.C., both cities were deserted. What caused this? Was it a flood? Was it an earthquake? Did the climate suddenly change? No one knows for sure.

About the same time, a group of warriors arrived from western and central Asia. They were called Aryans. Aryan means "noble one." These people brought the horse and the chariot to the Indus River valley. They also brought the Aryan language and religion throughout the Indian subcontinent. The Aryans mixed with the local people to produce a new way of life.

## Aryan Beliefs

At first, Aryans passed down their religious beliefs by word of mouth. Later they wrote down their religious stories and poems in a collection of books. It took hundreds of years to finish them. These books are called the **Vedas**.

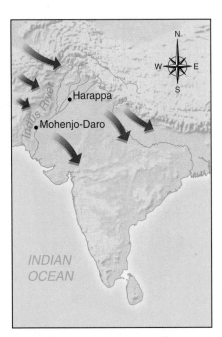
Aryan Movement into India

The oldest book is the Rig-Veda. One part tells how people were born into different classes, or **castes**. At the top was the priest, or **Brahman**. Then came the warrior. Next came the trader, or merchant. The bottom person was the worker.

Below the caste system were a group called the **untouchables**. These people were thought to be dirty and not pure. They had to do the worst jobs in the city. They had to pick up garbage and clean the dirty streets.

Another part of the Rig-Veda teaches people not to be greedy. It encourages them to give food to the hungry.

A Brahman

66When the needy [man] comes . . . begging for bread to eat, [he who] hardens his heart against him . . . [will find no one] to comfort him.99

# Lesson 2 Review

Choose words from the list that best complete the paragraphs. One word will not be used.

India is often called a __1__. Civilizations there developed along the Indus River. The city of __2__ had organized streets. The people there also made pottery, jewelry, and cotton crafts.

Harappa and Mohenjo-Daro came to an end around 1500 B.C. No one knows why. The __3__ were the next group to enter the region. They came from western and central Asia. They wrote religious books called the Vedas. The Vedas taught that everyone belonged in a certain caste. The highest caste was the __4__. Below all the castes were the untouchables.

**Word List**

Harappa

citadel

subcontinent

Aryans

Brahman

### Summary

- China was separated from other civilizations by deserts, mountains, and the Pacific Ocean.

- Early Chinese civilization began along the Huang He. Yangshao and Longshan were two early Chinese cities.

- The Shang Dynasty came to power around 1750 B.C. The Zhou Dynasty ruled by the Mandate of Heaven.

- India is surrounded by two mountain ranges and the Indian Ocean.

- Harappa and Mohenjo-Daro were two cities on the Indus River.

- The Aryans brought their language and religion to India around 1500 B.C.

## Find Out More!

After reading Chapter 4, you're ready to go online. **Explore Zone**, **Quiz Time**, and **Amazing Facts** bring this chapter of world history alive.

Visit www.exploreSV.com and type in the chapter code 1-Ch4.

### Vocabulary

Number your paper from 1 to 6. Write the word or words from the list that best complete the paragraphs. One word will not be used.

The history of early Chinese civilization is mixed with __1__. Archaeologists now know about the history of China from objects they have found. Some of these objects are made from __2__, a hard metal made by mixing copper and tin. The Chinese believed their gods put the ruling family in power. This special right was called the __3__.

India is sometimes called a __4__ because it is a huge piece of land. The ancient Indian cities of Harappa and Mohenjo-Daro had __5__, or forts. Each city also had a __6__ where grain was kept.

**Word List**

legends

granary

bronze

Mandate of Heaven

citadels

millet

subcontinent

## Comprehension

Number your paper from 1 to 4. Write the letter of the correct answer.

1. Where did the Chinese build their first civilization?
   **a.** along the Huang He        **c.** in a desert
   **b.** on a subcontinent         **d.** in high mountains

2. Who took power away from the Shang Dynasty in China?
   **a.** Aryans                    **c.** Tang
   **b.** Zhou                      **d.** Philistines

3. Where did the early civilizations of India begin?
   **a.** in Longshan               **c.** in the Indus River valley
   **b.** in the Himalayas          **d.** in the Hindu Kush

4. Which group of people were in the highest caste?
   **a.** warriors                  **c.** untouchables
   **b.** Brahmans                  **d.** workers

## Critical Thinking

**Fact or Opinion**   Number your paper from 1 to 5. For each fact, write **Fact**. Write **Opinion** for each opinion. You should find three sentences that are opinions.

1. Early farming villages appeared in China around 5000 B.C.
2. Archaeologists find Yangshao more interesting than Longshan.
3. Harappa was the best city of all early civilizations.
4. The people of Mohenjo-Daro traded with civilizations far away.
5. The Vedas contain the most beautiful ancient stories and poems.

## Writing

Write a paragraph explaining how the Shang used oracle bones to try to tell the future.

## Skill Builder: Reading a Timeline

A **timeline** shows the order in which events happened. A timeline also helps us see how much time there was between events. Dates tell us when events in history happened.

We say that events happened before or after the birth of a man called Jesus. Jesus was a religious leader you will read about in Chapter 9. Events that happened before Jesus' birth are marked **B.C.** Events that happened after Jesus' birth are marked **A.D.** When counting years before Jesus' birth, the highest number tells the oldest event. When counting years after Jesus' birth, the lowest number tells the oldest event. Read the timeline from left to right.

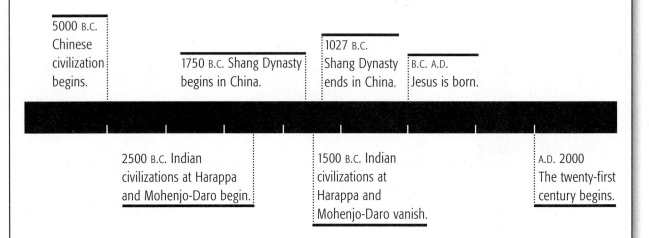

5000 B.C. Chinese civilization begins.

1750 B.C. Shang Dynasty begins in China.

1027 B.C. Shang Dynasty ends in China.

B.C. A.D. Jesus is born.

2500 B.C. Indian civilizations at Harappa and Mohenjo-Daro begin.

1500 B.C. Indian civilizations at Harappa and Mohenjo-Daro vanish.

A.D. 2000 The twenty-first century begins.

**Number your paper from 1 to 5. Answer each question with a complete sentence.**

1. Did the events in ancient China and ancient India happen before or after Jesus' birth?

2. Which is older: 1500 B.C. or 2500 B.C.?

3. Did China or India have the first civilization?

4. In what year did the Harappa and Mohenjo-Daro civilizations vanish?

5. Between which dates did the Shang Dynasty rule?

**LESSON 1**

# The First Americans

## Before You Read

- How did early people get to the Americas?
- Why would a nomad become a settler?

You might have heard that Christopher Columbus reached the Americas in 1492. But he wasn't the first person to see the Americas. The first people arrived thousands of years earlier. Today these people are called Native Americans. We don't know exactly when they first arrived. Many scientists think it was around 13,000 B.C. Others think it was as early as 30,000 B.C.

## Crossing the Bering Strait

The first people in the Americas crossed the Bering Strait from Asia into North America. A **strait** is a thin body of water. It connects two larger bodies of water. Today, the Bering Strait connects the Pacific Ocean with the Arctic Ocean. It is 60 miles of open water.

**New Words**
strait
land bridge
migration
maize
population

**People and Places**
Americas
Native Americans
Bering Strait
Central America
Mexico

Ice floats in the cold water of the Bering Strait.

Early humans crossed the Bering Strait between Asia and North America.

During an Ice Age, the Pacific and Arctic oceans were 300 feet lower than they are now. Much of the water was trapped in glaciers. During that time, there was no water in what is now the Bering Strait. It was dry land. It served as a **land bridge** between Asia and North America.

Like all of the earliest humans, the people who used the land bridge were nomads. They were traveling from Asia, looking for animals to hunt and plants to eat. They took only what they could carry. They didn't make clay pots or build temples. They left few clues about their lives.

Over thousands of years, the nomads spread out to the south and east. This is called a **migration**. They lived in small groups. Some groups stayed in North America. Others kept moving. Some settled in Central America. Others kept going until they reached South America.

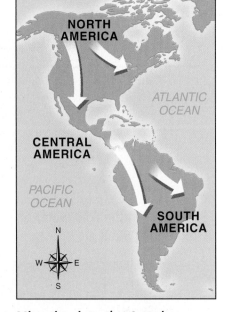

Migration into the Americas

## First Farming

The men hunted most of the time. Like other Stone Age people, the early Americans hunted using sharp spears made from stones. They hunted mammoths and other animals. The women and children gathered berries, nuts, and seeds.

Around 8000 B.C., the climate changed. The mammoth and other large animals did not survive. Hunters could only hunt smaller animals such as foxes, deer, and rabbits.

Some people began to put seeds into the ground. These Americans began farming in the area we call Mexico. They began farming around the same time as people in Egypt, Mesopotamia, China, and the Indus River valley. The early Americans planted beans, potatoes, squash, pumpkins, and peppers.

The most important crop was corn. The Americans called it **maize**. They learned how to mix wild maize with other grasses. They could grind the corn to use it in cooking.

Farming gave the Americans a steady food supply, which allowed the **population** to grow. Villages developed and grew. A steady food supply allowed for the building of cities and the beginning of civilization in the Americas.

Corn is still a common food in Central America.

# Lesson 1 Review

Choose words from the list that best complete the paragraphs. One word will not be used.

People came to North America many thousands of years ago. They walked from Asia across the ___1___ . There was a land bridge between Asia and North America. These early Americans were ___2___ who moved from place to place.

Early Americans hunted for food and gathered plants. The first farms developed in the modern country of ___3___ . An important crop was ___4___ . Farming gave the early Americans a steady food supply. American civilizations soon followed.

**Word List**

maize

population

nomads

Mexico

Bering Strait ·

## LESSON 2

# Early American Civilizations

## New Words

basalt
calendar
shamans
jaguar

## People and Places

Olmecs
Caral
Gulf of Mexico
La Venta
Peru
Supe River

## Before You Read

- How do scientists learn about early people?
- How are games important to people?

For a long time, no one knew about the early American civilizations. Many of their cities and objects were buried under deep grasses and hard clay. One group, the Olmecs, lived in the area that is now Mexico. In South America, an old city named Caral was discovered only recently. Both early American civilizations are some of the most mysterious of the ancient world.

## The Olmecs

The Olmec civilization began about 1500 B.C. Like all early civilizations, it developed in an area that supported farming. The Olmecs settled along the Gulf of Mexico and built large religious centers. One such center was La Venta.

The Olmecs built huge statues of heads.

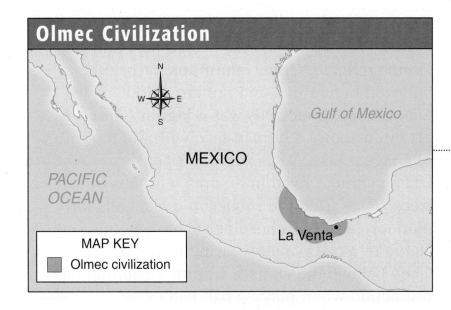

## Olmec Civilization

MAP KEY
■ Olmec civilization

The Olmecs settled in modern-day Mexico. Along what body of water did they settle?

The Olmecs are most famous for their huge statues of heads. The heads were probably those of kings. They ranged in height from 5 feet to 11 feet. They weighed as much as 20 tons. The Olmecs made the heads out of a volcanic rock called **basalt**. But there was no basalt where the Olmecs lived. They had to bring the rock from as far as 80 miles away. How they did that is a mystery.

They might have carved the heads and then hauled them over land. But that would have been difficult since the Olmecs didn't use wheels. They also didn't use animals to pull heavy loads. Maybe the Olmecs floated the basalt heads on rafts down rivers. Then they could have placed the carved heads on land. But how would they have gotten them up the hills? No one really knows.

The Olmecs might have floated their statues on rafts.

### Life for the Olmecs

The Olmecs built farms and made pottery. They studied the stars and made a **calendar**. They knew mathematics. They developed a writing system, too. The Olmecs used hieroglyphics. The Olmec hieroglyphics were very different from Egyptian hieroglyphics. Scientists have learned only recently what some of the Olmec pictures mean. One stone tells of a leader who could turn himself into an animal.

This statue has both human and jaguar features.

Early Americans playing an outdoor ball game

Animals played a big role in the lives of the Olmec people. They were even a part of the Olmec religion. Olmec **shamans**, or priests, believed the animal and human worlds mixed. One of the Olmec gods was a **jaguar**. Olmec art often shows a human face with the mouth of a jaguar.

The Olmecs lived in an area with lots of rubber trees. They used the rubber to make balls for outdoor games. Archaeologists have found a statue of a ball player wearing heavy padding. They believe the Olmecs wore the padding for protection when playing ball games.

The Olmecs disappeared around 300 B.C. No one knows why this civilization disappeared. It is another mystery. But many of the arts and skills of the Olmecs were passed on to the civilizations that followed.

## Discovery in South America

Archaeologists continue to learn more about ancient civilizations. They used to think that the Olmecs were the oldest civilization in the Americas. But in 2001, they announced that an older city had been found in Peru. This city is called Caral.

Archaeologists are still learning about the ancient city of Caral in Peru.

Caral was in the Supe River valley not far from the Pacific Ocean. It dates back to 2627 B.C., which means it is 1,100 years older than any Olmec city.

For its time, Caral was a large city. As many as 10,000 people might have lived there. Caral had six great pyramids. The people in Caral were building pyramids around the same time as people in the Old Kingdom of Egypt. But the pyramids in Caral were not as tall as those in Egypt. The biggest pyramid in Caral was 60 feet high and 500 feet long. The people of Caral built the pyramids with stones and mud. They did all this without using wheels or metal tools.

The people of Caral grew a few vegetables. They ate a lot of fish. They also used dried fish as money. They traded with people who lived in small fishing villages on the coast. One thing they traded was cotton. The villagers used the cotton to make fishing nets.

Fish hung up to dry

# Lesson 2 Review

Choose words from the list that best complete the paragraphs. One word will not be used.

The Olmec civilization was located in modern-day __1__. It dates back to 1500 B.C. The Olmecs are known for their huge statues of heads. These heads were made from __2__. The Olmecs made fine pottery and developed their own calendar and writing system. Their shamans believed the human and animal worlds were mixed.

The oldest known city in the Americas is Caral, located in __3__. It dates back to 2627 B.C. The people there built pyramids. Their pyramids were built with stones and __4__. The people of Caral ate vegetables and fish.

**Word List**

basalt

Peru

rafts

Mexico

mud

## Summary

- The first people to come to the Americas were nomads. They crossed a land bridge from Asia to Alaska, where the Bering Strait is today.

- Over thousands of years, these nomads spread out across North America and South America. In time, they settled and learned to farm.

- The Olmecs built a civilization in ancient Mexico about 3,500 years ago. They are known for building giant stone heads. They also developed a calendar and played ball games.

- In 2001, archaeologists learned that the city of Caral in Peru is the oldest known civilization in the Americas.

## Find Out More!

After reading Chapter 5, you're ready to go online. **Explore Zone**, **Quiz Time**, and **Amazing Facts** bring this chapter of world history alive.

Visit www.exploreSV.com and type in the chapter code **1-Ch5**.

## Vocabulary

Number your paper from 1 to 6. Write the word or words from the list that best complete each sentence. One word will not be used.

1. A thin body of water that connects two larger bodies of water is called a _____.

2. Early people came to the Americas across a _____.

3. People moving across a large area is called a _____.

4. The most important crop for early farmers in ancient Mexico was _____.

5. The Olmecs studied the stars and developed a _____.

6. Olmec priests were called _____.

### Word List

shamans

calendar

maize

basalt

land bridge

migration

strait

## Comprehension

Number your paper from 1 to 5. Write the word from the list that best completes the paragraph. One word will not be used.

The first people in the Americas crossed the Bering Strait. A __1__ is a thin body of water that connects two larger bodies of water. The early people who came to North America from Asia were __2__ who traveled looking for food. The early Americans hunted __3__. Around 8000 B.C., some Americans began to farm in the area now called __4__. Archaeologists think that the city called Caral is the oldest __5__ in the Americas.

**Word List**

civilization

domesticate

strait

nomads

mammoths

Mexico

## Critical Thinking

**Main Idea**  Number your paper from 1 to 4. Write the sentence that is the main idea in each group.

1. Many scientists think people came to the Americas in 13,000 B.C.
   Some think people came to the Americas in 30,000 B.C.
   We don't know exactly when people first arrived in the Americas.

2. Farming gave early people in the Americas a steady food supply.
   More people began to live in villages and cities.
   A steady food supply helped villages and cities in the Americas grow.

3. La Venta was an important early Olmec religious center.
   Two of the earliest civilizations in the Americas were La Venta and Caral.
   Caral, an old city in South America, was found just recently.

4. One of the Olmec gods was a jaguar.
   Animals played an important part in the lives of the Olmecs.
   Olmec art often shows animals such as the jaguar.

## Writing

Write a paragraph describing a day in the life of a person living in an Olmec civilization.

# Vast Empires and World Religions

## 600 B.C.–A.D. 500

These years in history are marked by new ideas. Some people changed the way they thought about government. Others made discoveries in science and medicine. Still others began practicing new religions.

This unit tells about the rise and fall of some of the world's greatest empires. These empires gained vast lands from 600 B.C. to A.D. 500. Each empire helped shape our modern world. They gave us modern religions and modern languages. They brought us closer to the way of life we know today.

| B.C. | 600 | 500 | 400 | 300 | 200 | 100 |
|------|-----|-----|-----|-----|-----|-----|

**500 B.C.**
**The city of Monte Albán is built on a mountaintop in Central America.**

**338 B.C.**
**Alexander the Great starts his journey to rule the world.**

B.C. A.D.    100    200    300    400    500    A.D. ▶

**44 B.C.**
**Julius Caesar is**
**killed in Rome.**

**A.D. 200**
**Outsiders cross**
**the Great Wall**
**of China and end**
**the Han Dynasty.**

**A.D. 476**
**Visigoths and other**
**groups bring the**
**Roman Empire to**
**an end.**

63

## LESSON 1

# Africa After the New Kingdom

**New Words**

culture

iron ore

caravans

resources

artifacts

terracotta

**People and Places**

Kerma

Napata

Meroe

Sudan

Ezana

Axum

Ethiopia

Nok

West Africa

Nigeria

**Before You Read**

- Why do we study civilizations that have ended?
- Why are trade routes important to a civilization?

You have read how some early civilizations came to an end. Some were taken over by nearby civilizations. Others fell because the people fought one another for power.

Even when civilizations fall, however, they remain important. People today can enjoy the art, writings, and buildings of civilizations from long ago. People also can learn from the mistakes of past civilizations. That is one reason to study history—to learn from the past.

Students look at King Tut's mummy case in the Egyptian Museum.

This Egyptian art was created during Kushite rule.

## Kush Rule Over Egypt

The Egyptian pharaohs began losing power during the New Kingdom. As the pharaohs lost power, Egypt became weak. It could no longer control the lands of Kush, to the South.

The trouble in the New Kingdom gave the people of Kush a chance to rule themselves. About 1100 B.C., they moved their capital from Kerma to a city further south called Napata. The Kush people thought of themselves as Egyptians. They shared much of Egyptian **culture**. They had the same gods. The Kushites even called their leaders pharaohs.

Kush got stronger while Egypt got weaker. Around 710 B.C., a Kushite pharaoh took over much of Egypt. Kushite pharaohs ruled Egypt for almost 50 years. They learned Egyptian hieroglyphics and repaired Egyptian temples.

Kushite rule of Egypt came to an end in 671 B.C. The Assyrians, who had already taken control of Mesopotamia, invaded Egypt. The Assyrians defeated the Kushites. The Assyrians used powerful iron weapons. They had learned how to use iron from the Hittites.

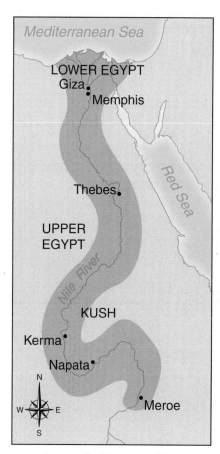

Area Controlled by Kingdom of Kush, 710 B.C.–671 B.C.

The Kushite civilization did not end when the Assyrians took over Egypt. The Kushite people moved their capital even further south to a city called Meroe. There they began building a new kingdom.

## New Capital at Meroe

The Kingdom of Kush was located in the area of modern-day Sudan. The city of Meroe was at a meeting point for many of the old Nubian trade routes. Meroe became a leading trading center. It was such an important city that this time in African history is called the Meroitic Period. The Meroitic Period lasted from about 270 B.C. to A.D. 330.

The Kushite people learned how to make iron from the Assyrians. They found that there was a great amount of **iron ore** in Meroe. During the Meroitic Period, Meroe became the East African leader in iron making.

**Caravans**, or groups of people traveling through the desert, stopped in Meroe. Some came from Southwest Asia and India. Others came from areas in western and southern Africa. The groups came to trade gold, spices, and other goods and **resources**.

Meroitic bowl

These iron tools were made by the people of Meroe.

The Kushite people kept many of their old Egyptian ways. But Meroe was far away from Egypt. So the Kush also developed a culture of their own. For example, the Meroitic women were much more involved in government than Egyptian women were. Some Meroitic carvings even show women holding swords in battle.

## The Rise of Axum

Meroe was a strong trading center when trading was done by land. But around A.D. 200, people began building ports along the Red Sea. Many traders used the sea routes instead of land routes.

Around A.D. 300, Ezana, the king of Axum, invaded the Kush kingdom. Axum was a kingdom on the Red Sea. Axum was located in the part of eastern Africa that is Ethiopia today. When Ezana defeated the Kushites, Axum took the place of Meroe as a leading trading center.

The people of Axum grew rich. As a trading center, people in Axum learned about the many changes happening in the world. Meroe, on the other hand, lost its importance as Axum grew. By A.D. 500, the Kushite culture had disappeared.

Meroitic silver with jewels

Around A.D. 200, people began trading across the Red Sea. Which kingdom was located along the Red Sea?

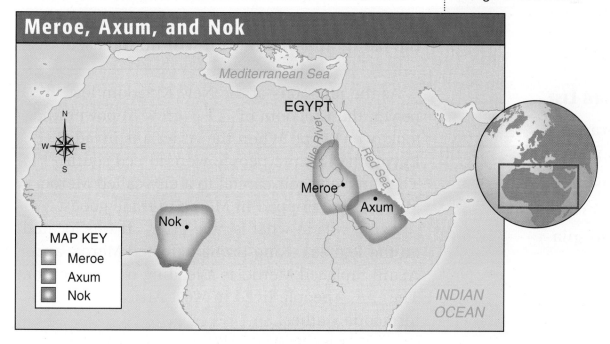

Meroe, Axum, and Nok

MAP KEY
Meroe
Axum
Nok

## The Nok People

There were other civilizations in Africa, but scientists today know little about them. The Nok civilization was in West Africa in what is now Nigeria. The Nok people lived sometime between 900 B.C. and A.D. 200. Very little is known about this group. Scientists don't even know what they called themselves. The name *Nok* comes from the present-day Nigerian town of Nok. That is where many of the Nok **artifacts** have been found.

The Nok people probably knew how to work with iron and tin. They also knew how to bake clay with sand to make **terracotta**. The Nok people shaped this clay to make statues. The most famous Nok artifacts are terracotta statues that show human faces.

Nok terracotta statue

# Lesson 1 Review

Choose words from the list that best complete the paragraphs. One word will not be used.

**Word List**

caravans

Nok

Kush

Nigeria

Ethiopia

As the pharaohs of the New Kingdom lost power, the Kingdom of __1__ grew in power and took over Egypt. When the Assyrians invaded Egypt, the Kushite people were forced south. They moved their capital to a city called Meroe. Many __2__ stopped in Meroe to trade goods.

Axum was in what is now __3__. It was located on the Red Sea. King Ezana defeated Meroe, and Axum replaced Meroe as a leading trading center. The __4__ people lived in West Africa and made terracotta statues.

## LESSON 2

# Central America

Monte Albán
funerary urn

### Before You Read

- Why did early civilizations want to please their gods?

- How did they try to please their gods?

A city called Monte Albán began in Central America around 500 B.C. Another city called Teotihuacán formed north of Monte Albán around 200 B.C. These two cities had much in common. They both had pyramids and temples. They both had great **plazas**, or big open areas. Both cities continued to grow for several centuries. Both cities began to disappear around A.D. 700.

### Monte Albán

A group called the Zapotec built the city of Monte Albán. They built it on flat land at the top of a mountain. The city looked over the area now called the Oaxaca Valley. The Zapotec stayed in the city for around 1,200 years.

### New Words

plazas
bas-reliefs
terraces
sacrifice
peninsula
slash-and-burn

### People and Places

Monte Albán
Teotihuacán
Zapotec
Oaxaca Valley
Maya
Yucatan Peninsula

The ruins of Monte Albán are in modern-day Mexico.

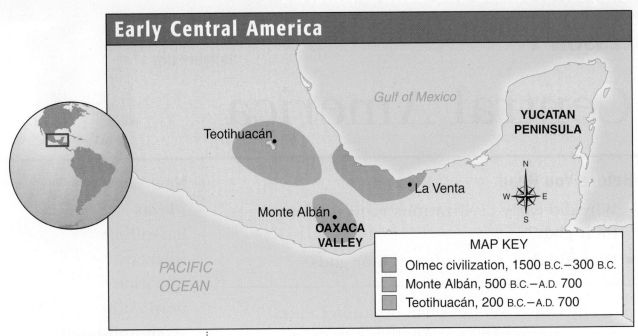

## Early Central America

Teotihuacán

Gulf of Mexico

YUCATAN PENINSULA

La Venta

Monte Albán

OAXACA VALLEY

PACIFIC OCEAN

N W E S

MAP KEY
Olmec civilization, 1500 B.C.–300 B.C.
Monte Albán, 500 B.C.–A.D. 700
Teotihuacán, 200 B.C.–A.D. 700

Early Central America was home to some of the first American civilizations. Which civilization began around 500 B.C.?

Bas-relief from the Building of the Dancers

A huge plaza filled the center of Monte Albán. Temples, homes, and tombs surrounded the plaza. The king's palace was also there. There was even a courtyard where they played ball games.

One place was the Building of the Dancers. The name comes from the **bas-reliefs**, or carvings made on a flat surface. The bas-reliefs show human figures in twisted shapes. A long time ago, someone called the figures dancers. Today, scientists don't know whether the figures really were dancers. The human figures look very similar to those in Olmec art. The people of Monte Albán probably traded with the Olmecs.

Monte Albán was high and dry. It was not a good place to grow crops. Zapotec farmers went to the valley below to grow corn, squash, and beans. The valley farmers grew enough food each year to feed the 17,500 people in the city.

The Zapotec left the city of Monte Albán around A.D. 700. No one knows why. There might have been a climate change. The soil might have stopped producing crops. Perhaps there was a disease or war that destroyed the city.

## Teotihuacán

Teotihuacán was built about 200 miles northwest of Monte Albán. It was a huge city that covered more than seven square miles. By A.D. 400, more than 100,000 people lived there.

*Teotihuacán* means "City of the Gods." The people of Teotihuacán believed in many gods. These included gods of the sun, rain, corn, and fire. The people believed these gods controlled the crops. They worked hard to please the gods so that the land would produce good crops.

The city of Teotihuacán had a large plaza and wide streets. One two-mile road was called the Avenue of the Dead. It was lined with pyramids, temples, and palaces.

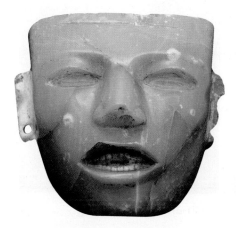

Mask from Teotihuacán

One pyramid was the Pyramid of the Sun. It had five **terraces**, or levels, and was 216 feet high. It was one of the largest pyramids in the world.

The people of Teotihuacán believed that one way to please the gods was to offer human **sacrifice**. This killing of people was not done to be cruel. The people felt that without human sacrifice, the gods would die. Then all the crops would fail, and all the people would die.

Around A.D. 650, invaders attacked Teotihuacán and burned the city. Who attacked the city and why they did so remain a mystery.

The Pyramid of the Sun was the largest building in Teotihuacán.

## Early Maya

Around 200 B.C., people called the Maya settled in an area now called the Yucatan Peninsula. A **peninsula** is a large piece of land that is mostly surrounded by water. The Maya had good farming methods. They used a **slash-and-burn** method to clear lands for farming. They cut down the plants and burned the fields. This kept the soil rich for long periods of time. Also, fields in lower areas sometimes had large puddles of standing water. So, the early Maya built raised fields. This kept their crops from rotting.

These farming methods helped the Maya become wealthy. They started building stone temples to honor their gods. By A.D. 250, many Mayan villages had grown into organized cities with massive temples. This was the beginning of one of the most remarkable civilizations of Central America.

Slash-and-burn farming

# Lesson 2 Review

Choose words from the list that best complete the paragraphs. One word will not be used.

**Word List**

Sun
bas-reliefs
sacrifice
slash-and-burn
Teotihuacán

Monte Albán was an ancient city in Central America. It is known for its __1__. These carvings show human figures in twisted shapes.

The largest city in Central America at this time was __2__. It had as many as 100,000 people. The people of Teotihuacán honored many gods. They felt they needed to please the gods in order to stay alive. The Pyramid of the __3__ had five terraces. It was one of the tallest pyramids in the world.

Another civilization, the Maya, began to grow. They used a __4__ method for farming and built raised fields.

### Summary

- Meroe, the last capital of the Kingdom of Kush, was an important trading center.

- Ezana of Axum defeated the Kush kingdom around A.D. 300. Axum became the main trading center in Africa.

- The Nok lived in West Africa between 900 B.C. and A.D. 200. Very little is known about the Nok culture.

- Monte Albán and Teotihuacán were two large cities in early Central America. Both cities had temples and pyramids. Both cities began to disappear around A.D. 700.

## Find Out More!

After reading Chapter 6, you're ready to go online. **Explore Zone**, **Quiz Time**, and **Amazing Facts** bring this chapter of world history alive.

Visit www.exploreSV.com and type in the chapter code **1-Ch6**.

### Vocabulary

Number your paper from 1 to 5. Finish the sentences from Group A with words from Group B. Write the letter of the correct answer.

**Group A**

1. The _____ of the Kush people was like that of the Egyptians.

2. Meroe was a trading center where _____ stopped to trade gold, spices, and other goods.

3. The Nok people made _____ by baking clay with sand.

4. Cities in ancient Central America had big open areas called _____.

5. The Pyramid of the Sun had five _____, or levels.

**Group B**

a. terracotta

b. caravans

c. terraces

d. plazas

e. culture

## Comprehension

Number your paper from 1 to 5. Write one or more sentences to answer each question below.

1. What did the Assyrians use to defeat Egypt?

2. Why did Axum become a leading trading center?

3. What are two things the cities of Monte Albán and Teotihuacán had in common?

4. What are two possible reasons that the Zapotec left Monte Albán?

5. Why did the people of Teotihuacán work hard to please their gods?

## Critical Thinking

**Categories**   Number your paper from 1 to 5. Read the words in each group below. Think about how they are alike. Write the best title for each group.

| Monte Albán | Meroe | Nok | Teotihuacán | Axum |

1. Kushite capital
   iron-making center
   early trading center

2. port on Red Sea
   King Ezana
   located in what is
      Ethiopia today

3. civilization in West Africa
   little is known about
   made terracotta statues

4. built by Zapotec
   Building of the Dancers
   built on the top of a mountain

5. "City of the Gods"
   Avenue of the Dead
   Pyramid of the Sun

## Writing

Write a paragraph describing how the Egyptian and the Kushite cultures were alike and how they were different.

## Skill Builder: Using a Map Key and Map Directions

**Map Key**  Sometimes a map uses colors or symbols to show important things on the map. A **map key** tells what the colors or symbols mean. Study the map key on the map below.

Number your paper from 1 to 3. Write the answers to the questions.

1. What symbol is used to show a river? Name a river shown on the map.

2. What is the symbol for a city? Name a city shown on the map.

3. What color is used to show where the Olmecs lived?

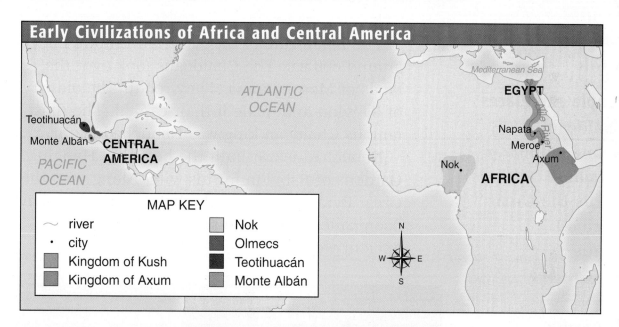

**Early Civilizations of Africa and Central America**

ATLANTIC OCEAN

Teotihuacán

Monte Albán  **CENTRAL AMERICA**

PACIFIC OCEAN

Mediterranean Sea

**EGYPT**

Napata

Meroe

Nok

Axum

**AFRICA**

MAP KEY
~ river
· city
Kingdom of Kush
Kingdom of Axum
Nok
Olmecs
Teotihuacán
Monte Albán

**Map Directions**  The four main directions are **north**, **south**, **west**, and **east**. Maps use a **compass rose** to show these directions. The compass rose shortens the directions to **N**, **S**, **W**, and **E**.

Number your paper from 1 to 4. Write **north**, **south**, **west**, or **east** to complete each sentence.

1. The Kingdom of Kush is _____ of the Mediterranean Sea.

2. The Olmecs lived _____ of Teotihuacán.

3. Meroe is _____ of Axum.

4. Central America is _____ of Africa.

## LESSON 1

# The Persian Empire

### New Words

conquered
tolerance
tribute
provinces
daric
Zoroastrianism
revolt

### People and Places

Chaldeans
Nebuchadnezzar
Persians
Cyrus the Great
Darius I
Sardis
Aegean Sea
Susa
Zoroaster
Greece
Marathon
Athens
Xerxes

### Before You Read

- Why might a large empire be difficult to hold together?
- How might a smaller army defeat a larger army?

The harsh rule of the Assyrian Empire ended around 600 B.C. The Chaldeans took over the lands of Mesopotamia. They rebuilt the old city of Babylon and made it their capital. The most famous Chaldean king was Nebuchadnezzar.

Nebuchadnezzar built the beautiful Hanging Gardens of Babylon for his wife. Along with the Great Pyramid at Giza, the hanging gardens have been called one of the seven wonders of the ancient world.

The Hanging Gardens of Babylon

Like the Assyrians, the Chaldeans were harsh rulers. But in 539 B.C., the Persians attacked Babylon and ended the Chaldean Empire.

## The Persian Empire

The Persians came from lands in what is today the country of Iran. From about 600 B.C. to 500 B.C., they **conquered** a huge area of land. The first king of the Persians was Cyrus the Great.

Cyrus the Great practiced **tolerance**. He told his soldiers not to harm the people they conquered and not to burn their temples. He also was kind to the Jews. The Chaldeans had attacked Judah and forced the Jews to work as slaves in Babylon. Cyrus let them go back to their homes. He allowed conquered people to keep their customs. They could keep their religions and their languages. In return, the people paid **tribute**, or a kind of tax, to the king.

Cyrus the Great returned objects to the Jewish temple.

## Controlling the Empire

In 522 B.C., Darius I became the leader of the Persians. Darius was a strong king. He rewarded his friends and punished his enemies. This is shown by the words carved into the side of a cliff in Persia.

**"The man who was loyal, him I rewarded well, [but he] who was evil, him I punished well."**

**Voices**
**In History**

The Persian Empire stretched from Egypt to India. Darius needed to find a way to control such a large empire. He divided his empire into **provinces**. He put a noble in charge of each province. He gave the nobles a lot of power. But he didn't trust them completely. He sent spies to each province to watch over the nobles. The spies were called the "Eyes and Ears of the King."

## The Persian Empire

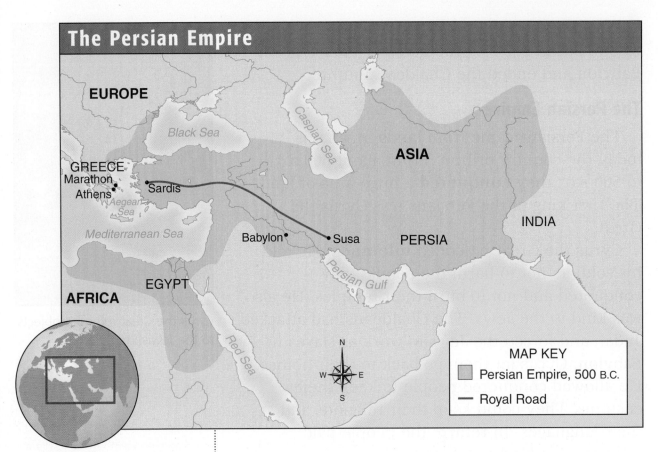

The Persian Empire controlled lands in Europe, Africa, and Asia. Which two cities did the Royal Road connect?

Persian daric

It took many months to get a message from one end of the empire to the other. To solve this problem, the Persians built roads. The longest was the Royal Road. It went from Sardis, near the Aegean Sea, to Susa, near the Persian Gulf. It was nearly 1,700 miles long.

The Persians used horses to travel on the Royal Road. A rider would run a horse as fast and as far as the horse could go. Then the rider chose a new horse and rode off again. The Royal Road had 111 stops for riders to change horses. Before using the system of horses, it took traders three months to travel the Royal Road. But with the horses, a message could reach the king in one week.

People traveling along the Persian roads would sometimes have to pay taxes. The Persians developed a money system based on a gold coin called the **daric**. The Persian daric became the coin used by traders from Southwest Asia, Egypt, and Europe.

## Religion in Persia

Like other ancient people, the Persians had many gods. But around 600 B.C., a new religious leader appeared in Persia. His Greek name was Zoroaster. His religion became known as **Zoroastrianism**.

Zoroaster told people there were two gods in the world. The highest god, Ahura Mazda, stood for goodness and light. The lesser god, Ahriman, stood for evil and darkness. Zoroaster also taught that there was life after death. Good people were rewarded. Bad people were punished. The teachings of Zoroaster spread. His ideas about good and evil were adopted by other religions.

Ahura Mazda

## The Persian Wars

Most of the time, the Persians enjoyed one victory after another. But they could not conquer the people of Greece. The Greeks had little land and a much smaller population. But they had strong fighters.

The Persian Wars started when Greek city-states within the Persian Empire refused to pay tribute to Darius, the Persian king. Greek city-states outside the Persian Empire helped in a **revolt** against Darius. The Persian army was able to stop the revolt. But Darius wanted to punish the Greeks.

The Greeks and the Persians fought in the Persian Wars.

In 490 B.C., Darius sent an army into the town of Marathon, Greece. The Persians had more men than the Greeks. But the Greeks did not give up.

The Greeks fought well and defeated the Persian army. According to legend, a runner raced 26 miles from Marathon to the Greek city-state of Athens with the news. This is why today we use the word *marathon* to describe a very long race.

In 480 B.C., Xerxes, the son of Darius, attacked the Greeks again. He sent a huge army and navy to Greece. The Persians captured Athens. But the Greeks fought hard. They defeated Xerxes and sent him back to Persia. The Greeks prevented the Persians from taking any more land. By around 350 B.C., the Persian Empire had lost most of its power.

Persian guards

## Lesson 1 Review

Choose words from the list that best complete the paragraphs. One word will not be used.

**Word List**

Cyrus

Greeks

Marathon

Zoroaster

Darius

The Chaldeans ruled after the Assyrians. They were followed by the Persians. The first Persian king was __1__. He was known for his tolerance. He let people keep their customs. Another king, __2__, divided the Persian Empire into provinces. He put nobles in charge of the provinces.

The Persians built roads to improve travel. __3__ introduced the Persians to new religious ideas. The Persians tried to defeat the __4__ in 490 B.C. and 480 B.C., but they failed. The Persian Empire lost power over the next century and lost control of its vast lands.

## LESSON 2

# Ancient Greece

### Before You Read

- How were most early civilizations ruled?
- Why did early civilizations need strong armies?

Greece is on a peninsula that extends into the Mediterranean Sea. Some of the first civilizations in Europe began in Greece. The Greeks, like the Phoenicians, were a **maritime** people. Their way of life depended on the sea.

Greece had many mountains and few rivers. The soil of Greece was rocky and poor. The Greeks could not grow enough food. So they became traders and developed colonies. Their way of life spread to their many colonies.

### New Words
maritime
myth
epic
democracy
philosophy

### People and Places
Minoans
Crete
Mycenaeans
Troy
Homer
Sparta
Socrates
Plato
Aristotle
Pericles
Macedonia
Alexander the Great

This Greek city was built on the rocky soil of an erupted volcano.

## Did You Know?

### Dressing Up

Ancient Greeks liked to look good. They often wore clothes with symbols from their own city-state. Some of their clothes were dyed with bright colors. But white was also popular. The Greeks often added a jeweled ring or hair pin. As a final touch, they also wore perfume made from boiled flowers and herbs.

The Minoans and the Mycenaeans are the oldest known Greek civilizations. On what island did the Minoans live?

## Early Greek Civilizations

The first Greek civilization, the Minoan, began on the island of Crete. Around 1500 B.C., the Minoans were destroyed by a volcano. For a long time, people didn't know if the Minoans really existed. People thought the Minoan civilization was just a **myth**, or legend. Then archaeologists found the ruins of the Minoan civilization.

The Mycenaean civilization followed the Minoans. Around 1200 B.C., the Mycenaeans attacked Troy, a city across the Aegean Sea. Homer, a Greek poet, told the story of this battle in two **epic**, or long story, poems. The poems are called the *Iliad* and the *Odyssey*.

## Athens and Sparta

By around 500 B.C., Athens and Sparta were the most famous city-states of ancient Greece. The Athenians and the Spartans had much in common. They spoke the same language and believed in the same gods. They both enjoyed sports.

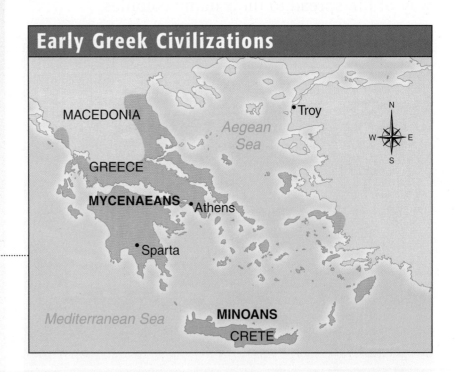

Early Greek Civilizations

The Greeks built huge outdoor theaters.

In other ways, Athens and Sparta were not alike. Athens had a direct **democracy**. The people ruled themselves. They could vote on issues facing the city. The Athenians enjoyed going to the theater. They also went dancing.

Athens was famous for **philosophy**. A philosopher is someone who likes to think and learn about life and its values. Socrates was a Greek philosopher who gained wisdom by asking many questions. Two other well-known philosophers from Greece were Plato and Aristotle.

Life in Sparta was different. Spartans did not have the same freedoms that the Athenians had. In Sparta, everyday life was centered around the army. Boys were taken from their homes at the age of seven. From then on they were taught to be warriors. They learned some reading and writing. But the main goal was to build their strength. The young boys lived under harsh rules.

Spartan soldier

## The Peloponnesian War

During the Persian Wars, Athens and Sparta joined together against the Persians. But by 431 B.C., Athens and Sparta both wanted to rule Greece. That year, Sparta attacked Athens, beginning the Peloponnesian War.

The leader of Athens was Pericles. He gave a speech praising the city of Athens, as well as those who died in battle.

**Voices**
**In History**

"Such is the city for whose sake these men . . . fought and died. They could not bear the thought that [Athens] might be taken from them."

The Peloponnesian War lasted 27 years. Athens had a strong navy. Sparta had a strong army. In the end, Sparta won the war and gained control of Greece.

## Alexander the Great

Macedonia was a kingdom north of the Greek city-states. It adopted much of the Greek culture. Around 357 B.C., King Phillip II of Macedonia began to take over the Greek city-states. He then planned to attack Persia. But Phillip was killed

Alexander the Great led his army from Macedonia and conquered the Persian Empire. Where did Alexander end his journey?

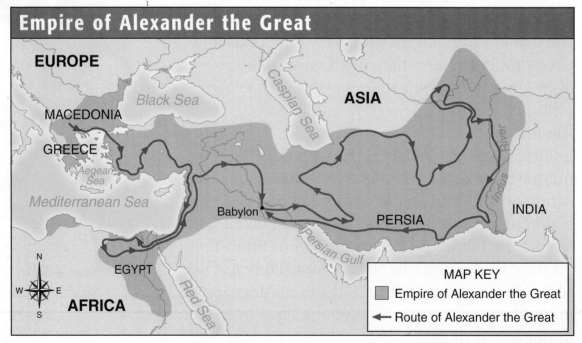

**Empire of Alexander the Great**

EUROPE

Black Sea

Caspian Sea

ASIA

MACEDONIA

GREECE

Aegean Sea

Mediterranean Sea

Babylon

PERSIA

Indus River

INDIA

Persian Gulf

EGYPT

Red Sea

AFRICA

N W E S

MAP KEY
▢ Empire of Alexander the Great
◄— Route of Alexander the Great

before he could attack. In 338 B.C., Phillip's 20-year-old son, Alexander, decided to carry out his father's plan. Alexander wanted more than Greece and Persia. He wanted to conquer the world.

Alexander first gained complete control of Greece. He then crossed into Asia and won battles in the western Persian Empire. Then he took control of Egypt. From there, he traveled east, conquering the rest of Persia. He continued all the way to the Indus River. But his tired army refused to go any further. Alexander and his army left India and headed home. In just over ten years, Alexander conquered and ruled one of the largest empires the world had ever seen. He died in Babylon three years later.

Without Alexander, the empire fell apart. But Greek culture spread throughout the vast lands. Many people admired the Greeks. They wanted to be like them. Greek culture remained strong for 300 years, until the rise of Rome.

Alexander the Great

# Lesson 2 Review

Choose words from the list that best complete the paragraphs. One word will not be used.

The Minoans and the __1__ were early Greek civilizations. Later, Athens and Sparta were two powerful city-states. The Athenians had a direct __2__ . They had much more freedom than the Spartans had.

After fighting the Persians, Athens and Sparta fought each other in the __3__ War. Sparta won and ruled Greece. Later, Alexander the Great conquered and ruled a huge empire. Greek __4__ spread and remained strong for 300 years.

**Word List**

culture

philosophy

Mycenaeans

democracy

Peloponnesian

### Summary

- Cyrus the Great and Darius I were two early Persian kings. The Greeks defeated the Persians twice in the Persian Wars.

- Two early Greek civilizations were the Minoan and the Mycenaean.

- The Athenians enjoyed philosophy and art, while the Spartans trained for war.

- Sparta and Athens fought each other in the Peloponnesian War. Sparta won and took control of Greece.

- Alexander the Great built a huge empire. After his death, Greek culture continued to spread.

### Find Out More!

After reading Chapter 7, you're ready to go online. **Explore Zone**, **Quiz Time**, and **Amazing Facts** bring this chapter of world history alive.

Visit www.exploreSV.com and type in the chapter code **1-Ch7**.

### Vocabulary

Number your paper from 1 to 5. Write the letter of the correct answer.

1. Cyrus practiced **tolerance**. He let conquered people _____.
   - **a.** keep their customs
   - **b.** play sports
   - **c.** pay taxes
   - **d.** vote for their leaders

2. **Tribute** is a kind of _____.
   - **a.** body of water
   - **b.** running race
   - **c.** statue
   - **d.** tax

3. The Persian _____ was based on the **daric**.
   - **a.** number system
   - **b.** writing system
   - **c.** land system
   - **d.** money system

4. An **epic** is a _____.
   - **a.** trade route
   - **b.** long story poem
   - **c.** big open area
   - **d.** method to clear lands

5. In a **democracy**, _____ rule themselves.
   - **a.** the people
   - **b.** warriors
   - **c.** pharaohs
   - **d.** shamans

## Comprehension

Number your paper from 1 to 5. Read each sentence below. Then write the name of the person or people who might have said each sentence. One name from the list will not be used.

1. "I was the Chaldean king who built the Hanging Gardens of Babylon."

2. "My ideas about good and evil were adopted by other religions."

3. "Our civilization was destroyed by a volcano around 1500 B.C."

4. "My long poems, the *Iliad* and the *Odyssey*, told about the Mycenaean's attack on Troy."

5. "I was a Greek philosopher who gained wisdom by asking questions."

### Word List

**Socrates**

**Zoroaster**

**Darius**

**Homer**

**Minoans**

**Nebuchadnezzar**

## Critical Thinking

**Points of View**   Number your paper from 1 to 5. Read each sentence below. Write **Sparta** if the point of view is from someone in Sparta. If the point of view is from someone in Athens, write **Athens**.

1. Every-day life should center around the army.

2. People should rule themselves and vote on issues about the city.

3. People should go to the theater.

4. It is important for boys to build their strength.

5. People should think and learn about life and its values.

## Writing

Write a paragraph that explains at least three ways that Cyrus practiced tolerance toward the people he conquered.

# LESSON 1

# Early Roman Republic

## New Words

republic
representatives
consuls
senate
dictator
patricians
plebeians
tribunes

## People and Places

Italy
Po River
Tiber River
Etruscans
Latins
Rome
Carthage
Hannibal
Alps

## Before You Read

- How might people take part in government?
- Why might early civilizations have wanted to control the Mediterranean Sea?

Like Greece, Italy is on a peninsula. The Italian Peninsula is shaped like a boot. Also like Greece, Italy has many mountains. Unlike Greece, however, Italy has two large rivers. The Po River is in the north. The Tiber River is in the center. Italy also has much more land that can be used for farming.

In ancient times, different people settled on and around the Italian Peninsula. Phoenicians set up colonies in the area. The Greeks built more than 50 city-states, passing their culture on to the local people. The Greeks taught the local people to grow grapes and olives. They showed them how to build with stone. They also shared the Greek alphabet. This was the beginning of the Latin language.

Some letters of the Greek alphabet look like letters in today's English language.

## The Early Roman Republic

A group of people called the Etruscans settled in northern Italy around 800 B.C. No one knows exactly where they came from. They began to expand their territory. Around 600 B.C., the Etruscans conquered the Latins who lived in the central part of the peninsula. One Latin village was called Rome. The Etruscans drained the marshes near Rome. This gave them more land on which to build. Under Etruscan rule, Rome grew into a city.

The Etruscan kings were often cruel. In 509 B.C., the Romans rebelled. They sent the Etruscan king out of Rome and set up a new kind of government. They called the new government a **republic**. It was similar to the government in Athens because the people could vote.

But Athens had a direct democracy. The people voted on each issue. Rome, however, set up an indirect democracy. The people voted for leaders. The leaders then voted on different issues. The leaders were called **representatives** because they represented the people. Different forms of representative government are still used today in the United States and other countries.

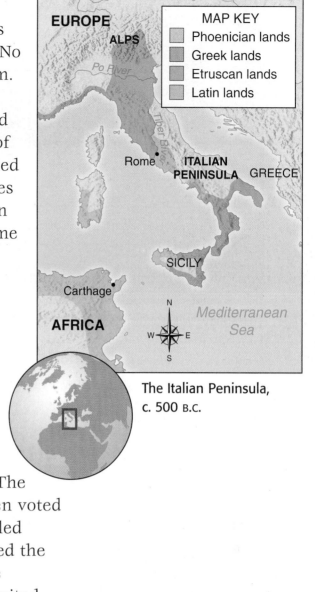

The Italian Peninsula, c. 500 B.C.

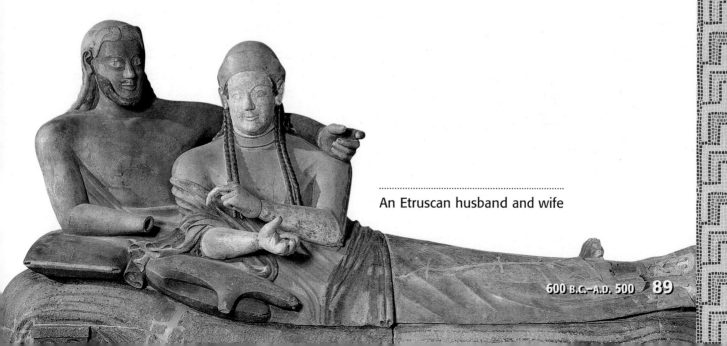

An Etruscan husband and wife

The senate was made up of 300 patrician men.

## Early Roman Government

The new Roman government had two leaders. They were called **consuls**. They had the power of a king, but only if they agreed with each other. Each consul had the power to stop what the other wanted to do. Also, the consuls served for just one year. This kept them from becoming too powerful.

The consuls were advised by a **senate**. The senate was made up of 300 men. They helped the consuls make decisions. In times of war, the senate could choose a **dictator**. A dictator is a leader with absolute power. But even the dictator could hold power for only six months.

Roman citizens were divided into two classes. Wealthy people who owned land were called **patricians**. The farmers and other common people were called **plebeians**.

## The Plebeians Gain Power

Plebeians had little power. Only patricians could be consuls. Only patricians could serve in the senate. Often the plebeians didn't even know what the laws were. The plebeians fought for change. They wanted the laws to be put in writing.

Roman plebeians

In 450 B.C., the laws were written down on tablets called the Twelve Tables. They were hung up for everyone to see. One of the laws made it clear that plebeians and patricians were not equal.

**"Marriages should not take place between plebeians and patricians."**

Once the plebeians learned the laws, they began demanding changes. Over time, plebeians gained more rights and had laws changed. They even demanded representatives of their own. They were allowed to vote for their own leaders. Those leaders were called **tribunes**. The plebeians even helped make a law that said one of the two consuls had to be a plebeian.

## Life in the Roman Republic

In Roman homes, the father was in charge. No one in the home could question him. The family's possessions belonged to the father alone. In the early years of the republic, when the father died, his possessions went to his oldest son.

Women took care of the home and cared for the children. In poorer families, the wife might have worked in a shop or a field with her husband.

Boys and girls of the patrician class went to school together. Girls often married by the age of 13. Boys stayed in school longer and usually did not marry until the age of 20.

## The Growth of the Roman Republic

The Romans were skilled soldiers. Their strong army took control of the entire Italian peninsula by about 270 B.C. Rome's next goal was to control trade in the Mediterranean Sea.

However, the people of Carthage, a city on the northern coast of Africa, also wanted this control. Carthage went to war against Rome in 264 B.C. This was the first of three wars known as the Punic Wars.

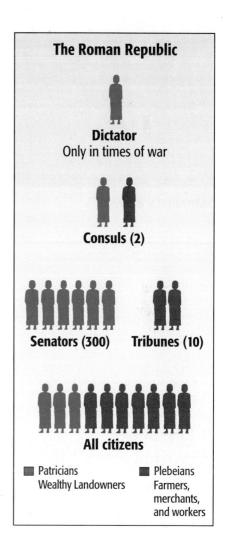

**The Roman Republic**

**Dictator**
Only in times of war

**Consuls (2)**

**Senators (300)**  **Tribunes (10)**

**All citizens**

■ Patricians
Wealthy Landowners

■ Plebeians
Farmers, merchants, and workers

After 23 years of fighting, Rome won the first war. Then in 218 B.C., Hannibal led the army of Carthage over the Alps. His army included elephants that each carried around 15 soldiers. The Romans were taken by surprise. They didn't think any army could get through the mountains. Then the Romans attacked Carthage, forcing Hannibal to return home. Rome won the second Punic War in 202 B.C.

The third Punic War began in 149 B.C. Roman soldiers attacked Carthage. They surrounded the city and cut off the food supply. The Romans burned the city of Carthage to the ground. By the end of the Punic Wars, Rome controlled Greece, northern Africa, and other lands around the Mediterranean Sea.

Hannibal's army

# Lesson 1 Review

Choose words from the list that best complete the paragraph. One word will not be used.

**Word List**

**Persia**

**Carthage**

**consuls**

**republic**

**plebeians**

The Etruscans conquered the Latins and controlled Rome for about 100 years. In 509 B.C., the Romans set up a __1__ . Two __2__ ruled the new government. They were advised by a group of 300 men called the senate. The new form of government was a representative government. The __3__ were not a part of government in the beginning. In time, they gained more rights. The Romans took control of the Italian Peninsula. They then went to war three times with the city of __4__ . Rome won all three of the Punic Wars.

## LESSON 2

# From Republic to Empire

### Before You Read

- What makes a good leader?
- What problems might come from two people ruling the same republic?

After Carthage fell, Rome ruled the Mediterranean Sea. With all its new lands, Rome grew rich. Some Romans grew richer than others. There was trouble in the government. The patricians wanted more power. They tried to limit the role of the plebeians. Army generals fought for control of Rome. At last, one general won. His name was Julius Caesar.

### New Words
senators
triumvirate
emperor

### People and Places
Julius Caesar
Marcus Brutus
Octavian
Lepidus
Mark Antony
Cleopatra
Actium
Augustus

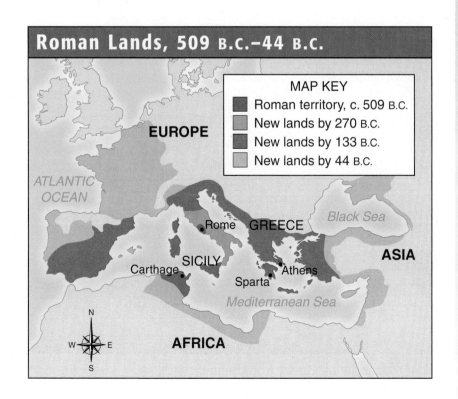

**Roman Lands, 509 B.C.–44 B.C.**

MAP KEY
- Roman territory, c. 509 B.C.
- New lands by 270 B.C.
- New lands by 133 B.C.
- New lands by 44 B.C.

EUROPE

ATLANTIC OCEAN

Rome  GREECE  Black Sea

ASIA

Carthage  SICILY  Athens

Sparta

Mediterranean Sea

N
W  E
S

AFRICA

## The Life and Death of Julius Caesar

Caesar was a powerful general. He won many battles. After one easy victory, he wrote back to Rome, *"Veni, vidi, vici."* In English, that means, "I came, I saw, I conquered."

Many Romans loved Julius Caesar. He replaced bad officials with good ones. He allowed people in conquered lands to become Roman citizens. Caesar tried to give Romans a government that was fair. He also had plans to help the poor and to offer free land to farmers. In 44 B.C., the senate changed the Roman law and made Caesar a dictator for life, not just six months.

But Caesar had some enemies in Rome. They feared Caesar would make himself king. They didn't want to see an end to the republic. On March 15, 44 B.C., a group of **senators** stabbed Caesar to death. One of the killers, Marcus Brutus, was an old friend of Caesar.

Julius Caesar

This painting shows Marcus Brutus about to stab Julius Caesar from behind.

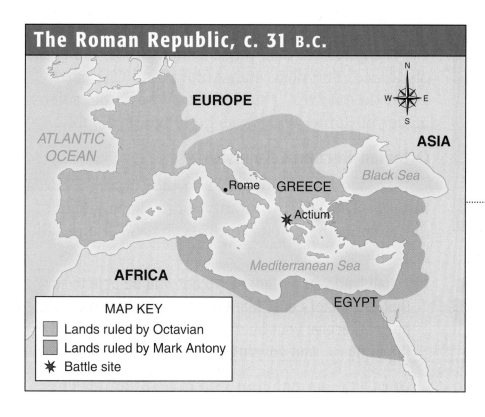

## The Roman Republic, c. 31 B.C.

EUROPE

ATLANTIC OCEAN

ASIA

Black Sea

Rome · GREECE

✴ Actium

Mediterranean Sea

AFRICA

EGYPT

**MAP KEY**
- ☐ Lands ruled by Octavian
- ☐ Lands ruled by Mark Antony
- ✴ Battle site

This map shows the Roman Republic divided between Octavian and Mark Antony. The city of Rome was under whose rule?

## The Struggle for Control

Caesar's death led to more trouble. Who would take his place? At first, three men worked together to rule Rome. They formed a **triumvirate**, or group of three rulers. One of these men was Caesar's adopted son, Octavian. The other two were the generals Lepidus and Mark Antony.

The three men divided up Rome's lands. Lepidus took lands in Africa. Octavian controlled the West, including Rome. Mark Antony ruled the East, including Egypt. Then Lepidus decided to give up his lands. For ten years, Octavian and Mark Antony shared control of the republic.

In the western half of the republic, Octavian increased his power. In the eastern half, Mark Antony was spending much time in Egypt. He had fallen in love with Cleopatra, the queen of Egypt. Octavian did not approve. He told the senate that Antony was giving Roman lands to Cleopatra. Octavian declared war against Mark Antony and Cleopatra.

Mark Antony

Octavian

In 31 B.C., Octavian's navy beat the Egyptian navy. The battle took place at Actium off the coast of Greece. The next year, Antony and Cleopatra killed themselves. That left Octavian as the sole leader of Rome. Rome was no longer a republic.

## Octavian Becomes Augustus

In 27 B.C., Octavian spoke to the senate. He was humble. He didn't want any more fighting. He didn't want the senate to think that he wanted to be king.

**Voices**
**In History**

**"I shall lead you no longer. No one will be able to say that [the victory over Mark Antony] was to win absolute power. Receive your liberty and the republic. Take over the army . . . and govern yourselves as you will."**

But Octavian did continue to lead Rome. The senators were grateful to him and trusted him. In fact, they made Octavian an **emperor**.

Octavian became the ruler of the Roman Empire. The senate also gave him the name *Augustus*, which means "respected one." For 41 years, Augustus ruled Rome. This period became known as "The Age of Augustus."

Like Caesar, Augustus did many good things. He chose honest people for leaders. He improved the schools and raised the pay for teachers. He put people to work making Rome a better place.

Rome became a better place under Augustus.

## Cleopatra (69 B.C.–30 B.C.)

Cleopatra was the queen of Egypt, but she was actually Greek. How was that possible? Earlier, Alexander the Great made a Greek family the rulers of Egypt. Cleopatra came from that family. She became queen in 51 B.C. Julius Caesar fell in love with Cleopatra. They had one child together.

Later, Mark Antony fell in love with Cleopatra. They had three children. Their story is one of the most famous love stories in history. It is also a sad story. After being defeated by Octavian, Antony heard a false story that Cleopatra had died. He was filled with sorrow and killed himself by falling on his sword. Cleopatra also killed herself. She allowed a deadly snake to bite her.

## Lesson 2 Review

Choose words from the list that best complete the paragraphs. One word will not be used.

In 44 B.C., the Roman senate named __1__ a dictator for life. He made some good changes and had plans to do more. But on March 15, he was killed. After a while, two men took control of the Roman Empire. __2__ ruled Roman lands in the West while Mark Antony ruled Roman lands in the East.

Mark Antony fell in love with Cleopatra, the queen of Egypt. This led to a war between Octavian and Antony. Octavian won a battle off the coast of __3__ . The Roman senate made Octavian an emperor. After that, he became known as __4__ . Under his long rule, Romans had honest leaders and better schools.

**Word List**

Greece

Octavian

Egypt

Julius Caesar

Augustus

## Summary

- The Latins and the Etruscans lived on the Italian Peninsula.

- Early Romans had a republic. Citizens voted for their own leaders.

- There were two groups of Roman citizens. The patricians owned land. The plebeians were workers.

- Rome defeated Carthage in the Punic Wars and won control over the lands surrounding the Mediterranean Sea.

- In 44 B.C., the Roman senate named Julius Caesar dictator for life. He was killed the same year.

- The senate made Octavian emperor in 27 B.C. He became known as Augustus.

## Find Out More!

After reading Chapter 8, you're ready to go online. **Explore Zone**, **Quiz Time**, and **Amazing Facts** bring this chapter of world history alive.

Visit www.exploreSV.com and type in the chapter code **1-Ch8**.

## Vocabulary

Number your paper from 1 to 5. Finish the sentences from Group A with words from Group B. Write the letter of the correct answer.

### Group A

1. The Roman people voted for leaders called _____.

2. In the Roman Republic, wealthy people who owned land were called _____.

3. Farmers and other common people in the Roman Republic were called _____.

4. After Caesar's death, a group of three rulers called the _____ ruled Rome together.

5. Rome became an empire when the senate made Octavian _____.

### Group B

a. patricians

b. triumvirate

c. representatives

d. emperor

e. plebeians

## Comprehension

Number your paper from 1 to 5. Write the word from the list that best completes each sentence. One word will not be used.

1. The leaders of the Roman government were advised by a _____.

2. The plebeians voted for their own leaders, or _____.

3. _____ led the army of Carthage over the Alps.

4. After Caesar's death, _____ ruled the East, including Egypt.

5. Rome under Octavian's rule is known as "The Age of _____."

**Word List**

Cleopatra

senate

Augustus

tribunes

Hannibal

Mark Antony

## Critical Thinking

**Sequencing**   Number your paper from 1 to 5. Write the sentences below in the correct order.

The Punic Wars began in 264 B.C.

In 450 B.C., the Roman laws were written down on tablets called the Twelve Tables.

Octavian became the emperor of Rome.

A group of senators stabbed Caesar to death.

The Etruscans conquered Rome around 600 B.C.

## Writing

Do you think Augustus was a good ruler? Write a paragraph to explain your answer.

## Skill Builder: Reading a Chart

A **chart** lists a group of facts. Charts help you learn facts quickly. Read the chart below to learn about the Punic Wars.

| The Punic Wars | | | |
|---|---|---|---|
| **Punic War** | **Dates Fought** | **Reason Fought** | **Results of War** |
| First Punic War | 264 B.C.–241 B.C. | Rome and Carthage wanted control of the Mediterranean Sea. | ■ Romans won the war and gained Sicily.<br>■ Carthage paid Rome for damages. |
| Second Punic War | 218 B.C.–202 B.C. | Carthage and Rome wanted to control lands in Spain. | ■ Rome defeated Hannibal and gained land in Spain.<br>■ Rome also received money and ships from Carthage. |
| Third Punic War | 149 B.C.–146 B.C. | Carthage fought against the agreement resulting from the Second Punic War. | ■ Rome won and gained control of the Mediterranean Sea.<br>■ Carthage was destroyed. |

Number your paper from 1 to 5. Write the letter of the correct answer.

1. To read the names of the wars, read the chart from _____.
   **a.** left to right  **b.** top to bottom  **c.** the middle

2. To learn about the First Punic War, read the chart from _____.
   **a.** left to right  **b.** top to bottom  **c.** bottom to top

3. The _____ was the shortest Punic War.
   **a.** First Punic War  **b.** Second Punic War  **c.** Third Punic War

4. The _____ was fought to control lands in Spain.
   **a.** First Punic War  **b.** Second Punic War  **c.** Third Punic War

5. One result of the Third Punic War was that Rome _____.
   **a.** gained Sicily  **b.** defeated Hannibal  **c.** destroyed Carthage

## LESSON 1

# Life in the Roman Empire

## Before You Read

- What kinds of forces could have stopped the Roman Empire from growing?
- What might a nation need to have a long period of peace?

You have read how Rome grew from a village to a city. You also have learned how Rome became a republic. The Roman Republic lasted for almost 500 years. In 27 B.C., Augustus became the emperor of Rome. The Roman Republic was over. But the Roman Empire was only beginning. The Roman Empire also lasted about 500 years.

**New Words**
Pax Romana
aqueducts
gladiators

**People and Places**
Germania
Rhine River
Danube River
Black Sea
Pompeii
Mount Vesuvius
Pliny the Younger

This image shows citizens of the Roman Empire.

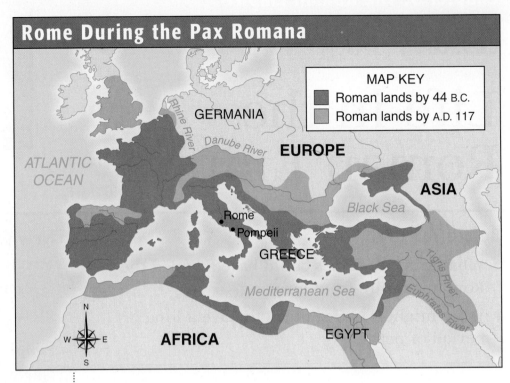

## Rome During the Pax Romana

MAP KEY

- Roman lands by 44 B.C.
- Roman lands by A.D. 117

GERMANIA

EUROPE

ATLANTIC OCEAN

ASIA

Rhine River

Danube River

Black Sea

Rome

Pompeii

GREECE

Tigris River

Euphrates River

Mediterranean Sea

AFRICA

EGYPT

Rome controlled a vast empire during the Pax Romana. What large sea was in the middle of the empire?

## Extending the Empire

Augustus increased the size of the Roman Empire. However, he had trouble extending into the area called Germania. The Germans forced the Romans back to the Rhine River in A.D. 9. The river remained the border for 300 years.

The Romans controlled the lands south of the Danube River. They extended their control around the Black Sea to the Euphrates River. The Romans also controlled lands in northern Africa. Within these borders, the Romans had full control. The Roman Empire was divided into provinces. Each province had its own governor.

The rule of Augustus began a peaceful time for Rome. Romans enjoyed good government and open trade. This time in Roman history is called the **Pax Romana**, or the "peace of Rome." It lasted from 27 B.C. to A.D. 180.

Augustus died in A.D. 14. He was 76 years old. He had made many good changes. He had united the Roman people. Some people thought he was a god, and they even built temples to honor him.

## Enjoying Life in Ancient Rome

Ancient Rome was an exciting city. There was always something to do. There was horse racing at a place called Circus Maximus. This was a huge race track. It could hold up to 250,000 people. At night, theaters in Rome offered plays and music.

Then there was the Roman Forum. This was where the senate met. People came to the Forum to talk and to hear the latest news. In some ways, the Forum was like a mall today. It had shops offering goods from all over the empire. It had food stalls. Entertainers sang, danced, and even charmed snakes in the Forum.

Rome had more than 100 public baths. Building a new bath was one way an emperor could please the Roman people. The baths were open to the rich and the poor. Men and women bathed in them. People even had a choice of water temperature.

At the baths, people could exercise. They could read books. They could walk through gardens of flowers and herbs.

Circus Maximus

The Forum was a busy place in ancient Rome.

Roman bath

Fresh water for the baths came into Rome through **aqueducts**. Many of these were arched channels built high above the ground. The water ran downhill to Rome. Many aqueducts still exist today even though they are 2,000 years old.

## The Colosseum

The Colosseum was built in Rome. It was made with stone and concrete. The oval-shaped Colosseum held as many as 50,000 people. In the Colosseum, the Romans watched people battle wild animals, such as lions, bears, and leopards, to the death.

Sometimes, people came to see warriors kill one another. These warriors were known as **gladiators**. They were usually slaves or prisoners of war.

Sometimes, the Romans flooded the Colosseum with water. Then they would have battles using ships. Like the aqueducts, much of the Colosseum is still standing.

Roman aqueduct

Today, visitors can see what is left of the Roman Colosseum.

## Life and Death in Pompeii

Many cities in the Roman Empire wanted to be like Rome. One such city was Pompeii. Pompeii was a busy town with 20,000 people. Traders bought and sold such items as wine, cloth, fruits, and oil. Pompeii had its own forum. It had its own gladiator games. It had ten temples and a theater with 20,000 seats.

Mount Vesuvius stood six miles away from Pompeii. On August 24, A.D. 79, this volcano erupted. For two days, white ashes and hot rocks fell on the city. The whole city, along with about 2,000 people, was buried in the ash. Pliny the Younger saw it from a safe distance and wrote about what he saw.

Mount Vesuvius destroyed the city of Pompeii.

**"**You could hear women [praying], children crying, men shouting . . . . Many believed that there were no gods any longer. This was one unending night for the world.**"**

**Voices**
In History

# Lesson 1 Review

Choose words from the list that best complete the paragraphs. One word will not be used.

The Roman Empire ruled many lands. Augustus tried to extend the empire. But his forces were defeated by the __1__ . Still, his rule started a time of peace called the __2__ . It lasted for about 200 years.

Romans liked to be entertained. They had race tracks and public baths. Fresh water flowed to the baths through __3__ . The Roman Colosseum held up to 50,000 people. One Roman city, __4__ , was destroyed by a volcano, Mount Vesuvius, in A.D. 79. About 2,000 people died.

**Word List**

aqueducts

Germans

gladiators

Pompeii

Pax Romana

**LESSON 2**

# Religion in Rome

## New Words

Christianity
Messiah
Gospels
crucified
disciples
resurrection
Edict of Milan
edict

## People and Places

Jesus
Bethlehem
Judea
Nazareth
Paul
Constantine
Theodosius
Byzantium
Constantinople
Western Roman
  Empire
Eastern Roman
  Empire

Jupiter was the main
Roman god.

## Before You Read

- Why might some people be scared by a new religion?
- How do religions spread?

Religion was an important part of life in Rome. The Romans, like most ancient people, believed in many gods. Jupiter was the most powerful Roman god. Some other gods were Mars, Venus, and Cupid. Romans also believed in the Roman emperor as a god.

The Romans punished Christians and others who believed in someone or something higher than the Roman gods or the Roman emperor. So, some new religions began in secret. People were interested in these religions because they offered hope for a better life in the next world. One of these religions, **Christianity**, grew and spread throughout the world.

## Christianity Begins

Christianity grew out of Judaism. The Hebrew Bible told that a **Messiah**, or chosen one, would come to the Jews. He would bring them peace and freedom. Some Jews believed that a man named Jesus was that Messiah. They became known as Christians.

Followers of Jesus wrote about his life in four books called the **Gospels**. The Gospels and other books were added to the Hebrew Bible to make the Christian Bible. According to the Bible, Jesus was born in Bethlehem in the province of Judea. He grew up in the town of Nazareth. As he grew older, people said he was teaching new ideas and performing miracles. Jesus said he was the son of God. He taught that God loved all people.

Jesus

Some people were concerned about Jesus. Some Jews thought Jesus was not the Messiah. They were angry that he claimed to be the son of God. The Romans also were worried. They thought people might be more loyal to Jesus than to the empire.

In A.D. 33, the Romans **crucified** Jesus by nailing him to a cross and leaving him there to die. The Gospels say that three days later Jesus rose from the dead and appeared to his **disciples**. The story of the **resurrection** became an important message of Christianity.

This famous painting is called "The Last Supper." It shows Jesus and his disciples the night before Jesus was crucified.

## The Spread of Christianity

A Jewish Roman citizen named Paul helped spread Christianity throughout the Roman Empire. Paul never actually met Jesus. At first, he was against Christianity. Then, the Bible says, he saw and spoke to the resurrected Jesus. After that, he began to teach about Jesus. For 30 years, Paul traveled from city to city spreading Christianity.

The Christians believed in only one God. They refused to believe that the Roman gods were the highest power. This angered some Roman emperors. Some Roman emperors ordered the killing of Christians.

For nearly 300 years, Christians lived in fear. But their religion continued to grow. In A.D. 313, life changed for Christians in Rome. Emperor Constantine had a vision before going to battle. He saw the Christian sign of the cross. When he won the battle, he said it was because of the Christian God. He became a Christian.

Constantine then issued the **Edict of Milan**, which made it legal to be a Christian. An **edict** is an order. Around A.D. 392, an emperor named Theodosius made Christianity the official religion of the Roman Empire.

Emperor Constantine

This map shows Christian lands before and after the Edict of Milan in A.D. 313. Did the Edict of Milan help or hurt the spread of Christianity?

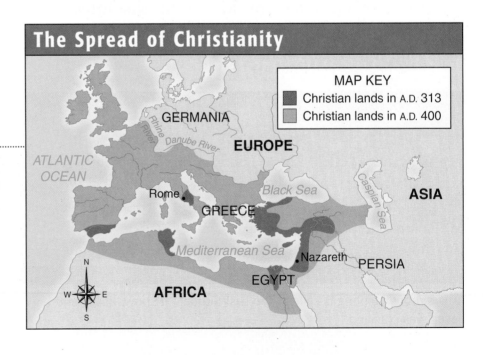

### The Spread of Christianity

MAP KEY
Christian lands in A.D. 313
Christian lands in A.D. 400

GERMANIA

EUROPE

ATLANTIC OCEAN

Rhine River

Danube River

Rome

GREECE

Black Sea

Caspian Sea

ASIA

Mediterranean Sea

Nazareth

PERSIA

EGYPT

AFRICA

## East and West

Constantine moved from Rome to a Greek town called Byzantium. Later, Byzantium became known as the city of Constantine, or Constantinople.

The Roman Empire then had two capitals. Rome was in the West, while Constantinople was in the East. After A.D. 395, the Roman Empire had two emperors as well. One ruled the Western Roman Empire; one ruled the Eastern Roman Empire. In time, the Christian church also split in two. The Roman church stayed in Rome. The Greek, or Eastern, church was based in the city of Constantinople. Christianity spread throughout the Roman Empire and beyond. Today, there are around 1.9 billion Christians in the world.

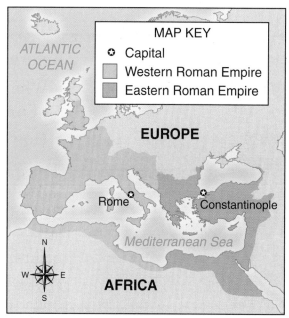

MAP KEY
⊙ Capital
▢ Western Roman Empire
▢ Eastern Roman Empire

The Two Roman Empires

# Lesson 2 Review

Choose words from the list that best complete the paragraphs. One word will not be used.

The Romans believed in many gods. The most powerful of their gods was __1__ . Christianity began under the rule of Augustus. Some Jews believed that Jesus was the __2__ . Jesus taught that God loved all people. In A.D. 33, the Romans crucified Jesus.

Christians refused to worship the Roman gods. Many emperors ordered the killing of Christians. But Emperor __3__ changed that. He made it legal to be a Christian. He moved his capital to __4__ in the East. The Roman Empire split in two.

**Word List**

**Byzantium**

**Jupiter**

**Constantine**

**Gospels**

**Messiah**

## LESSON 3

# The Fall of Rome

## New Words
bribes
looted
pope
sanctuary
invasions

## People and Places
Huns
Visigoths
Angles
Saxons
Franks
Vandals
Valens
Edward Gibbons

## Before You Read
- What qualities of a leader might cause the fall of an empire?
- How might religion cause an empire to fall?

When Emperor Constantine moved to Byzantium, he knew the Roman Empire was not as strong as it once was. But it was just the beginning of a slow fall. In A.D. 476, about 150 years after Constantine, German invaders defeated the last Roman emperor in the West. They put a German king in his place. This is known as the fall of Rome.

## Outside Trouble

Before the fall of Rome, the Germans had been trying to cross the northern border of the empire.

The city of Rome was destroyed by German invaders.

## Invasions into Rome

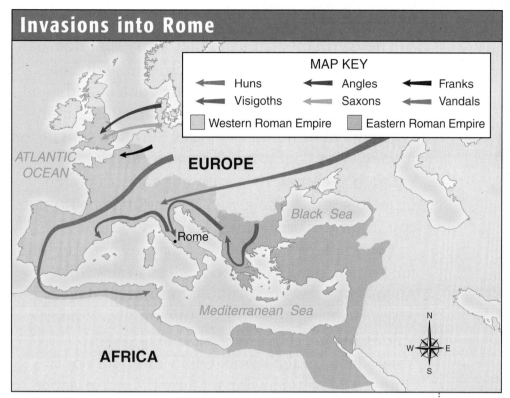

**MAP KEY**

| ← Huns | ← Angles | ← Franks |
| ← Visigoths | ← Saxons | ← Vandals |
| ☐ Western Roman Empire | ☐ Eastern Roman Empire |

ATLANTIC OCEAN

EUROPE

Black Sea

•Rome

Mediterranean Sea

AFRICA

N W E S

Several German tribes invaded the Western Roman Empire. Which tribe invaded the city of Rome?

Roman emperors sent armies to defeat the Germans. Sometimes, they won. Other times, they lost. At times, there was peace.

In the fourth century, a group called the Huns was moving toward the Roman Empire. They were from central Asia. The fierce Huns conquered Germans in eastern Europe. The Visigoths, a German tribe, begged Rome for help. The Romans allowed the Visigoths to come inside Roman borders and settle on empty land. The Visigoths had to promise to leave their weapons behind.

But some Romans charged the Visigoths high prices for the land. Some Romans also took **bribes**, or money, to let the Visigoths keep their weapons.

Soon, fighting broke out. In A.D. 378, the Visigoths beat the Romans. The defeat left Rome very weak. Four other German groups crossed the border into the Roman Empire. They were the Angles, Saxons, Franks, and Vandals. These groups invaded different parts of the empire. In A.D. 410, the Visigoths **looted**, or robbed, the city of Rome.

Attila the Hun

## Inside Trouble

The Germans had a smaller army than the Romans did. But they were still able to defeat Rome. The Germans had strong leaders and good soldiers. By A.D. 400, the Roman army had more Germans than Romans. These Germans fought for money. They did not feel loyal to Rome.

Often the emperor could not collect enough taxes to support the army. When Rome could not pay, the Germans soldiers refused to fight.

The emperors themselves were also a problem for Rome. Some were good rulers. A few, like Augustus, were great rulers. But not all the emperors were able to rule the empire. Emperor Valens made the bad decision to allow the Visigoths to enter Rome. Other emperors of this time made bad decisions. Many did not practice tolerance. In 1776, Edward Gibbons wrote a history of the fall of the Roman Empire. He wrote about how some of the Roman emperors were weak and dishonest.

**Roman soldier**

### Voices
**In History**

"The [emperors], if they were stripped of their purple [robes] . . . would immediately sink to the lowest rank of society."

The fierce Huns conquered lands in eastern Europe.

## The Growing Power of the Church

Meanwhile, the power of the western Christian church grew. The **pope**, who was head of this church, helped the poor and the weak. People who were in trouble could find safety in any church. This protection was called **sanctuary**. The pope set up church courts. He began to collect taxes. The pope controlled the army and even made repairs to the aqueducts. The growing power of the church took some power away from the Roman emperors.

The German **invasions**, weak emperors, and the growing power of the church all led to the fall of Rome. In A.D. 476, the last Roman emperor in the West was replaced by a German king. By A.D. 500, the Western Roman Empire had split into several German kingdoms.

The pope gained power during the 400s.

# Lesson 3 Review

Choose words from the list that best complete the paragraphs. One word will not be used.

In the fourth century, the __1__ attacked the Germans in eastern Europe. Rome offered protection to one of these German groups, the Visigoths. But the Visigoths did not leave their __2__ behind. Once inside the empire, the Visigoths looted the city of Rome.

Germans fought in the Roman army. They had no loyalty to Rome. They fought for __3__ . The Roman Empire failed to support its army. Too many emperors were weak. Also, the __4__ gained more and more power. All of this led to the fall of Rome in A.D. 476.

**Word List**

sanctuary

weapons

Huns

money

pope

### Summary

- The Roman Empire was divided into provinces. Each province had its own governor.

- The period when the Roman Empire was most peaceful is called the Pax Romana.

- A volcano buried the city of Pompeii in A.D. 79, killing 2,000 people.

- Christianity was started by Jews who believed that Jesus was their Messiah. In A.D. 392, Christianity became the official religion of the Roman Empire.

- The Roman Empire fell in A.D. 476, when German invaders defeated the last Roman emperor in the West.

## Find Out More!

After reading Chapter 9, you're ready to go online. **Explore Zone**, **Quiz Time**, and **Amazing Facts** bring this chapter of world history alive.

Visit www.exploreSV.com and type in the chapter code **1-Ch9**.

### Vocabulary

Number your paper from 1 to 6. Write the word from the list that best completes each analogy. One word will not be used.

1. Roads are to people and goods as _____ are to water.

2. Judaism was to Hebrews as _____ was to Romans.

3. The Vedas were to Aryans as the _____ were to Christians.

4. Visigoths were to eastern Europe as _____ were to Asia.

5. An emperor is to an empire as a _____ is to the church.

6. Shelter is to a house as _____ is to a church.

**Word List**

Gospels
aqueducts
Christianity
pope
Huns
sanctuary
gladiators

## Comprehension

Number your paper from 1 to 5. Write **True** for each sentence that is true. Write **False** for each sentence that is false.

1. The rule of Augustus began a peaceful time in Roman history called the Pax Romana.

2. In some ways, the Roman Forum was like a mall today.

3. Christians believed in many gods, including Jupiter, Mars, and Venus.

4. The Romans did not allow the Visigoths to come inside Roman borders.

5. The pope was the head of the western Christian church.

## Critical Thinking

**Cause and Effect**   Number your paper from 1 to 4. Read the causes in the left column. Then choose the correct effect from the right column. Write the letter of the correct effect.

| **Cause** | **Effect** |
|---|---|
| 1. Mount Vesuvius was six miles away from Pompeii, so _____ | a. the power of the western Christian church grew. |
| 2. The Romans thought Jesus might take over the empire, so _____ | b. it was easier for other German groups to invade Rome. |
| 3. In A.D. 378, the Visigoths beat the Romans, so _____ | c. they crucified him. |
| 4. The pope began to collect taxes and control the Roman army, so _____ | d. Pompeii was buried in ash when Mount Vesuvius erupted. |

## Writing

Write a paragraph describing a day in the life of a person living during the Pax Romana.

**LESSON 1**

# Indian Empires

## New Words

assassinate
Buddhism
Hinduism
gravity
ahimsa

## People and Places

Chandragupta
  Maurya
Pataliputra
Ganges River
Asoka
Gupta
Faxian
H.G. Wells

## Before You Read

- Why might an emperor be nervous?
- What happens during the Golden Age of an empire?

In 327 B.C., Alexander the Great arrived at the Indus River. Alexander's army fought battles against the people there. His army conquered a part of India. But the army grew tired. They wanted to return home to Greece. Alexander and his army turned around in 326 B.C.

Alexander left some Greeks behind, however. They ruled the conquered lands in India. The Indian people feared more Greeks might come back to conquer all of India. They needed a strong empire of their own to protect them.

Alexander the Great arrived in India in 327 B.C.

## Mauryan Empire

It wasn't long before India had such an empire. A new leader came to power in 322 B.C. He was Chandragupta Maurya. He united the many smaller kingdoms in India. Chandragupta built a huge army. Some say he had as many as 700,000 men and 9,000 elephants. His army defeated the Greeks that had stayed in India. The Mauryan Empire became the first empire in India.

The Mauryan Empire was divided into three provinces. The capital was Pataliputra in the Ganges River valley. Pataliputra was a rich and beautiful city. Merchants sold jewelry, silk, and leather there. Emperor Chandragupta built a massive palace. He planted various trees and plants. Beautiful parrots were brought to live among the trees.

Chandragupta was a nervous emperor. He lived in fear that someone would **assassinate**, or kill, him. He did not trust men. So, he had female soldiers watch over him. He had servants taste his food before he would eat it. He even slept in a different place every night.

The Mauryan Empire, c. 320 B.C.–232 B.C.

Chandragupta Maurya began the first empire in India.

## Did You Know?

### Fun and Games

Ancient Indians were the first to play cards. The cards they used didn't look like the ones we use today. The cards were made of cloth. The highest card showed a king riding a horse. The next highest card showed a general riding a horse. The rest of the cards showed a number of horses from one to ten. Today, there are 52 cards in a deck. In ancient India, they had 144 cards. Can you imagine shuffling 144 cloth cards?

In 273 B.C., Asoka, the grandson of Chandragupta, became the third ruler of the Mauryan Empire. Asoka was a fierce warrior who won many bloody victories. But after one battle, he realized that killing was wrong. He spent the rest of his life encouraging peace. He began to follow the teachings of **Buddhism**. Asoka began to spread Buddhism throughout the empire.

### Gupta Empire

Asoka died in 232 B.C. His sons fought for control of the empire. Invaders attacked the northern provinces, and the Mauryan Empire fell apart by 180 B.C.

Once more, India became a land of small kingdoms. Over the next 500 years, the invaders became part of Indian society. The Indian people were good at bringing new people into their culture. They were able to live peacefully with many different people.

The Gupta Empire started around A.D. 320 and lasted more than 200 years. Like the Mauryan Empire, the Gupta Empire was centered in the Ganges River valley. The new emperors supported the old religion of the Aryans. They felt

This monument was built to honor Asoka.

it was India's true religion. The religion became known as **Hinduism**.

## The Golden Age of the Gupta

The Gupta Empire is known as the Golden Age of India. Before, the Indian artists mostly copied the Greeks. But during the Gupta Empire, they developed their own style. Using stone, metal, and clay, they made images of gods. Indians also created a famous peaceful image of the Buddha. It shows him sitting down with his eyes closed. His legs are crossed and his hands are at his chest.

During the Gupta Empire, Indians developed a number system using the numbers 1 through 9 and zero. Along with the Maya in Mexico, they were one of the first people to use the zero.

Indian scientists studied the stars and the movement of planets. They knew the true size of the moon. They learned about **gravity**. They learned these things more than 1,000 years before Europeans did. Indian doctors made many medical discoveries during this Golden Age. They learned to heal broken bones and to prevent diseases. Traders spread the Indian ideas of science and medicine to areas around the world.

Faxian, a Chinese monk, traveled to India in A.D. 400. He wrote about the people.

Statue of the Buddha

Chinese traveling monk

**"**The people are . . . happy beyond comparison. When people of other countries come to [India], they . . . supply them with what they need.**"**

The Gupta Empire ended slowly. The Huns who invaded Rome also invaded India. In A.D. 480, just after the fall of Rome, the Huns took over northern India. By A.D. 500, the Huns had conquered western India. Fifty years later, the Gupta controlled no more land. But their science, mathematics, and art from the Golden Age have lived on.

## Asoka (c. 299 B.C.–232 B.C.)

When Asoka became emperor, he fought for more land. But after a particularly bloody battle, Asoka turned against war. Why did Asoka suddenly change his mind about killing? It was because he learned the teachings of the Buddha.

Asoka began doing everything he could to preserve life. He believed in **ahimsa**, or never hurting others. Asoka said he was sorry for the deaths he had caused. He built hospitals. He stopped the killing of animals. He told his people to be kind. He sent people throughout India to teach about Buddhism. Asoka had a huge round stone monument built to honor the Buddha.

The author H.G. Wells wrote about Asoka in 1920. He said that of all the kings in history, "the name of Asoka shines, and shines almost alone, a star."

# Lesson 1 Review

Choose words from the list that best complete the paragraphs. One word will not be used.

**Word List**

Golden Age

ahimsa

Huns

Ganges River

Asoka

The Mauryan Empire began in 322 B.C. Its first leader was Chandragupta Maurya. He lived in fear that someone would assassinate him. Another Mauryan emperor, __1__, changed his life after a terrible battle. From then on, he spent his life doing good.

Both the Mauyran and the Gupta empires were centered in the __2__ valley. The Guptas were in power during the __3__ of India. They made discoveries in math, science, and medicine. The Gupta Empire ended after the __4__ invaded India.

## LESSON 2

# Religion in India

## Before You Read

- How do people use religion to explain suffering?
- What are some major world religions?

In Chapter 4, you read how the Aryans brought their ideas of the Brahmans and the caste system to the Indian subcontinent. You also learned about the holy books called the Vedas. These Aryan beliefs became known as Hinduism. Followers of Hinduism are called Hindus.

You read a little about Buddhism, too. You learned how its teachings changed the life of Asoka. Buddhism also changed the lives of many other people. Both Hinduism and Buddhism are still practiced today.

## New Words

reincarnation
reborn
rebirth
enlightenment
Four Noble Truths
Eightfold Path
nirvana

## People and Places

Siddartha Gautama

This Buddhist temple is called the Marble Temple.

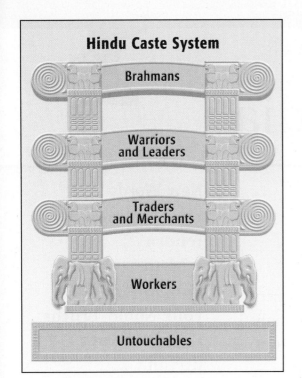

**Hindu Caste System**

Brahmans

Warriors and Leaders

Traders and Merchants

Workers

Untouchables

## Hinduism and the Caste System

The Aryans brought the idea that people were divided into castes. The caste system became a part of Hinduism. Brahmans, or priests, were in the top caste. The second caste was the warriors and leaders. Traders and merchants made up the third caste. The lowest caste was for workers. Some people did not fit in any of these castes. They were called outcastes. They became known as untouchables.

People were born into the caste of their parents. They stayed in that caste until death. A member of one caste could not marry someone from another caste.

## Life and Death

In Hinduism, there is a way to enter a higher caste, even for untouchables. Hindus believe in **reincarnation**. They believe that after death, a person's soul is born again in a new body. If a person lives a good life, he or she will be **reborn** into a higher caste. If a person lives a bad life, he or she will be reborn into a lower caste. Some

A Hindu god is shown holding up a mountain.

people could be reborn as animals. Hindus believe that animals have human souls. That is why most Hindus do not kill animals.

This pattern of birth, death, and **rebirth** continues. A person may live many lives. The pattern only ends when a person lives a perfect life. Then the soul is not reborn. Instead, it becomes part of one great spirit.

Hinduism has many gods. The three most important are Brahma, Vishnu, and Shiva. Brahma created the world. Vishnu preserves life. Shiva is the destroyer.

No one person started Hinduism. It developed over many years. It spread throughout India. However, around 500 B.C., many people became interested in a different religion—Buddhism.

Vishnu

## The Life of Buddha

Buddhism began with the teachings of a man known as the Buddha. But Buddha was not his real name. He was born Siddartha Gautama around 567 B.C. in northern India. He was a prince. His father wanted to protect Siddartha from the sadness of the world. So, the father kept Siddartha inside the palace.

When Siddartha was 30 years old, he left the palace for the first time. He wanted to see the real world. Siddartha was shocked by what he saw. He saw a dead body. He saw a sick man. He saw a beggar. Everywhere he looked, he saw suffering.

Siddartha wanted to know what caused all this pain. He left the palace for good. He threw out his silk robes and put on beggar's clothes. He ate very little food. He nearly starved to death. He wandered around India and read many books. He studied the holy Vedas. But still he found no answers.

Siddartha Gautama cuts his hair with a sword.

Buddha reaches a state of peace.

Then one day he decided not to move until he found the secret of life. After many days of sitting under a tree, **enlightenment** came at last. He felt he saw the truth for the first time. He became known as the Buddha, or the "Enlightened One."

## The Beliefs of Buddhism

The Buddha spent the rest of his life as a teacher. He taught what he called the **Four Noble Truths**: (1) Life is full of pain and suffering. (2) Pain is caused by greedy desire. (3) Pain will end when we stop being greedy. (4) This can be done by living the right way.

To live right, the Buddha said that people must follow the **Eightfold Path**. The first step in the path is to have the right beliefs or views about life. The next step is to have the right wishes and thoughts. The next three steps are to act, speak, and work in the right way. The final three steps are to always try, to always be mindful, and to stay calm.

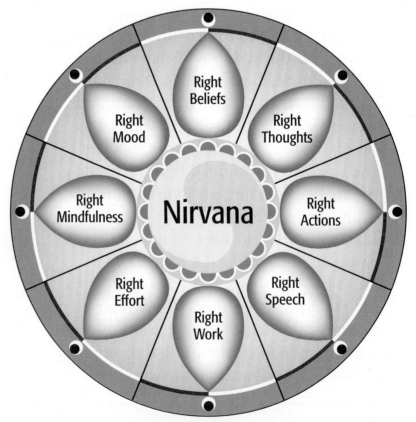

**The Eightfold Path**

If a person follows the eight steps of the path, the person enters **nirvana**. This is a state of mind where there is no desire or greed. There is only true peace.

## The Spread of Indian Religions

Buddhism spread over much of India. Some people saw it as a challenge to Hinduism. The Buddha said that the caste system was wrong. He thought all people should be treated equally.

Over time, both Hinduism and Buddhism grew. Hinduism became the major religion of the Indian subcontinent. Today, Hinduism has about 750 million followers.

Buddhism faded in India. But it spread to other areas in Asia, including Japan, China, and Southeast Asia. Today, Buddhism is practiced by about 335 million people.

This flower is a symbol of Buddhism.

# Lesson 2 Review

Choose words from the list that best complete the paragraphs. One word will not be used.

The Aryans brought the caste system to the Indian subcontinent. There were four major castes. Those below the caste system became known as __1__. The Aryan caste system became a part of Hinduism. Hindus believe in __2__. That means that when people die, their souls are reborn.

The __3__ first saw the outside world at the age of 30. He was shocked by the suffering he saw. He wanted to find out why there was so much pain in the world. In time, __4__ came to him. The Buddha taught the Four Noble Truths and the Eightfold Path. Today, both Hinduism and Buddhism are important world religions.

**Word List**

nirvana

untouchables

enlightenment

reincarnation

Buddha

# LESSON 3

# Chinese Empires

## New Words
civil war
peasants
examination system
bureaucracy
porcelain
Silk Road

## People and Places
Shi Huangdi
Qin
Han

## Before You Read

- How do people get government jobs?
- How can trade help spread ideas?

In Chapter 4, you learned that in 771 B.C., the Zhou Dynasty fell. The new Eastern Zhou period began. This was a weak dynasty because no one had real control. A series of wars broke out. This time often is called the period of the Warring States. Large kingdoms fought one another for control of China.

At last, in 256 B.C., the Eastern Zhou fell. But fighting continued. Then in 221 B.C., one kingdom won control and united China. Shi Huangdi ruled the Qin Dynasty. The dynasty lasted just 15 years.

Different kingdoms fought for control of China during the period of the Warring States.

## The Qin Dynasty

Shi Huangdi won new lands. He made the laws the same for all of China. Shi Huangdi had everyone use the same weights and measures. He built fine roads and further developed the Chinese language. Shi Huangdi also linked a series of walls on the western border into one long wall. This became known as the Great Wall of China. It was meant to protect China from any enemy who might attack from northern or western areas.

Shi Huangdi was a cruel leader. He felt books might put bad ideas into people's heads. So, he burned all the books he could find. He also had people killed for the smallest reasons. If a general was late for a meeting, Shi Huangdi had him killed.

Shi Huangdi's cruelty led to **civil war**. In 210 B.C., Shi Huangdi died. He was buried in a huge tomb that was cut into the side of a mountain. It had taken thousands of **peasants** many years of hard work to build the tomb.

The Great Wall of China

Shi Huangdi ordered the burning of books during the Qin Dynasty.

Shi Huangdi's tomb is guarded by thousands of life-size clay soldiers.

Shi Huangdi had about 7,500 life-size clay soldiers buried with him. Each one was at least six feet tall. Each one had a different look on his face. The civil war continued after Shi Huangdi's death. Four years later, the Qin Dynasty fell.

## The Han and Good Government

The Han Dynasty took control in 206 B.C. This dynasty lasted more than 400 years. Han emperors were more gentle than Shi Huangdi. They gave nobles back some of their power. Peasants did not have to work as hard.

Chinese officials taking tests

The Han changed how the government worked. They did not give jobs to their friends or family. Instead, the Han set up an **examination system**. A person had to pass a difficult test to become a government official. Students went to special schools to prepare for the test.

By 206 B.C., China was a huge country of about 60 million people. China had many more people than any other country at the time. Who would manage all this land and all these people? Who would keep the peace? China needed a large

**bureaucracy**, or many well-trained officials. All the dynasties that followed the Han used the examination system. Those who passed the tests became a part of the bureaucracy. Future dynasties continued using the examination system until the 1900s.

## Han Inventions

The Han invented many new things. They made a new and better plow. They also wrote the first dictionary and the first history of China. The Han were the first to use water mills to grind rice into flour. They put a special coating on pottery to make **porcelain**. Centuries later, when Europeans saw the porcelain, they liked it. Because of where it came from, they called it "china."

The Han were the first Chinese empire to trade with Southwest Asia and Europe. They developed a famous trade route called the **Silk Road**. This road ran through deserts and mountains. It stretched all the way from China to the Mediterranean Sea. The Chinese sold silk, spices, and furs. The Silk Road was the first major link between Asia and Europe. Ideas and goods were shared across the continents.

Han statue of a tower

The Silk Road was built during the Han Dynasty. What mountain range did it cross?

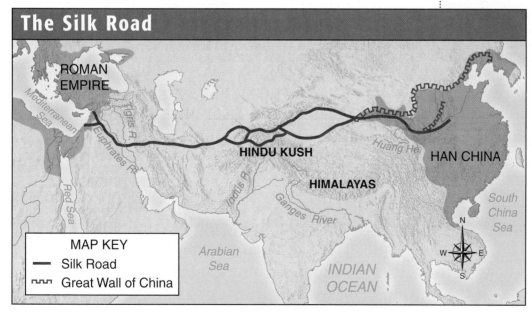

**The Silk Road**

ROMAN EMPIRE

Mediterranean Sea

Tigris R.

Euphrates R.

Red Sea

HINDU KUSH

Indus R.

Ganges River

HIMALAYAS

Huang He

HAN CHINA

South China Sea

Arabian Sea

INDIAN OCEAN

MAP KEY
— Silk Road
᠊ᠣᠣᠣ Great Wall of China

## The Fall of the Han Dynasty

The inventions of the Han did not always help the poor people. The gap between the rich people and the poor people grew wide.

The Chinese made silk using the threads of silkworms.

Around A.D. 200, outside groups, including the Huns, attacked China. They broke through the Great Wall of China. The Han Dynasty began to lose power. The emperors were too weak to keep the country together. In A.D. 220, the Han Dynasty came to an end. Without a steady government, the flow of ideas slowed. China went from a time of much invention to a time of little or no invention. This lasted about 350 years.

# Lesson 3 Review

Choose words from the list that best complete the paragraphs. One word will not be used.

## Word List

Mediterranean
  Sea

cruel

protection

Europe

bureaucracy

The Qin Dynasty lasted only a short time. Shi Huangdi did many good things. He built the Great Wall of China to give __1__ to China. As a ruler, though, he was known for being __2__. Shi Huangdi had thousands of life-size soldiers buried with him in a mountain tomb.

The Han Dynasty lasted more than 400 years. To become a government official, a person needed to pass a test. China needed a __3__ because it was so large and had millions of people. The Silk Road stretched from China to the __4__. It allowed Chinese ideas to spread. The Han Dynasty ended in A.D. 220.

# LESSON 4

# Religion in China

## Before You Read

- Why might a ruler want to burn religious books?

- What lessons can be learned from nature?

During the Chinese period of the Warring States, several new ideas developed. This is considered one of the best times in Chinese philosophy. People needed to make sense out of the troubled time. One important idea to come out of this time was the idea of the **yin and yang**. Yin was darkness and weakness. Yang was brightness and strength. The Chinese believed that when yin and yang were balanced, there would be peace.

## New Words
yin and yang
Confucianism
sage
Daoism

## People and Places
Kong Fuzi
Confucius

Yin and yang symbol

The yin and yang symbol is popular in Chinese art.

### The Beginning of Confucianism

Another idea from this time became a major philosophy—**Confucianism**. A man named Kong Fuzi was born during the time of the Warring States, around 550 B.C. Today, we know this **sage**, or wise teacher, as Confucius.

Few people listened to the ideas of Confucius during his lifetime. But over time, his ideas became more popular. Teachers continued spreading his ideas. The Qin Dynasty did not approve of Confucianism. Shi Huangdi had hundreds of teachers killed. He ordered all books on Confucianism burned. But some people hid many of these books. In this way, the ideas of Confucius were saved.

### The Ideas of Confucius

What did Confucius teach? Why would his ideas upset a ruler such as Shi Huangdi? Confucius lived in a time of many wars. He wanted law and order. He thought that keeping the peace was the highest goal of government.

Confucius said that the best rulers were fair and just. They first learned to rule themselves. Good rulers, Confucius said, should be like fathers are to their families. They should be loving and set a good example.

Confucius

66When a [leader's] personal conduct is correct, his government [works well] without the issuing of orders. If his personal conduct is not correct, he may issue orders but they will not be followed.99

Confucius did not write any books. His followers collected his sayings and wrote them down. The most famous book of sayings is called the *Analects*. Confucius taught about how people should behave. He said that society would be at peace if people behaved in the right way. People should treat others the way they want to be treated.

Confucius put a high value on family life. In China, most families were large. They included the grandparents as well as the parents. There were clear rules to follow. If everyone followed these rules, the family would have peace and good fortune. Confucius believed the same was true of the government. Countries needed strong leaders in order to keep harmony and peace.

Confucianism continued to grow even though the Qin Dynasty did not approve of it. During the Han Dynasty, Confucianism became the official philosophy of China.

Confucius with students

## Daoism

The Han also supported a religion called **Daoism**. Daoism began around 500 B.C., also during the period of the Warring States. The book of Daoism is called the *Dao de Jing*. Daoism teaches people to follow the way of nature. In other words, people should look to nature to see how to live.

For example, think of a river. How does the water behave? The water follows the easiest route. It moves around rocks. It always heads for the lowest point. Over time, the river is powerful enough to wear away the hardest rocks.

Daoism teaches people to follow the way of nature.

Daoist charm

Daoism teaches that people should follow that example. They shouldn't work too hard. They should not worry about having power. They should not worry about getting rich. Instead, people should be patient. Good things will come if they move through life the way water moves in a river.

Both Confucianism and Daoism became important in China. Confucianism appealed to those looking for clear rules. Daoism was followed by people wanting more freedom and fewer rules.

Hinduism, Buddhism, Confucianism, and Daoism all have survived over the centuries. They are sometimes called Eastern religions because they began in Asia. These religions are still practiced mostly in Asia. But people in all parts of the world have been affected by these teachings.

## Lesson 4 Review

Choose words from the list that best complete the paragraphs. One word will not be used.

**Word List**

nature

Qin

Han

peace

Asia

Confucius thought the highest goal of government was to keep the __1__. He said the best rulers were fair and just. Centuries after Confucius died, his ideas became more popular. Under the __2__ Dynasty, Confucianism became the official philosophy of China.

Daoism began around 500 B.C. It taught that people should look to __3__ to see how to act. Hinduism, Buddhism, Confucianism, and Daoism all began in __4__. They are still practiced today by people all over the world.

## Summary

- The Mauryan empire of India began in 322 B.C. in the Ganges River valley. The Gupta empire began around A.D. 320. The Gupta empire was the Golden Age of India.

- Hinduism and Buddhism began in India. Hinduism has many gods and a caste system. Buddhism teaches people to seek peace.

- During the Han Dynasty, the Chinese improved government and invented many things. They also expanded trade.

- Confucianism and Daoism began around 500 B.C. Confucianism teaches people to be fair and just. Daoism teaches people to follow nature.

## Find Out More!

After reading Chapter 10, you're ready to go online. **Explore Zone**, **Quiz Time**, and **Amazing Facts** bring this chapter of world history alive.

Visit www.exploreSV.com and type in the chapter code **1-Ch10**.

## Vocabulary

Number your paper from 1 to 6. Write the word or words from the list that best complete the paragraphs. One word will not be used.

Around 273 B.C. in India, Asoka began to follow the religious teachings of __1__. This religion says that to live right, people must follow the __2__. If a person follows these steps, the person enters a state of mind called __3__. Asoka believed in __4__, or never hurting others.

The Gupta Empire supported __5__, a religion based on the beliefs of the Aryans. The followers of this religion were divided into castes. A person could be __6__ into a higher caste if he or she lived a good life.

### Word List

**Eightfold Path**

**ahimsa**

**gravity**

**nirvana**

**reborn**

**Hinduism**

**Buddhism**

## Comprehension

Number your paper from 1 to 4. Write the word or words from the list that best complete each sentence. One word will not be used.

1. During the Qin Dynasty, the _____ was linked together to protect China.

2. The Han used a _____ to manage their large kingdom.

3. The trade route called the _____ linked Asia and Europe.

4. The Chinese believed that balancing _____ created peace.

**Word List**

yin and yang
Great Wall
porcelain
Silk Road
bureaucracy

## Critical Thinking

**Conclusions**   Number your paper from 1 to 3. Read each pair of sentences below. Then look for a conclusion that follows from these sentences. Write the letter of the correct conclusion.

1. The Huns invaded Rome.
   They also took over northern and western India.

2. Shi Huangdi burned books about Confucianism.
   He also killed hundreds of teachers of Confucianism.

3. Asoka did everything he could to preserve life.
   He built hospitals and stopped the killing of animals.

### Conclusions

a. Asoka believed in ahimsa, or never hurting others.

b. The Qin Dynasty did not approve of Confucianism.

c. The Huns conquered large areas of land in Europe and Asia.

## Writing

Write a short paragraph explaining why the Gupta Empire is known as the Golden Age of India.

## Skill Builder: Reading a Diagram

A **diagram** is a picture that helps you understand information. The diagram on this page helps you understand the Great Wall of China.

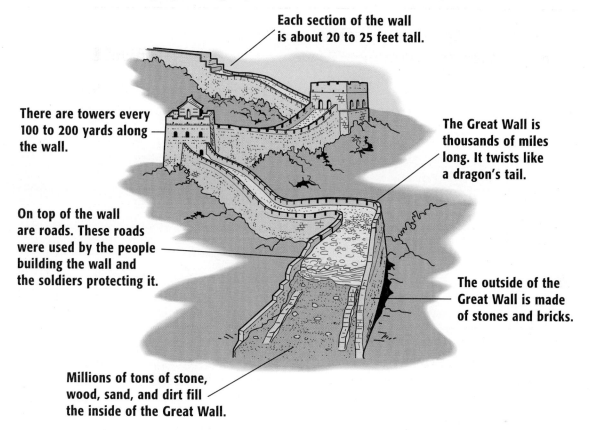

**Each section of the wall is about 20 to 25 feet tall.**

**There are towers every 100 to 200 yards along the wall.**

**The Great Wall is thousands of miles long. It twists like a dragon's tail.**

**On top of the wall are roads. These roads were used by the people building the wall and the soldiers protecting it.**

**The outside of the Great Wall is made of stones and bricks.**

**Millions of tons of stone, wood, sand, and dirt fill the inside of the Great Wall.**

Number your paper from 1 to 5. Write the word or number that best completes each sentence.

|   |   |   |   |   |
|---|---|---|---|---|
| 25 | 200 | roads | thousands | millions |

**1.** The Great Wall twists like the tail of a dragon for _____ of miles.

**2.** There are towers every 100 to _____ yards along the wall.

**3.** The inside of the Great Wall is filled with _____ of tons of stone, wood, sand, and dirt.

**4.** Each section of the wall is about 20 to _____ feet tall.

**5.** There are _____ on top of the wall.

# UNIT 3

# Rise and Fall of Civilizations

## 500–1000

Every early civilization had a story of its own. As you have seen, some made a brief appearance and then faded. Others stayed longer and affected future generations. Civilizations in one part of the world might have struggled. At the same time, civilizations in another part of the world might have been very powerful.

This unit tells about the 500 years following the fall of Rome. Europe suffered through some hard times. Other civilizations, however, experienced some of their greatest years. Civilizations in Asia, for example, took giant steps forward in art, science, and medicine.

A.D.           500                         600                       700

**A.D. 500**
The Byzantine Empire and the Sassanid Dynasty become two of the most powerful kingdoms.

**A.D. 609**
A six-year-old boy named Pacal becomes king of a Mayan city.

**A.D. 700**
The Soninke people rule Ghana in West Africa and control the gold trade.

138

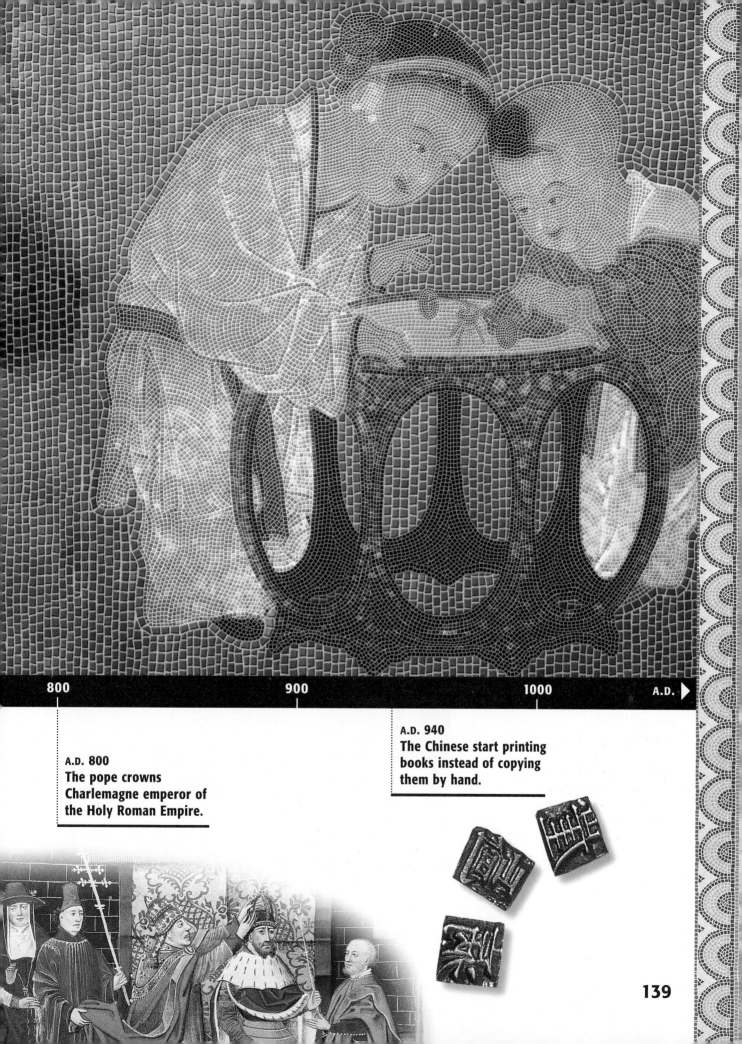

800        900        1000    A.D.

A.D. 940
The Chinese start printing
books instead of copying
them by hand.

A.D. 800
The pope crowns
Charlemagne emperor of
the Holy Roman Empire.

# LESSON 1

# After the Fall of Rome

## New Words

Middle Ages
barbarians
mayor of the palace
Islam
Muslims
Papal States
Vikings
sagas

## People and Places

Clovis
Merovingians
Charles Martel
Arabs
Tours
Pepin
Carolingians
Lombards
France
Normans
Normandy

## Before You Read

- How might the church help a ruler?
- How might invaders affect the culture of the people they invade?

The Western Roman Empire fell in A.D. 476. For the next 500 years, no strong kingdom or empire ruled the area. The German invaders set up several kingdoms. Europe entered the **Middle Ages**. For Europe, this was a time between the ancient world and the modern world.

The Germans were very different from Romans. They wore rough clothes and animal skins. They carried weapons and fought often. They did not write books or build temples or paint pictures. Romans called them **barbarians**.

Barbarians were fierce warriors.

Clovis became a Christian in 496.

## Merovingians

The Franks were one group of barbarians. A 15-year-old boy named Clovis became king of the Franks in 481. For ten years, he went to war with neighboring barbarians. He conquered lands and became the first king of the Merovingian Dynasty.

In 496, Clovis became a Christian. He forced all his followers to become Christians, too. The church leaders then supported Clovis and allowed the Merovingian kings to continue as rulers of the kingdom.

The Merovingians stayed in power for about 275 years. Most of the kings were weak. They became known as the "do-nothing kings." Power shifted to the king's officials. The most powerful official was the **mayor of the palace**.

In 732, Charles Martel was the mayor of the palace. That year, he led his army against Arab attackers. These Arabs practiced a new religion called **Islam**. Charles Martel defeated the **Muslims**, or believers of Islam, at the Battle of Tours. The church then supported Charles Martel instead of the Merovingian king.

Charles Martel defeated the Muslims at the Battle of Tours.

Pepin

Charles Martel held the power of a king without the title. His son Pepin changed that. Pepin wanted to take the title of king away from the powerless Merovingians. He asked the pope to choose either him or the Merovingian king to be the ruler. The pope chose Pepin. The Merovingian Dynasty ended in 751 when Pepin was crowned the new king of the Franks.

## Carolingians

Pepin's rule began the Carolingian Dynasty. The Carolingians and the church worked closely together. Since the pope chose Pepin to be king, Pepin felt loyal to the pope.

Shortly after becoming king, Pepin sent an army of Franks to defeat the Lombards, a German group who had invaded Rome. Pepin gave the pope the captured Lombard lands. These lands became known as the **Papal States**, or states of the pope.

## Trouble from the North

Few Europeans knew much about the clans living in far northern Europe. These clans lived in lands that are now Norway, Sweden, and Denmark. In 793, these **Vikings**, or "Northmen," began attacking the rest of Europe.

Vikings sailed from northern Europe in long, fast ships.

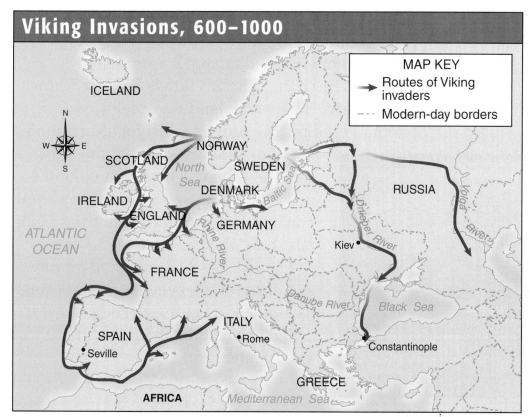

## Viking Invasions, 600–1000

MAP KEY
→ Routes of Viking invaders
- - - Modern-day borders

ICELAND

NORWAY

SCOTLAND

SWEDEN

North Sea

DENMARK

RUSSIA

IRELAND

Baltic Sea

ENGLAND

GERMANY

Rhine River

Dnieper River

Volga River

ATLANTIC OCEAN

Kiev

FRANCE

Danube River

Black Sea

ITALY

Rome

SPAIN

Seville

Constantinople

AFRICA

GREECE

Mediterranean Sea

Europeans became very afraid of the Vikings. The Vikings had fast ships. Using sails and long oars, they could cross the open seas or sail up rivers. They were skilled sailors. First, the Vikings attacked lands in the modern-day countries of England, Scotland, and Ireland. Later, they moved south and east, attacking areas in France, Italy, Spain, and Russia.

The Vikings attacked churches to steal gold and silver. They burned many churches to the ground. The Vikings often went to the same place more than once. They wanted to make sure they hadn't left anything valuable behind.

## Viking Settlers

Ruled by small German kingdoms, the Europeans could not stop the strong Vikings. Over time, the Vikings began to settle in the areas that they had invaded.

The Vikings began their invasions from what is now Norway, Sweden, and Denmark. What sea did they cross to reach England?

A Viking

In 911, one king gave some Vikings a huge piece of land in modern-day France. Many Vikings there learned to speak French and became Christians. These Vikings became known as Normans. Their new land was called Normandy, after the French word for "Northmen."

Viking carving

Other Vikings explored the North Atlantic Ocean. They built colonies in Iceland and Greenland. They even reached North America, but they did not settle there.

The Vikings had many adventures, and storytelling became an important part of Viking culture. Their stories, called **sagas**, told about the many Viking adventures.

## Lesson 1 Review

Choose words from the list that best complete the paragraphs. One word will not be used.

**Word List**

**Lombards**

**Tours**

**sagas**

**Vikings**

**Franks**

Clovis was king of the __1__. In 496, he became a Christian. He conquered lands and began the Merovingian Dynasty. In 732, Charles Martel won the Battle of __2__. His son, Pepin, ended the rule of the Merovingians when the pope chose him to be king. Pepin later gave the pope land that he captured in Italy.

The __3__ came from northern Europe. They were skilled sailors with fast ships. Some of them settled in France and became known as Normans. They told __4__ about their many adventures.

**LESSON 2**

# Life in the Early Middle Ages

## Before You Read

- Why might a time be called the "Dark Ages"?
- How could a ruler offer protection to the people of the kingdom?

The early Middle Ages in western Europe are sometimes called the **Dark Ages**. The Roman Empire was gone. There was no central government. Roads and bridges were not repaired. Schools closed. Trade slowed down, too. Most merchants didn't want to travel in Europe during this time. They worried that robbers or invaders might attack them. People left the cities and moved to the country.

### New Words
Dark Ages
feudalism
fief
lord
vassal
manor
serfs
monasteries
convents

### People and Places
Charlemagne
Gaul
Leo III
Holy Roman Empire

Many people moved to the country during western Europe's early Middle Ages.

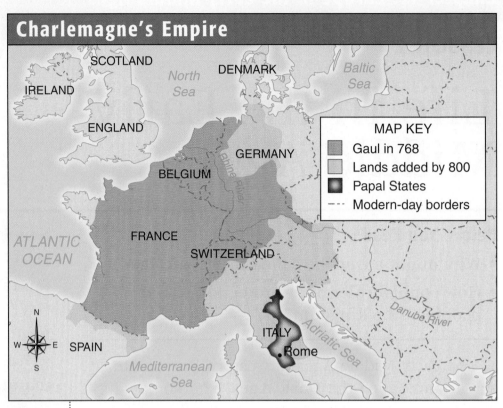

## Charlemagne's Empire

MAP KEY
- Gaul in 768
- Lands added by 800
- Papal States
- - - Modern-day borders

Charlemagne ruled much of western Europe. Did Charlemagne gain control of much of the Papal States before or after 768?

## Charlemagne

One man tried to bring Europe together again. Charles the Great, or Charlemagne, was the son of Pepin. In 768, Charlemagne became king of the Franks. He ruled an empire called Gaul. His empire covered all of modern-day France and parts of Germany, Belgium, and Switzerland. Charlemagne added lands to his kingdom. By 800, he had gained control over much of western Europe, including the Papal States.

The poem *The Song of Roland* celebrates the greatness of Charlemagne. No one knows who wrote the poem. The opening lines tell of Charlemagne's victories in Spain.

## Voices
**In History**

"Charles the King, our Lord and [emperor]
Full seven years [he traveled] in Spain,
Conquered the land, and won the [West],
Now no [fort] against him [does] remain,
No city walls are left for him to gain.""

Charlemagne tried to bring Europe out of the Dark Ages. Although he did not know how to write, he knew the importance of education. He opened new schools and hired the best teachers. He supported artists and writers.

## The Holy Roman Empire

Charlemagne also worked closely with the church to spread Christianity. On Christmas Day in the year 800, Pope Leo III crowned Charlemagne and declared him emperor of the Holy Roman Empire. Three hundred years after the fall of Rome, the idea of a Roman Empire still existed. When Pope Leo crowned Charlemagne, it suggested that the pope had more power than the emperor. This was only the beginning of a long struggle. For centuries, popes and rulers in Europe would fight over who had the most power.

Charlemagne died in 814. His three grandsons divided up the land, but they could not stop invaders such as the Vikings from taking over many parts of the empire. Europe once again became a land of small kingdoms.

Pope Leo III crowned Charlemagne as emperor of the Holy Roman Empire.

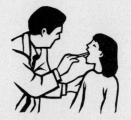

## Did You Know?

**Say "Ahhhh"**

It's never fun to be sick. But it was really tough in Europe's Dark Ages. People thought diseases were caused by evil spirits. To get rid of a fever, people were told to swallow spiders wrapped in raisins. To stop an aching tooth, they had to touch a dead man's tooth. For stomach problems, they tied an eel skin around their knee. If their leg was bothering them, the leg might have been cut open so that evil spirits would pour out along with the blood.

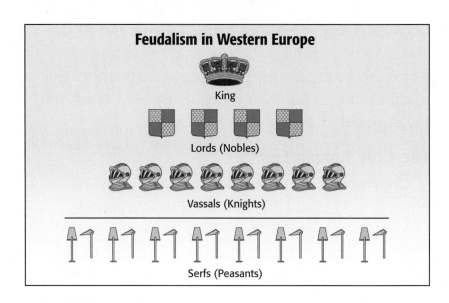

**Feudalism in Western Europe**

King

Lords (Nobles)

Vassals (Knights)

Serfs (Peasants)

## Feudalism

Charlemagne's death ended any hope for a strong central government. The local kings needed to protect the people. Wealthy nobles could offer that protection by providing knights and soldiers. The knights and soldiers served the nobles in exchange for land. This began the system of **feudalism**.

In feudalism, nobles gave each knight a **fief**, or large piece of land. In return, the knights promised to be loyal to the noble. Under this system, the noble who gave the land was a **lord**. The knight who received the land was a **vassal**. It was possible for a lord to be a vassal to an even more powerful lord.

## Life on the Manor

The fief that the lord ruled over was his **manor**. The manor usually included peasants who farmed the land. The peasants, or **serfs**, were bound to the land. They had to work on the manor where they were born.

Serfs grew all the food for themselves, the lord, and the lord's family. They cut down trees to make lumber. They chopped wood for fires. They raised animals for meat and wool. Serfs made almost everything the manor needed.

Serfs often worked in the fields of a manor.

## Religion and Culture

Life in the Middle Ages centered around the church. There were even religious communities. Men sometimes joined **monasteries** and became monks. Women sometimes joined **convents** and became nuns. These people lived for God alone and promised never to marry. They spent their days working, reading the Bible, and praying.

The power of the church affected culture, too. Most art from this time was about religion. Music was written for church services. Plays were written about Bible stories. Monks began decorating religious books with colorful paintings. They often painted pictures inside the first letter of a story.

This religious work is decorated with colorful paintings.

# Lesson 2 Review

Choose words from the list that best complete the paragraphs. One word will not be used.

The early Middle Ages are sometimes called the __1__. It was a time of invasions and no central government. In 768, __2__ became king of the Franks. In 800, Pope Leo III crowned him emperor of the Holy Roman Empire.

After Charlemagne's death, Europe was ruled by local kings. The system of __3__ developed. A knight who promised to fight for a lord was a __4__. Serfs lived on a lord's manor. They worked the land and provided food for the lord and the lord's family.

The culture and art of the Middle Ages was centered on the church. Some people joined religious communities.

### Word List

**Charlemagne**

**feudalism**

**noble**

**vassal**

**Dark Ages**

## LESSON 3

# Eastern Europe

### New Words
Justinian Code
mosaics
icons
Catholic Church
Orthodox Church

### People and Places
Byzantine Empire
Justinian
Theodora
Russia
Kiev
Kievan Russia
Zoe
Romanus III
Michael IV
Michael V

### Before You Read
- Why might one culture want to copy another?
- What might cause one church to separate into two churches?

The fall of the Western Roman Empire in A.D. 476 sent western Europe into the Dark Ages. But the Eastern Roman Empire continued another one thousand years. It became known as the Byzantine Empire. The Byzantines wanted to gain back the glory of the Roman Empire. They built aqueducts, roads, and beautiful churches in the capital city of Constantinople. One church still stands today—the Hagia Sophia. When it was built, it was the world's largest and most magnificent church.

Hagia Sophia was the largest building in Constantinople.

The inside of Hagia Sophia is richly decorated.

## The Byzantine Empire

In 527, Emperor Justinian set out to make the Byzantine Empire as mighty as the ancient Roman Empire. He conquered lands in the West, including Athens, Rome, and Carthage. He took the Roman laws and made them easier to understand. This new set of laws became known as the **Justinian Code**.

Justinian's wife, Theodora, played a large role in Justinian's government. She helped him choose army officials. She encouraged Justinian to make laws that were fair to women. One law allowed parents to leave property to their daughters. Before this change, they could only leave property to their sons.

The Byzantine Empire became known for its art. The Byzantine people filled churches with paintings and **mosaics**, or pictures made from small pieces of colored stone or glass.

Constantinople was the largest city in Europe. The city dazzled visitors. Most people had never seen so many markets or so many beautiful buildings. One man wrote of the city, "We knew not whether we were in heaven or on Earth."

This mosaic shows Theodora.

## One Religion, Two Churches

After 476, there was little communication between the two capital cities, Rome and Constantinople. The church in the East developed different ideas from the church in the West.

One difference involved **icons**. In the West, few people could read or write. The church used icons so people could learn Bible stories. In the East, church leaders felt it was wrong to pray to icons. They ordered that all the icons be destroyed. The two churches did not agree on other issues. By 1054, they had split into two separate groups. The **Catholic Church** was based in Rome. The **Orthodox Church** was based in Constantinople.

## Beginning of Russia

The Vikings invaded the lands of Russia during the 800s. Together with the local people, the Vikings captured Kiev and other cities. The new lands became known as Kievan Russia.

There were many trade routes between Russia and the Byzantine Empire. The Russians began to copy the Byzantine style of writing and painting. They also copied the customs of the Byzantines.

Church leaders in the East ordered that all icons be destroyed.

Many trade routes between Kievan Russia and the Byzantine Empire followed rivers. Which river ran from Kiev to the Black Sea?

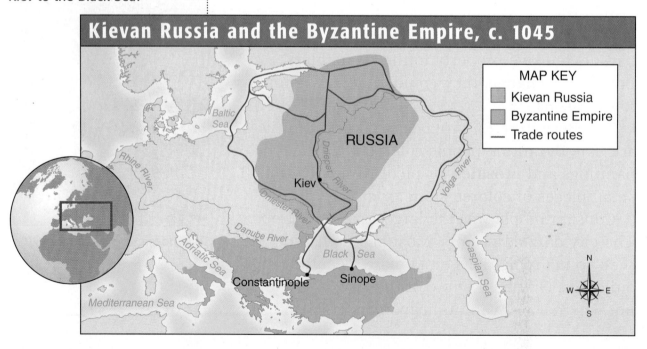

Kievan Russia and the Byzantine Empire, c. 1045

MAP KEY
- Kievan Russia
- Byzantine Empire
- Trade routes

Baltic Sea

Rhine River

RUSSIA

Dnieper River

Volga River

Kiev

Dniester River

Danube River

Caspian Sea

Adriatic Sea

Black Sea

Constantinople     Sinope

Mediterranean Sea

N
W    E
S

## Empress Zoe (978–1050)

In 1028, the Byzantine emperor was dying. He had no sons. His 50-year-old daughter, Zoe, was in line to take over the throne. The emperor didn't think Zoe could successfully rule the empire. So he arranged for her to marry Romanus III.

Zoe didn't love Romanus, and Romanus didn't love Zoe. After six years, Zoe had Romanus killed. She then married the man she did love— Michael IV.

When Michael died in 1041, his nephew, Michael V, ruled with Zoe. Michael V did not want to share power with Zoe. He tried to send her to a convent. But the Byzantine people rose up against him. They brought Empress Zoe back to power. For a few months, Zoe ruled with her sister. Then she married a third husband. Together, Zoe, her sister, and her husband ruled the Byzantine Empire until Zoe's death in 1050.

## Lesson 3 Review

Choose words from the list that best complete the paragraphs. One word will not be used.

The Western Roman Empire fell in 476. But the Eastern Roman Empire continued. It became known as the __1__ Empire. Under the rule of __2__, the empire gained back some western lands.

There was little communication between Rome and Constantinople. Church leaders argued over the use of icons and other issues. The church split in two. The church in the West became known as the __3__ Church. The church in the East became known as the __4__ Church.

**Word List**

Justinian

Byzantine

Orthodox

Catholic

Russian

### Summary

- The period when western Europe was between the ancient and modern worlds is called the early Middle Ages, or "Dark Ages."

- Vikings invaded western Europe in 793. Some Vikings settled in France. Others continued to explore the North Atlantic Ocean.

- The Merovingians ruled western Europe for 275 years. The Merovingian Dynasty ended in 751 when Pepin became king of the Franks.

- Charlemagne tried to improve education and art. He also tried to spread Christianity.

- The Eastern Roman Empire became known as the Byzantine Empire. The Byzantine Empire produced beautiful churches and art.

## Find Out More!

After reading Chapter 11, you're ready to go online. **Explore Zone**, **Quiz Time**, and **Amazing Facts** bring this chapter of world history alive.

Visit www.exploreSV.com and type in the chapter code **1-Ch11**.

### Vocabulary

Number your paper from 1 to 5. Write the word or words from the list that best complete each analogy. One word will not be used.

1. Hot is to cold as _____ were to the Romans.

2. Epics were to the Greeks as _____ were to the Vikings.

3. The Code of Hammurabi was to the Babylonians as the _____ was to the Byzantines.

4. Bas-reliefs were to the Zapotecs as _____ were to the Byzantines.

5. The Catholic Church was to the Western Roman Empire as the _____ was to the Eastern Roman Empire.

**Word List**

mosaics

vassals

sagas

Orthodox Church

Justinian Code

barbarians

## Comprehension

Number your paper from 1 to 4. Write the letter of the correct answer.

1. Who was the first king of the Merovingians?
   - **a.** Leo III
   - **b.** Charles Martel
   - **c.** Clovis
   - **d.** Pepin

2. Who tried to bring Europe out of the Dark Ages?
   - **a.** Empress Zoe
   - **b.** Charlemagne
   - **c.** Theodora
   - **d.** Romanus III

3. What did culture in the Middle Ages center around?
   - **a.** the church
   - **b.** education
   - **c.** the theater
   - **d.** trade

4. What city was the capital of the Byzantine Empire?
   - **a.** Normandy
   - **b.** Kiev
   - **c.** Rome
   - **d.** Constantinople

## Critical Thinking

**Fact or Opinion**   Number your paper from 1 to 6. For each fact, write **Fact**. Write **Opinion** for each opinion. You should find two sentences that are opinions.

1. Charles Martel defeated the Muslims at the Battle of Tours.
2. Pepin should not have given the Papal States to the pope.
3. The Vikings who settled in France were called Normans.
4. *The Song of Roland* is the best poem about Charlemagne.
5. Justinian wanted his empire to be like the Roman Empire.
6. The Byzantine people brought Empress Zoe back to power.

## Writing

Write a paragraph explaining why western Europe's Middle Ages are sometimes called the Dark Ages.

## LESSON 1

# The Rise of Islam

### New Words

bedouins
Allah
idols
hijrah
Kaaba
Qur'an
Five Pillars of Islam
prophet
fast
hajj
mosques

### People and Places

Arabian Peninsula
Arabia
Mecca
Muhammad
Medina
Palestine
Syria

### Before You Read

- What do some religions have in common?
- Why do people often oppose new religions?

The Arabian Peninsula, or Arabia, is in Southwest Asia. The peninsula is almost entirely desert. Some people lived in this area as **bedouins**, or nomads. Others settled in the few places with water. But for most of early history, very few people lived in Arabia.

Trade routes connected Arabia with both Africa and the rest of Asia. The Arabian city of Mecca became a trade center. The leader of Islam, Muhammad, was born in Mecca around 570.

Bedouins use camels for travel in the deserts of Arabia.

This caravan is traveling to Mecca.

## The Life of Muhammad

Muhammad became a caravan manager. Meeting people along the trade routes, Muhammad probably heard the teachings of Judaism and Christianity.

Muslims believe that one day Muhammad went to a cave to pray. There, the angel Gabriel appeared. Gabriel told Muhammad he was to be the messenger of **Allah**. Gabriel also told Muhammad that there was only one God. The angel said that all people were equal. All people should share their wealth with the poor.

Muhammad started to teach this message. At first, few people listened. The people of Mecca had many gods. They did not like hearing that there was only one God. Merchants made money by selling **idols**, or statues of gods. They feared they would lose money if people believed in only one God. Some people in Mecca even wanted Muhammad killed.

Map of Mecca

A page from the Qur'an

In A.D. 622, Muhammad left Mecca. He went to the Arabian city of Medina, where people accepted him. This journey from Mecca to Medina is called the **hijrah**, which means a "journey from danger." It marks the first year of the Islamic calendar, just as the birth of Jesus marks the first year of the Christian calendar.

The people of Medina were more open to Muhammad's message. In 630, he returned to Mecca with an army. After several years of fighting, the people of Mecca accepted Islam. Muhammad went to the **Kaaba**. This was a temple where many idols were stored. He destroyed the idols. Two years later, in 632, Muhammad died.

## The Beliefs of Islam

Muslims believe that Gabriel spoke to Muhammad many times. Muhammad wrote down the words of Allah as spoken through Gabriel. These writings became the **Qur'an**, or holy book of Islam.

The Qur'an states the five duties of all Muslims. These are called the **Five Pillars of Islam**. The

Muslims built beautiful buildings throughout Southwest Asia.

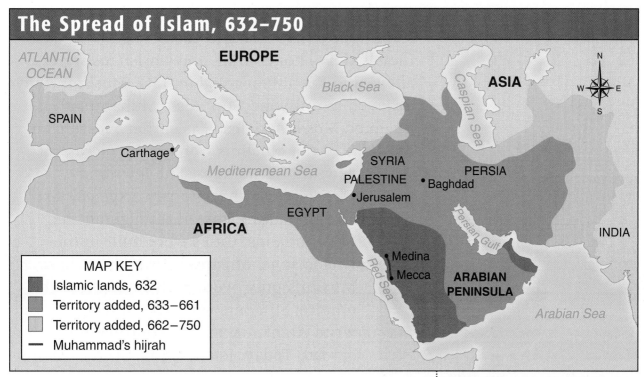

## The Spread of Islam, 632–750

ATLANTIC OCEAN

EUROPE

Black Sea

ASIA

Caspian Sea

SPAIN

Carthage

Mediterranean Sea

SYRIA
PALESTINE

PERSIA

Baghdad

Jerusalem

EGYPT

AFRICA

Persian Gulf

INDIA

Red Sea

Medina

Mecca

ARABIAN
PENINSULA

Arabian Sea

**MAP KEY**
- ■ Islamic lands, 632
- ■ Territory added, 633–661
- ☐ Territory added, 662–750
- — Muhammad's hijrah

first pillar is to believe there is only one God and that Muhammad is his **prophet**, or inspired teacher. The second pillar is to pray five times a day. Muslims must turn toward Mecca during prayer. Muslims in Mecca turn toward the Kaaba.

The third pillar is to help the poor. The fourth pillar is to **fast**, or not eat food for a period of time. This is done during the daylight hours of one month every year. The fifth pillar is to make a **hajj**, or trip to Mecca. The Qur'an says that Muslims should do this once during their life if at all possible.

## The Spread of Islam

Muhammad said that Muslims had a duty to spread Islam. After Muhammad's death, Muslims spread the religion throughout Arabia. Within a few years, Muslim armies conquered Palestine, Syria, Persia, and Egypt. Muslims spread across North Africa and into Spain. They also moved into India and central Asia.

Islam began in the Arabian Peninsula around 630. Between what years did Islam spread to Palestine and Jerusalem?

Muslims making a hajj

Many of the conquered people welcomed Islam. But others changed their religion because they had no choice. Jews and Christians were allowed to keep their religion. Like Muslims, they believed in only one God. Also, Muhammad accepted Moses and Jesus as earlier messengers of Allah. So the Muslims were more tolerant of Jews and Christians. But Jews and Christians did have to pay a special tax.

Arab culture spread throughout the Muslim lands. Cities were built in the Arabic style. **Mosques**, or places where Muslims pray, were built throughout the empire. Students were taught to speak and write Arabic. Islam has continued to spread. Today, Islam is practiced by more than a billion people around the world.

Muslims in Mecca face the Kaaba when they pray.

# Lesson 1 Review

Choose words from the list that best complete the paragraphs. One word will not be used.

**Word List**

hajj

fast

Medina

Mecca

Kaaba

Muhammad was born in __1__ in Arabia. Muslims believe that an angel appeared to Muhammad and gave him a message from Allah. Some people did not agree with the message and wanted Muhammad killed. Muhammad went to __2__ in 622. That marked the first year in the Islamic calendar. Later, Muhammad destroyed the idols at the __3__ in Mecca.

The Qur'an teaches Muslims the Five Pillars of Islam. One pillar is to make a __4__ to Mecca. After Muhammad's death, Islam continued to spread. Today, Islam is practiced around the world.

## LESSON 2

# Empire in Southwest Asia

## Before You Read

- How can religion affect government?
- Why are scientific discoveries important to civilizations?

In Chapter 7, you learned that Alexander the Great conquered the Persian Empire. After Alexander the Great died, Persia fell under the control of several different groups. The Sassanids rose to power around A.D. 200. The Sassanid Dynasty lasted 400 years. After the fall of Rome in 476, the Byzantine Empire and the Sassanid Dynasty were two of the most powerful kingdoms in the world.

This image shows a Sassanid king in battle.

## New Words

treason
relic
caliph
caliphate
bazaar
converted
calligraphy
Arabic numerals

## People and Places

Sassanids
Heraclius
Mu'awiyah
Damascus
Umayyads
Abbasids
Harun al-Rashid
Baghdad
Iraq

This container holds parts of the relic of the cross.

The Umayyads captured lands once held by the Byzantines and the Sassanids. Which two cities on this map were ruled by both the Byzantines and the Umayyads?

## The Sassanids

The Sassanids made Zoroastrianism the official religion of Persia. To practice any other religion was **treason**.

The Sassanids attacked the Byzantine Empire. They captured Syria, Palestine, and Egypt. In 619, the Sassanids burned down a Christian church in Jerusalem. They also captured a **relic** of the cross on which, many people believe, Jesus died. That angered Heraclius, the Byzantine emperor. He raised a new army and defeated the Sassanids in 628. Heraclius won back lands, as well as the relic of the cross.

The fighting, however, weakened both sides. A few years later, Muslim Arabs from the Arabian Peninsula attacked the Sassanids. In 642, the last Sassanid king died. The Arabs also captured the Byzantine lands of Syria, Palestine, and Egypt.

## The Umayyad Caliphate

In 661, Mu'awiyah became the leader of the Muslims. He was named **caliph**, or head of the Islamic communities. His rule began the

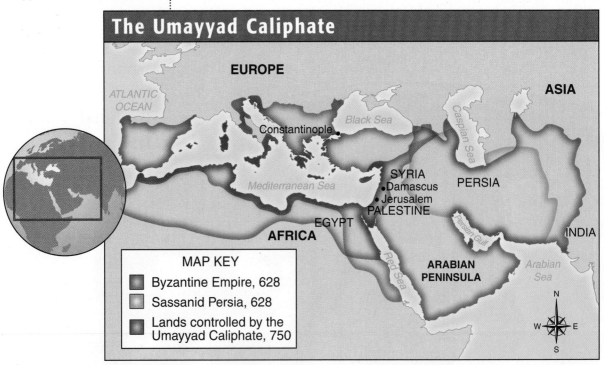

### The Umayyad Caliphate

MAP KEY
- Byzantine Empire, 628
- Sassanid Persia, 628
- Lands controlled by the Umayyad Caliphate, 750

Umayyad **Caliphate**. Mu'awiyah made the Syrian city of Damascus his capital. It became a center of trade in Asia, Europe, and Africa. Merchants from all over Southwest Asia came to the **bazaar**, or market, in Damascus.

The Umayyad Caliphate lasted less than 100 years. Arab victories continued during that period. Arabs won control of North Africa, most of Spain, Persia, and lands as far east as India. They had their only failure when they tried to capture Constantinople.

The Umayyads were poor governors. They lived a rich style of life, while the common people had nothing. The Umayyads didn't treat Muslims equally. Many non-Arabs had **converted** to Islam. But the Umayyads favored Arab Muslims. In 750, the Umayyads were replaced by the Abbasids. The Abbasids promised to treat all Muslims fairly.

Umayyad artifact

## The Golden Age of Harun al-Rashid

Harun al-Rashid ruled the Abbasids from 786 to 809. Charlemagne ruled the Holy Roman Empire around the same time. The two leaders admired each other. They exchanged gifts to help encourage peace. Harun al-Rashid even gave Charlemagne an elephant as a gift.

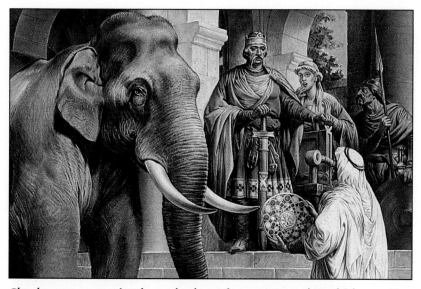

Charlemagne received an elephant from Harun al-Rashid.

Ancient Baghdad was filled with magnificent buildings.

Harun al-Rashid's capital was the new city of Baghdad. It took four years and 100,000 workers to build the city on the banks of the Tigris River. Like Damascus before it, Baghdad soon became a center for trade. Baghdad was filled with magnificent buildings and gardens. Today, Baghdad is the capital city of Iraq.

## The Abbasid Caliphate

The Abbasid Caliphate lasted 500 years. It was a time of much development. Muslim artists used designs and beautiful writing, called **calligraphy**, to decorate books and buildings. All writing was done in Arabic, which became the language for Muslim leaders. People from conquered lands such as Egypt gave up their old languages and learned Arabic. Sharing one language helped unite all Muslims.

Arabic calligraphy

Baghdad had many clean hospitals, and Muslim doctors during this time were among the world's most advanced. The doctors had to pass a difficult test before they could practice medicine. Muslim doctors were the first to add sugar to medicine. The sweet taste made people more willing to take medicine. Muslim doctors showed how a disease could be passed from one person to another. Muslim doctors also wrote books on different diseases and how to treat them.

Muslim scientists discovered that the earth was round. They also proved that the earth was about 25,000 miles around. Muslims made some of the most correct maps of the time. They also learned the movements of the moon and planets.

From India, Muslims learned to use the numbers 1 through 9. These numbers became known as **Arabic numerals**. They took the place of Roman numerals (I, II, III, IV, and so on), which were more difficult to use.

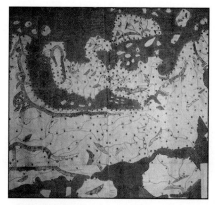

Muslim map

## Lesson 2 Review

Choose words from the list that best complete the paragraphs. One word will not be used.

The Byzantine Empire and the __1__ Dynasty were two of the most powerful kindoms after the fall of Rome. Arabs then took over the Sassanid Dynasty. Their leader, Mu'awiyah, became __2__ of the Umayyad Caliphate in 661. Soon, Muslims controlled land from Spain to India.

In 750, the Abbasids took over. They promised to treat all Muslims fairly. Their capital was __3__. The Abbasids used a form of writing called __4__. They made major advances in art, science, math, and medicine.

**Word List**

Damascus
Sassanid
Baghdad
caliph
calligraphy

## Chapter 12: Using What You've Learned

### Summary

- Muhammad was born in Mecca in A.D. 570. As an adult, he began teaching a new religion, Islam. Followers of Islam are called Muslims.

- Islam spread throughout North Africa, Spain, India, and central Asia.

- After the fall of Rome, the Sassanid Dynasty in Persia was one of the world's most powerful kingdoms.

- The Umayyad Caliphate began when Arab Muslims captured Sassanid Persia.

- In 750, the Abbasid rulers took control. Under the Abbasid Caliphate, Arab culture made advances in art, science, medicine, and mathematics.

### Find Out More!

After reading Chapter 12, you're ready to go online. **Explore Zone**, **Quiz Time**, and **Amazing Facts** bring this chapter of world history alive.

Visit www.exploreSV.com and type in the chapter code **1-Ch12**.

### Vocabulary

Number your paper from 1 to 6. Write the word or words from the list that best complete each sentence. One word will not be used.

1. The holy book of Islam is called the _____.

2. Places where Muslims pray are called _____.

3. Muslims believe that Muhammad is a _____, or inspired teacher.

4. The head of the Islamic communities was called a _____.

5. Muslim artists decorated books and buildings with designs and writing called _____.

6. The numbers 1 through 9 are called _____.

**Word List**

prophet

Arabic numerals

caliph

mosques

bazaar

Qur'an

calligraphy

## Comprehension

Number your paper from 1 to 5. Write one or more sentences to answer each question below.

1. At first, why did the people of Mecca not accept Muhammad's message?

2. What are the Five Pillars of Islam?

3. How did Islam spread to other countries?

4. What did Heraclius gain when he defeated the Sassanids?

5. What were two scientific discoveries made during the Abbasid Caliphate?

## Critical Thinking

**Main Idea**   Number your paper from 1 to 4. Write the sentence that is the main idea in each group.

1. Some people lived in Arabia as bedouins, or nomads.
   For most of early history, very few people lived in Arabia.
   Some people settled in the few places in Arabia with water.

2. Arab culture spread throughout Muslim lands.
   Cities in the Muslim empire were built in the Arabic style.
   Students were taught to speak and write Arabic.

3. Mu'awiyah made Damascus the capital of his lands.
   Merchants from all over Southwest Asia came to the bazaar in Damascus.
   Damascus was an important city in Southwest Asia.

4. The Umayyads were poor governors.
   The Umayyad leaders were rich, while the common people had nothing.
   The Umayyads did not treat all Muslims equally.

## Writing

Write a paragraph telling how the Umayyad and the Abbasid rulers of Persia were alike and how they were different.

## Skill Builder: Reading a Physical Map

A **physical map** shows what the land in an area looks like. This kind of map shows the features of the land. Some features are bodies of water, mountains, hills, and deserts.

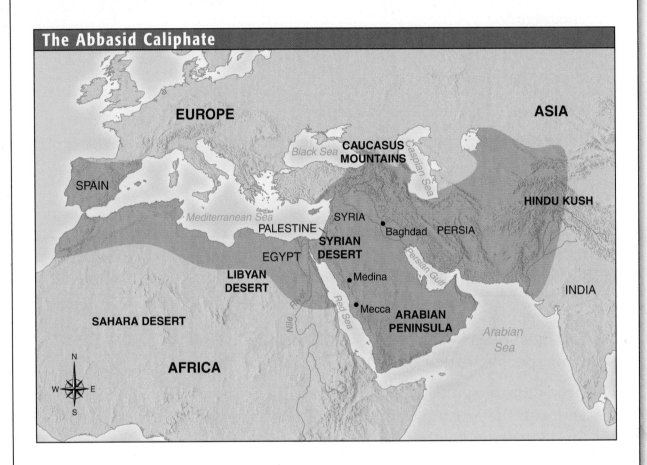

**The Abbasid Caliphate**

Number your paper from 1 to 5. Answer each question with a complete sentence.

1. What mountains are located in the Abbasid Caliphate?

2. What deserts are located in this empire?

3. What three bodies of water surround the Arabian Peninsula?

4. The Mediterranean Sea is what direction from the Syrian Desert?

5. Baghdad is located on what river?

## LESSON 1

# China Unites

## Before You Read

- Why might a ruler allow people to practice different religions?
- Do art and poetry make a civilization better?

When the Han Dynasty ended in A.D. 220, China was divided into small states. For more than 350 years, China remained divided. Then, in 581, the Sui Dynasty united China once more. This dynasty didn't last long, but it left an important mark on Chinese history.

The Sui had only two emperors. Both were harsh rulers. They made people pay high taxes. They made them work hard on **public works** projects. The first ruler, Wen Ti, made the people rebuild the Great Wall of China. The second ruler, Yang, made them dig the first **Grand Canal**. The canal connected the Huang He in the North to the Yangtze River in the South. This made it easier to trade goods throughout the kingdom.

## New Words

public works
Grand Canal
opera
movable type
gunpowder

## People and Places

Sui
Wen Ti
Yang
Yangtze River
Tang
T'ai Tsung
Empress Wu
Li Po
Song

The Grand Canal is still used today.

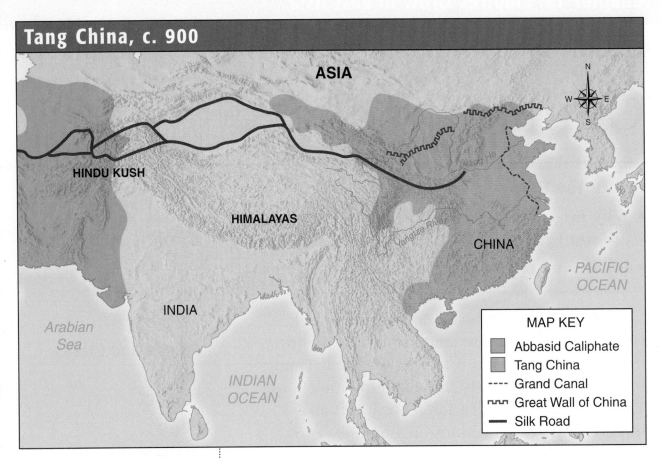

## Tang China, c. 900

ASIA

HINDU KUSH

HIMALAYAS

Yangtze River

CHINA

INDIA

Arabian
Sea

PACIFIC
OCEAN

INDIAN
OCEAN

**MAP KEY**
Abbasid Caliphate
Tang China
---- Grand Canal
ᴖᴖ Great Wall of China
— Silk Road

The Tang Dynasty ruled much of East Asia. What trade route connected the Tang Dynasty with the Abbasid Caliphate?

T'ai Tsung

## Two Tang Rulers

The Tang Dynasty replaced the Sui Dynasty in 617. The Tang kept the Mandate of Heaven for almost 300 years. China became powerful and wealthy under the Tang.

One Tang emperor, T'ai Tsung, ruled from 627 to 649. T'ai Tsung made China safe by defeating enemies. He added new lands to China. T'ai Tsung worked to make life better for the Chinese. He lowered taxes for peasants. T'ai Tsung chose strong leaders. He believed it was better to have good leaders than good laws.

T'ai Tsung accepted new ideas. Buddhism spread into China during the Tang Dynasty. Christianity, Zoroastrianism, and Islam were introduced to China through trade with the West. The local beliefs in Confucianism and Daoism also grew during the Tang Dynasty.

One of only a few female rulers in Chinese history was the Tang ruler Empress Wu. She came to power when her husband died in 690. She ruled for 15 years. Empress Wu was a stern ruler. She had many of her enemies killed. She taxed the peasants heavily. Empress Wu also wanted to spread Buddhism throughout China. She favored Buddhism because, unlike other religions, it allowed women to be rulers.

Empress Wu

## Art Under the Tang

Art and culture grew under the Tang. Poetry, for example, became popular. It was a sign of learning. Many people wrote poems. One of China's greatest poets was Li Po, who wrote about ordinary people and about nature.

Nature was a powerful force in Chinese art. One of Li Po's short poems was titled "Waterfall at Lu-Shan." It shows how Li Po felt about nature.

**"Sunlight streams on the river stones.
From high above, the river steadily plunges—
three thousand feet of sparkling water—
the Milky Way pouring down from heaven."**

## Voices
### In History

Chinese music and dance also developed. The Chinese created new musical instruments. They invented new dances. People began to sing poems and often sang several poems together. This was the beginning of Chinese **opera**. Poems were often sung in houses that served tea. The custom of drinking tea grew under the Tang.

## The Five Dynasties

The Tang Dynasty fell in 907. For the next 53 years, China had no central government. This time is known as the Five Dynasties. There were five small dynasties that came to power and fell during these years. Although there was no strong dynasty, China made progress in several areas.

Court ladies of the Tang Dynasty

Tea became an important trading good. Also, artists improved porcelain by making it harder and thinner. Around 940, the Chinese made the first attempts to print books instead of copying them by hand. Also, the first paper money was introduced in China during this time. China had few metals to make coins. Paper money made it easier for merchants to do business.

## The Song Dynasty

The Song Dynasty took control of China and ruled from 960 to 1279. The Song ruled a smaller area than the Tang did. But the Song kept tight control over the money coming in from taxes and trade. By 1000, the Song government was making three times more money than the Tang had made at the height of its dynasty.

Under the Song, the Chinese were the first to use **movable type** in printing. They cut Chinese symbols on blocks of wood. The blocks could be moved to make new sentences. Printing led to more books. More books led to more education for more people.

Printing blocks

This painting was made during the Song Dynasty.

Another new idea was the use of **gunpowder** in weapons. The Chinese had used gunpowder to make fireworks. In weapons, they used it to destroy enemy walls.

The Chinese also developed the compass, a tool for telling direction. Like compasses today, the early Chinese compass had a needle that always pointed north. The Chinese used the compass on ships when traveling long distances.

Art continued to develop under the Song. Some artists changed from using color to using black and white. This captured a special feeling in their paintings. The trees, mountains, and rivers almost seemed to move. If there were any people in a painting, they were small, suggesting that nature is more important than people.

Painting from the Song Dynasty

# Lesson 1 Review

Choose words from the list that best complete the paragraphs. One word will not be used.

Under the Sui Dynasty, the people rebuilt the Great Wall of China and built the __1__ . The Tang Dynasty leader, T'ai Tsung, lowered taxes for the peasants. He believed that good government was based on good leaders. __2__ was one of only a few female rulers in Chinese history.

The Chinese made progress during the Five Dynasties, although there was no central government. They continued that progress under the Song Dynasty. They were the first to use __3__ to print books. They used gunpowder in weapons. The Chinese also invented the __4__ to help tell direction.

**Word List**

compass

movable type

opera

Empress Wu

Grand Canal

## LESSON 2

# Korea and Japan

### New Words
mainland
ally
influence
archipelago
Shinto
shrines
Taika reforms
reforms

### People and Places
Korean Peninsula
Japan
Korea
Koguryo
Manchuria
Paekche
Silla
Koryo
Kotoku
Nara

### Before You Read
- How might living on an island affect a culture?
- Why do some cultures adopt foreign ideas?

The Korean Peninsula extends south from northeastern China. It is located between two larger neighbors—China and Japan. Around 108 B.C., the Han Dynasty of China conquered lands in Korea. Chinese culture spread to the peninsula. But three Korean kingdoms developed, which fought against the Chinese rule.

### The Three Kingdoms
The Kingdom of Koguryo controlled northern Korea. It also controlled a part of Manchuria, an

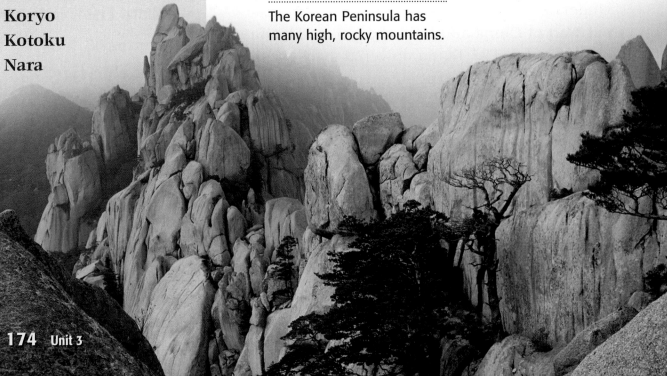

The Korean Peninsula has many high, rocky mountains.

## The Three Kingdoms

MANCHURIA

Koguryo

KOREA

Sea of Japan

Paekche — Silla

JAPAN

Yellow Sea

CHINA

N W E S

The Korean Peninsula is located between China and Japan. Which of Korea's Three Kingdoms was closest to Japan?

area on the **mainland** of Asia. The Kingdom of Paekche held the southwest corner of the peninsula. The Kingdom of Silla held the southeast corner. This time in Korean history is known as the Three Kingdoms period.

In A.D. 342, China attacked Koguryo. After several years of fighting, the Koreans kept the Chinese from taking over. Still, Chinese culture remained. The Koreans accepted Buddhism in 372. They also accepted Chinese ways in art, philosophy, and trading practices.

Around 610, the Chinese under the Sui Dynasty attacked Koguryo with a huge army. The Koreans once more held back the Chinese. Later, the Tang emperor T'ai Tsung tried three times to defeat Koguryo. Each time he failed.

Then in 668, the Chinese made the Kingdom of Silla an **ally**, or wartime friend. Silla joined with the Chinese in an attack on Koguryo and Paekche. Koguryo and Paekche were caught between the two armies and were defeated.

Earrings from Korea's Three Kingdoms period

## United Under Silla

Then Silla drove the Chinese out of Korea. By around 670, the Kingdom of Silla had united Korea for the first time. A time of peace and growth began for the Korean people. Trade with the Tang and Japan even increased under Silla control.

The Chinese had a strong **influence** on Korean culture. Both Buddhism and Confucianism grew steadily. Silla modeled its government after the Chinese government and used Chinese characters in writing.

About 200 years later, Silla leaders grew weak. Civil wars broke out. Then in 918, about the same time the Tang Dynasty ended in China, a new dynasty took over Korea. The Koryo Dynasty lasted nearly 500 years. The name *Korea* comes from this dynasty.

Bronze dragon from early Koryo Dynasty

## Early Japan

Japan is east of Korea. It is an **archipelago**, or chain of islands. It has more than 3,000 islands. Most are small, but a few are very large. In its early history, Japan was protected by the sea. No foreign army could invade and conquer it.

We know little about the early history of Japan. Scientists have found no written records before the fifth century A.D. Koreans came to Japan at that time. They brought Chinese writing with them. The Japanese then used Chinese characters to write their own language.

The Japanese adopted many other parts of Chinese culture. They studied Chinese art and wore Chinese clothing. They used Chinese ideas about government and copied the Chinese calendar. In 552, Buddhism was introduced into Japan. Many Japanese quickly accepted Buddhism, although they had their own native religion, **Shinto**. The people had no trouble practicing both religions.

Coast of Japan

This gate stands in front of a modern Shinto shrine.

## The Shinto Religion

The word *Shinto* means "the way of the gods." No one knows who started the religion. Shinto has no holy books like the Torah, the Bible, or the Qur'an.

Early Shinto **shrines** were plain buildings made from wood. They were built to honor a part of nature, such as a waterfall, some trees, or a large rock. Most Shinto gods come from nature. The most important is the sun goddess. The Japanese thought that all their emperors were related to the sun goddess. The belief that the emperor was a god lasted until the mid-1900s.

## Changes in Government

For a long time, Japan had no central government. It was divided into small states run by local clans. The Japanese did have an emperor. Although thought of as a god, the emperor was not a true leader of the government. Then, in 645, the Emperor Kotoku announced the **Taika reforms**. These **reforms** changed government in Japan.

Statue of an ancient Japanese warrior

Confucian teachers wrote the reforms. Confucianism taught that a strong central government was important. The teachers used the Tang Dynasty as a model for the reforms.

The Taika reforms made the emperor the true ruler of Japan. The power of the clan leaders was limited. The emperor ruled by the Mandate of Heaven and had total power. Unlike the Chinese emperor, however, a Japanese emperor could not lose the Mandate of Heaven.

With the Taika reforms, a central government was formed. All land came under the control of the emperor. In 710, the Japanese built a new capital at Nara. Nara looked like a small Chinese city. It had Buddhist temples and Chinese art. In time, the Japanese changed the Chinese ideas into a culture of their own.

Buddhist temple in Nara, Japan

# Lesson 2 Review

Choose words from the list that best complete the paragraphs. One word will not be used.

**Word List**

Koguryo

Silla

Shinto

ally

Taika reforms

The Koreans came under Chinese rule during the Han Dynasty. Then three kingdoms developed. Two of these kingdoms, __1__ and Paekche, fell when both China and Silla attacked. Then __2__ fought China and won control of Korea for more than 200 years.

Japan is an archipelago. The native religion of Japan was __3__. In 645, Emperor Kotoku began the __4__, which created a strong central government in Japan. The Japanese believed their emperors were gods. The emperors could not lose the Mandate of Heaven.

## LESSON 3

# Southeast Asia

### Before You Read

- How did China influence its neighbors?
- What might neighboring lands like and dislike about China?

China was so large and powerful that it influenced all of its neighbors. China's neighbors wanted to learn about Chinese inventions. They liked Chinese culture and art. They also liked Chinese writing and laws. But they did not want the Chinese to control their lives. That was why the Koreans fought the Chinese. It was also why Vietnam, China's southern neighbor, spent around 1,000 years fighting China.

Vietnamese farmers plant rice in wet fields.

### New Words
delta
guerrilla tactics
location

### People and Places
Vietnam
Red River Delta
Annam
Trung Trac
Trung Nhi
Indonesia
Sriwijaya
Sumatra
Strait of Melaka
Borobudur
Java
Prambanan

## Early Vietnamese History

More than 2,000 years ago, the Vietnamese grew rice in the rich soil of the Red River **Delta**. In 111 B.C., the Han army of China took over lands in Vietnam. At that time the land was called Annam. At first, the Chinese were kind rulers, allowing the local people to keep their customs. But then China began taxing the Vietnamese people and putting them to work for China. The Vietnamese didn't like this. They wanted to rule themselves.

In A.D. 40, the Vietnamese fought for their independence. Trung Trac and her sister Trung Nhi led the fight. Their armies defeated the Chinese, and they ruled as queens for three years. But stronger armies came back to conquer Vietnam. The Trung sisters drowned themselves rather than let the Chinese capture them. The Trung sisters became great heroes to the Vietnamese. They are still a symbol that Vietnam is free from foreign rule.

Vietnamese statue of a Hindu god

The Trung sisters led a fight for Vietnamese independence in A.D. 40.

The Vietnamese continued to fight against China. Vietnam finally won its freedom in A.D. 938. The Vietnamese used **guerrilla tactics**. They hid in jungles. They made surprise attacks at night. Then they slipped back into the jungle.

## Chinese Influence in Vietnam

The Chinese influenced the Vietnamese people and culture. The Chinese had roads, harbors, and waterways built in Vietnam. Every year, peasants were forced to give several days of free work to the government on these projects.

The Chinese trained a few Vietnamese as local officials. The Chinese taught the officials how to use the examination system. They shared the ideas of Confucius. They shared the Chinese language with the officials.

The Chinese also brought Buddhism to Vietnam. As in Japan, many Vietnamese began practicing Buddhism along with their own beliefs.

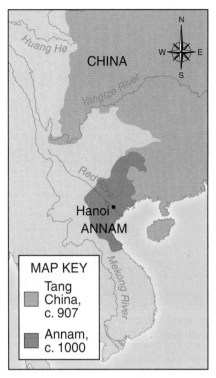

MAP KEY

Tang China, c. 907

Annam, c. 1000

Annam

This Buddhist temple was built in Vietnam in the 500s.

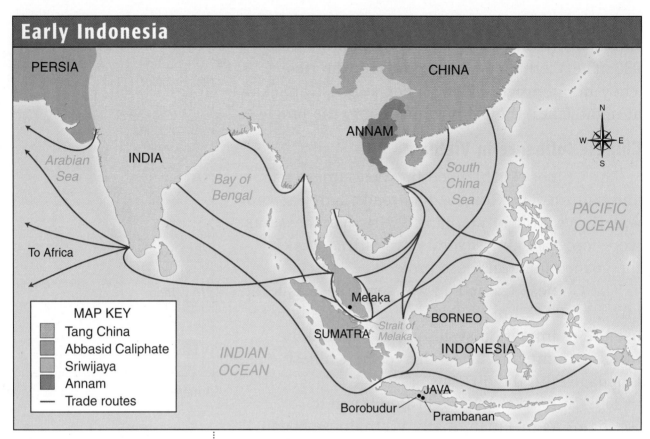

## Early Indonesia

PERSIA

CHINA

Arabian Sea

INDIA

ANNAM

Bay of Bengal

South China Sea

PACIFIC OCEAN

To Africa

Melaka

BORNEO

SUMATRA

Strait of Melaka

INDONESIA

INDIAN OCEAN

JAVA

Borobudur

Prambanan

MAP KEY

Tang China
Abbasid Caliphate
Sriwijaya
Annam
— Trade routes

Valuable trade routes ran through the Strait of Melaka. Which kingdom controlled this strait?

Statue at Borobudur

## Early History of Indonesia

Indonesia is a vast archipelago. Its more than 13,000 islands stretch 3,000 miles from the Indian Ocean to the Pacific Ocean. Long ago, traders from all parts of Asia came to Indonesia for its spices. These spices were used to flavor food. They also were used to make medicines.

One early Indonesian kingdom was Sriwijaya. It began in the seventh century on the island of Sumatra. Sriwijaya grew strong because of its **location**. It controlled the Strait of Melaka. Traders used this narrow waterway whenever they sailed from Arabia, Persia, or India to China.

## Religion in Indonesia

Trading brought many different cultures to Indonesia. Buddhism and Hinduism came from China and India. Around A.D. 800, Buddhist Indonesians built the monument called

Borobudur on the island of Java. Borobudur is the largest Buddhist monument in the world. Carvings on its eight levels show the Eightfold Path to enlightenment.

About the same time, Hindu Indonesians also built great temples on the island of Java. One temple was located on the plains of Prambanan. It was built to honor the god Shiva and stood 152 feet tall.

Both Buddhism and Hinduism spread throughout Indonesia. Like other people in Southeast Asia, the Indonesians successfully blended the new religions with their native beliefs.

Hindu temple at Prambanan

## Lesson 3 Review

Choose words from the list that best complete the paragraphs. One word will not be used.

The Vietnamese fought against China for 1,000 years. The __1__ sisters defeated the Chinese for a short time. The Vietnamese kept fighting. They used __2__ against the Chinese. Vietnam finally won its freedom in 938.

Many traders came to the islands of Indonesia for its spices. One early Indonesian kingdom was __3__ . Its location gave Indonesia contact with traders from Arabia, Persia, India, and China. Trading brought different cultures to Indonesia. Hinduism and Buddhism spread. The Buddhist monument __4__ has eight levels. It is the largest Buddhist monument in the world.

**Word List**

**guerrilla tactics**

**Melaka**

**Sriwijaya**

**Borobudur**

**Trung**

## Chapter 13: Using What You've Learned

### Summary

- The Sui Dynasty united China. China became powerful under the next dynasty, the Tang.

- Under the Song Dynasty, the Chinese invented many things.

- The Kingdom of Silla drove the Chinese out of Korea in 670.

- The first religion of Japan was Shinto. Shinto shrines were built to honor nature.

- Vietnam, or Annam, fought for around 1,000 years against China's rule.

- Trade brought many cultures to Indonesia.

### Find Out More!

After reading Chapter 13, you're ready to go online. **Explore Zone**, **Quiz Time**, and **Amazing Facts** bring this chapter of world history alive.

Visit www.exploreSV.com and type in the chapter code **1-Ch13**.

### Vocabulary

Number your paper from 1 to 5. Write the letter of the correct answer.

1. The Chinese developed the _____, a tool for telling direction.
   - **a.** compass
   - **b.** opera
   - **c.** porcelain
   - **d.** movable type

2. In 668, the Chinese made Silla an _____, or wartime friend.
   - **a.** icon
   - **b.** idol
   - **c.** ally
   - **d.** artifact

3. Japan is a chain of islands called an _____.
   - **a.** empire
   - **b.** archipelago
   - **c.** avenue
   - **d.** aqueduct

4. The _____ changed government in Japan.
   - **a.** Grand Canal
   - **b.** Trung sisters
   - **c.** Empress Wu
   - **d.** Taika reforms

5. The Vietnamese fought against the Chinese by using _____.
   - **a.** deltas
   - **b.** bedouins
   - **c.** guerrilla tactics
   - **d.** public works

## Comprehension

Number your paper from 1 to 5. Write the word or words from the list that best complete the paragraph. One word will not be used.

The __1__ Dynasty had only two emperors. These emperors made the Chinese people work hard on __2__, such as the Great Wall and the Grand Canal. In 617, the __3__ Dynasty came to power. This dynasty kept the Mandate of Heaven for almost 300 years. Then in 960, the __4__ Dynasty took control of China. During this dynasty, the Chinese started using __5__ in weapons.

**Word List**

**public works**

**movable type**

**Sui**

**gunpowder**

**Song**

**Tang**

## Critical Thinking

**Categories**  Number your paper from 1 to 5. Read the words in each group below. Think about how they are alike. Write the best title for each group.

**Korea    Indonesia    China    Vietnam    Japan**

1. built the Grand Canal
   first to use movable type
   first to use paper money

2. Kingdom of Koguryo
   Kingdom of Paekche
   Kingdom of Silla

3. Shinto religion
   small states run by local clans
   Taika reforms

4. Red River Delta
   Annam
   Trung sisters

5. spices
   island of Sumatra
   Borobudur

## Writing

Nature was a popular subject for poetry during the Tang Dynasty. Write your own short poem about nature.

## LESSON 1

# Kingdom of Ghana

**New Words**
Sahel
evaporate
monopoly
jihad

**People and Places**
Soninke
Senegal River
Niger River
Ghana
Kumbi
Al-Bakir
Wangara
Almoravids

## Before You Read

- Why might a desert make trade difficult?
- How might a kingdom's location bring it wealth?

There are no written histories from the early West African civilizations. Instead of writing, West Africans used stories and songs to pass their history from one generation to the next. Arab travelers reached West Africa in the eighth century. They were the first to write about people in West Africa.

### The Camel and the Desert

The Sahara Desert stretches across North Africa. It is so large, so dry, and so hot that traveling across it was nearly impossible. In ancient times, a few traders from Egypt made the

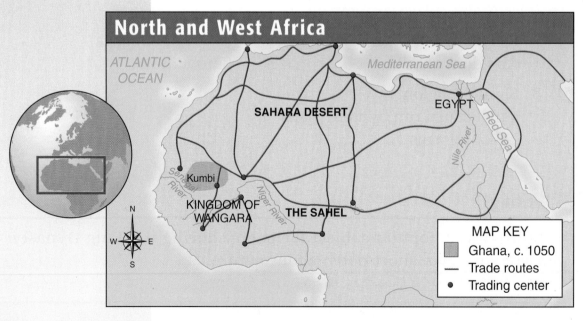

**North and West Africa**

ATLANTIC OCEAN

Mediterranean Sea

SAHARA DESERT

EGYPT

Nile River

Red Sea

Senegal River

Kumbi

Niger River

KINGDOM OF WANGARA

THE SAHEL

N W E S

MAP KEY
Ghana, c. 1050
Trade routes
Trading center

After crossing the Sahara Desert, traders came to the dry grasslands of the Sahel.

trip to West Africa. They brought back gold, ivory, and other valuable goods. But the trip was too long and hard to make it a regular trade route.

Around 750, traders from North Africa began to use camels to cross the Sahara Desert. The camels could carry heavy loads a long distance. They could walk over rough sand easily. The use of camels brought great changes to the **Sahel**, the region south of the Sahara Desert. The Sahel was a hot region of dry grasslands. It became an important trading area for goods going across the Sahara Desert.

## The Kingdom of Ghana

Around 400, people called the Soninke developed a kingdom between the Senegal River and the Niger River. By 700, the Soninke had taken over much of the West African Sahel. The leaders of the Soninke were called *Ghana*, which means "war chief." Later, their kingdom became known as Ghana. The Soninke set up a capital at Kumbi, a city on the edge of the Sahara Desert.

The kings of Ghana came from the female side of the family. When a king died, his son was not the next king. Instead, the son of the king's sister took over the throne.

The Kingdom of Ghana reached its greatest power around 1000. The Muslim traveler Al-Bakir wrote a book in 1067 called *Glimpses of Ghana*. He was greatly impressed by Ghana.

**Voices**
**In History**

66 [The king] is the master of a large empire . . . . The king of Ghana can put two hundred thousand warriors in the field . . . . [He is guarded by ten soldiers] holding shields and gold-mounted swords . . . . On his right hand are the sons of the princes . . . with gold [braided] into their hair. 99

## West African Trade

Ghana's location made it a perfect center for trade. The traders coming from North Africa and the Mediterranean Sea wanted gold. Gold was plentiful in a kingdom south of Ghana called Wangara. The people of Wangara needed salt,

Today, salt is still gathered by digging holes and letting the water evaporate.

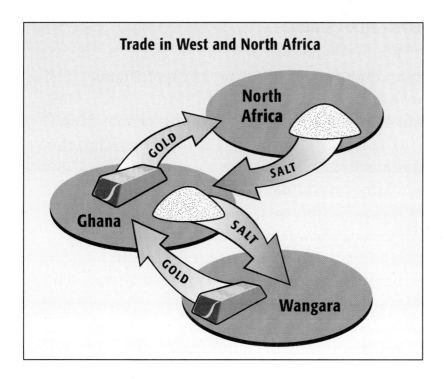

**Trade in West and North Africa**

which was gathered in North Africa. The Arabs of North Africa gathered salt by digging holes in the ground where there was salt. They filled the holes with water. Then they let the water **evaporate**, or dry up. A ring of salt was left behind. After doing this many times, a solid block of salt was created.

Along with salt, Arabs brought metals, cloth, and weapons to Ghana. In exchange, the Arabs got gold, ivory, nuts, animal skins, and slaves. The slaves worked in the homes of rich Arabs.

Ghana's location between Wangara and North Africa gave Ghana a **monopoly** over gold trade. The king owned all the gold. He could decide when to sell and when to wait for a better price.

The king of Ghana made money by taxing each load of goods coming into Ghana or going out. In addition, the Arabs and the people of Wangara paid a tribute to the king of Ghana. The king used the tax money to raise a huge army. The army kept West Africa peaceful. It also kept the trade routes safe.

### The Fall of Ghana

While Ghana was growing in power, Islam was spreading into Africa. The kings of Ghana welcomed the Muslims from North Africa. Most Muslims came as teachers. Many people from Ghana became Muslims. This helped to improve trade between North Africa and West Africa. But the kings of Ghana did not become Muslims.

In 1075, a group of Muslims called the Almoravids invaded Ghana. They came from north of Ghana. They declared a **jihad**, or struggle to protect the faith, against Ghana. The Almoravids destroyed Kumbi. They forced many people to accept Islam.

After ten years of fighting, Ghana won back its land. But the power of the king was broken. Ghana never gained back its power.

Muslim art

## Lesson 1 Review

Choose words from the list that best complete the paragraphs. One word will not be used.

**Word List**

Wangara

Sahara

monopoly

jihad

Sahel

Around 750, traders began to use camels to cross the __1__ Desert. Camels allowed them to carry heavy loads a long distance. The use of camels brought changes to the region south of the desert called the __2__.

Ghana began around 400. Ghana got gold from a kingdom south of Ghana. From the North Africans, Ghana got salt. The kings of Ghana grew rich by taxing all goods passing through the kingdom. Ghana had a __3__ on the gold trade. Muslims from the North declared a __4__ on Ghana in 1075.

## LESSON 2

# The Bantu Migrations

## Before You Read

- What causes groups to move to new areas?
- What can one culture share with another culture?

A little more than 2,000 years ago, many people from West Africa began to move. They headed south and east. They traveled to the rain forests of the Congo River. They also traveled to the **highlands** of East Africa.

The mass movement of these people is called the **Bantu migrations**. The West Africans spoke Bantu languages but left no written history. It has been difficult for scientists to learn why and how the West Africans moved.

## New Words

highlands
Bantu migrations
tones
Swahili
overpopulation
elders

## People and Places

Congo River

West Africans traveled to the highlands of East Africa.

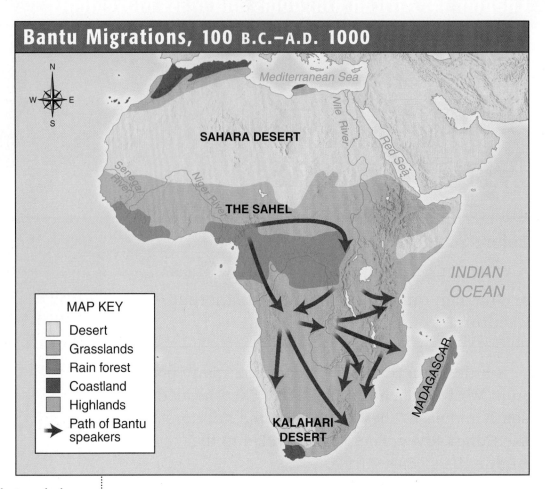

## Bantu Migrations, 100 B.C.–A.D. 1000

Mediterranean Sea

SAHARA DESERT

Nile River

Red Sea

Senegal River

Niger River

THE SAHEL

INDIAN OCEAN

MADAGASCAR

KALAHARI DESERT

**MAP KEY**
- Desert
- Grasslands
- Rain forest
- Coastland
- Highlands
- → Path of Bantu speakers

The Bantu people traveled over many different types of land. What type of land was around the northern part of the Congo River?

## The Bantu Languages

As the West Africans moved, they met other African groups. Some of these people adopted the Bantu languages. Others mixed Bantu with their own language. Bantu spread easily. Today, hundreds of languages in Africa have Bantu words. The word *Bantu*, which means "the people," is in nearly all modern African languages.

Many Africans today speak in the same way the first West Africans spoke. They use **tones** to give a word its meaning. That means one word can have several meanings, depending on how the word is spoken. If a word is spoken with a high voice, it has one meaning. If it is spoken with a low voice, it has a different meaning. The only major Bantu language that docs not use tones is **Swahili**.

## Causes for the Bantu Migrations

The Bantu migrations took place over a very long period of time—from about 100 B.C. to A.D. 1000. No one really knows why the West Africans left their homes. The reasons probably varied with different groups in different times.

Some West Africans might have left because there were too many people in their own area. Most West Africans at that time were farmers or herders. They needed open land to grow crops or raise animals. **Overpopulation** might have forced them to seek new lands. Drought or war also might have forced the West Africans to move.

A modern Bantu person from South Africa

## How They Moved

The Bantu migrations did not happen all at once. Most people believe the West Africans traveled as families or clans. Some families may have left hundreds of years after another family. Families traveled over the deserts, grasslands, and rain forests of Africa.

The Bantu people lived in huts made of dried grass.

African making iron tools

The West Africans were highly skilled and had strong iron tools. They had learned how to use iron long before many other people. They had plows that could easily prepare new lands for farming. As they moved, they could farm and find food rather easily.

Some West Africans went farther and faster than others. The herders, for example, could keep moving while their animals grazed along the way. It was easier for them to leave an old spot and move to a new one. Farmers had to wait to harvest their crops before they could move.

## Southern Africa and Eastern Africa

The West Africans shared more than their language with the people of southern and eastern Africa. They also shared their knowledge. They taught the people in other areas how to use iron. They also taught them how to plant crops such as yams and bananas.

The people of southern and eastern Africa learned new ways of farming from the West Africans.

More food led to an increase in population. More and more villages developed in southern and eastern Africa. Some villages joined together to form larger communities. Trade became more important.

As people settled in larger communities, they needed a government. Some communities grew and became states under the rule of a king. Others organized their villages under the leadership of a chief. Still others were led by a group of **elders**.

The Bantu migrations lasted more than 1,000 years. They changed southern and eastern Africa forever. They changed the languages people spoke and the tools people used.

African elders

## Lesson 2 Review

Choose words from the list that best complete the paragraphs. One word will not be used.

During the Bantu migrations, many people moved away from West Africa. The Bantu languages of West Africa spread throughout the continent. In most Bantu languages, the meaning of a word depends on its __1__. One of the reasons for the migrations might have been __2__.

The West Africans knew how to use __3__. They shared their language and knowledge with the local people. The Bantu migrations led to more organized communities. Older people called __4__ ruled some villages.

**Word List**

iron

overpopulation

elders

highlands

tone

### Summary

- Around 750, North African traders began to use camels to cross the Sahara Desert. The Sahel became an important trading area.

- The Kingdom of Ghana developed in West Africa. The kings of Ghana taxed all goods traded in the kingdom and grew rich.

- In 1075, the Almoravids invaded Ghana. After ten years of fighting, Ghana won back its land. It never gained back its power, however.

- From around 100 B.C. to A.D. 1000, the Bantu people slowly moved from West Africa to southern and eastern Africa.

- Many people in southern and eastern Africa adopted Bantu languages. They also learned farming and iron working skills from the Bantu.

## Find Out More!

After reading Chapter 14, you're ready to go online. **Explore Zone**, **Quiz Time**, and **Amazing Facts** bring this chapter of world history alive.

Visit www.exploreSV.com and type in the chapter code **1-Ch14**.

### Vocabulary

Number your paper from 1 to 5. Write the word or words from the list that best complete the paragraphs. One word will not be used.

The ___1___ was south of the Sahara Desert. It became an important trading area for goods going across the desert. Ghana's location between Wangara and North Africa gave it a ___2___ over the gold trade.

Around 2,000 years ago, the people of West Africa began a mass movement called the ___3___. Most of the Bantu languages use ___4___, such as a high or a low voice, to give a word its meaning. One possible reason for the mass movement was ___5___, or too many people living in an area.

**Word List**

Bantu
  migrations
Sahel
overpopulation
tones
jihad
monopoly

## Comprehension

Number your paper from 1 to 5. Write **True** for each sentence that is true. Write **False** for each sentence that is false.

1. West Africans used stories and songs to pass their history from one generation to the next.

2. The Sahara Desert was easy for traders to cross.

3. The kings of Ghana welcomed Muslims from North Africa.

4. The West Africans learned how to use iron long before many other people did.

5. After the Bantu migrations, some communities in southern and eastern Africa were led by elders.

## Critical Thinking

**Sequencing**   Number your paper from 1 to 5. Write the sentences below in the correct order.

By about 1000, the Bantu migrations had ended.

Traders from North Africa began to use camels to cross the Sahara Desert.

The Soninke developed a kingdom between the Senegal River and the Niger River around 400.

The Bantu migrations began.

In 1075, the Almoravids invaded Ghana and declared a jihad against the kingdom.

## Writing

Write a paragraph explaining how goods were traded in West Africa.

## Skill Builder: Reading a Flow Chart

A **flow chart** shows facts in their correct order. This flow chart shows how the Arabs of North Africa gathered salt. They traded this salt for other goods.

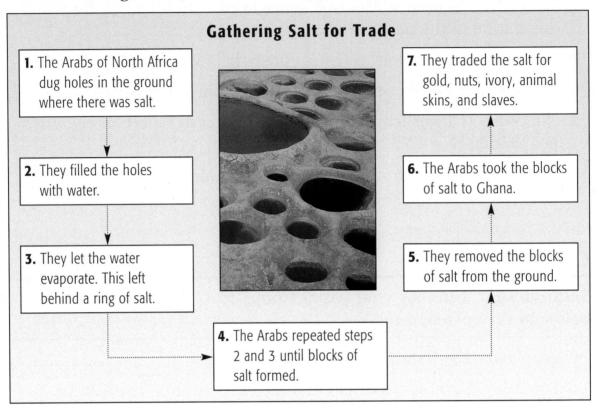

**Gathering Salt for Trade**

**1.** The Arabs of North Africa dug holes in the ground where there was salt.

**2.** They filled the holes with water.

**3.** They let the water evaporate. This left behind a ring of salt.

**4.** The Arabs repeated steps 2 and 3 until blocks of salt formed.

**5.** They removed the blocks of salt from the ground.

**6.** The Arabs took the blocks of salt to Ghana.

**7.** They traded the salt for gold, nuts, ivory, animal skins, and slaves.

Number your paper from 1 to 5. Write the letter of the correct answer.

1. In Step 1, the Arabs dug holes in the ground where there was _____.

   **a.** water        **b.** salt        **c.** gold

2. In Step 2, the holes were filled with _____.

   **a.** water        **b.** nuts        **c.** ivory

3. After the water evaporated, a ring of _____ was left behind.

   **a.** gold        **b.** animal skins        **c.** salt

4. To form blocks of salt, the Arabs repeated steps _____.

   **a.** 1 and 2        **b.** 2 and 3        **c.** 5 and 6

5. Step 6 was to bring the blocks of salt to _____ for trade.

   **a.** North Africa        **b.** Ghana        **c.** Wangara

## LESSON 1

# Classic Maya

### Before You Read

- Why did the Maya plant crops on raised fields?
- Why does the end of some cultures remain a mystery?

### New Words

Classic Maya
glyphs
mathematicians
smelt

### People and Places

Tikal
Toltec
Tula
Pacal
Palenque
Lady Zac-Kuk

The Maya settled on the Yucatan Peninsula in Central America around 200 B.C. Their civilization was at its height between A.D. 300 and A.D. 900. This time is called the **Classic Maya**.

The Maya were remarkable people. They drained water from marshes. They built raised areas to plant crops. They even built terraces on hillsides to gain more area for planting. The Maya also built cities, designed temples, and studied the stars.

These ruins are in the Mayan city of Palenque.

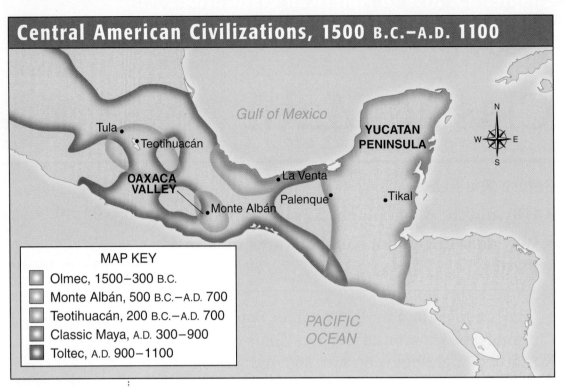

## Central American Civilizations, 1500 B.C.–A.D. 1100

Gulf of Mexico

Tula

Teotihuacán

YUCATAN PENINSULA

OAXACA VALLEY

La Venta

Palenque

Monte Albán

Tikal

PACIFIC OCEAN

**MAP KEY**
- Olmec, 1500–300 B.C.
- Monte Albán, 500 B.C.–A.D. 700
- Teotihuacán, 200 B.C.–A.D. 700
- Classic Maya, A.D. 300–900
- Toltec, A.D. 900–1100

This map shows the early Central American civilizations between 1500 B.C. and A.D. 1100. Which group lived in the Yucatan Peninsula?

## Mayan Writing

The Maya created their own form of writing. They used pictures, sometimes mixing animals and people. The Maya also used several hundred characters called **glyphs**. Each glyph stood for something. It could stand for an idea. Or it could stand for a sound, like an English letter.

The Maya wrote books. They made paper using tree bark. Then they folded the pages together to create a book. The books opened like a fan. Only four of these books remain.

The Maya wrote stories about their gods. They believed the god Heart-of-Sky created Earth because he was lonely. This is explained in one Mayan book, *The Book of Creation*.

**Voices**
**In History**

❝And so Heart-of-Sky thinks,
'Who is there to speak my name?
Who is there to praise me?'
. . . Heart-of-Sky only says the word 'Earth,'
and the earth rises, like a mist from the sea.❞

## Other Mayan Advances

The Maya were skilled architects. They built many cities, which became active centers for trade and religious services. The largest city was Tikal. Tikal had two massive stone temples next to a huge plaza. The temples looked like pyramids with flat tops.

The Maya were also **mathematicians**. Like the Gupta in India, they came up with the idea of zero. The Mayan number system was based on 20 rather than 10.

The Maya studied the stars and the night sky. They knew the movement of the sun, moon, and stars. They created two calendars. One showed when ceremonies should be held. The other was a yearly calendar. Both were as correct as any calendar today.

Each Mayan city had its own ruler and its own way of life. People living near mountains used precious stones to make knives and jewelry. People who lived on plains grew cotton and made pottery. Those along the coast traded salt.

The Maya studied the stars from this building.

This wall painting was found in the ruins of a Mayan city.

## Did You Know?

### Sparkling Teeth

Teeth were important to the Mayan people. They chewed with them, of course. But they also decorated them. Some Maya had jewels put into their teeth. First, a hole was drilled in a tooth. Then, a jewel was fit into the hole. The jewel could be a piece of gold, or it could be a shiny red, green, or blue stone. Getting a jewel put in wasn't easy. One slip, and the tooth could be destroyed.

## The Fall of the Maya

Something unexpected happened in the late 800s. The Maya simply stopped building temples and deserted their cities. In just a few years, nearly the entire Mayan civilization was gone. The age called the Classic Maya was over.

As with other early civilizations, it is not clear what happened to the Maya. Some say the Mayan cities fought wars against one another. Those who lived were perhaps too few and too weak to save the cities. Perhaps overpopulation caused the fall of the Maya because the food supply could not feed all the people. Diseases also might have killed the Mayan people.

## The Toltec

After 700, a group called the Toltec began building an empire in what is now Mexico. They were skilled stone builders. In fact, the word *Toltec* means "master builders." Little is known about the Toltec. Around 900, they settled in Tula. This city was near the ancient city of Teotihuacán. There they built a capital city. They collected tribute from nearby tribes. The Toltec knew how to **smelt**, or melt, metals. Like the Maya, they studied the stars.

The Toltec built massive temples. These temples honored their gods. Like the people of Teotihuacán, the Toltec believed in human sacrifice. The Toltec believed such sacrifice was necessary to keep their gods alive and happy.

Toltec armies conquered much of Mexico. Around A.D. 1000, they took over what was left of the Maya in the Yucatan. The Toltec spread their influence throughout Central America. But during the 1100s, the Toltec began losing control of their empire. In time, invading groups, such as the Aztec, replaced the powerful Toltec.

## King Pacal (603–683)

The young boy Pacal was named the Mayan king of Palenque, a Mayan city, in 609. But since he was only six years old, Pacal didn't have a strong claim to the throne. His mother, Lady Zac-Kuk, came from a family of rulers. She herself had ruled for more than ten years. She believed Pacal should be the next leader. So when he was 12 years old, she officially turned the kingdom over to him.

Pacal turned out to be a great leader. He ruled until his death at age 80. He improved the city of Palenque. He had a beautiful temple built there. It was called the Temple of the Inscriptions. Inside the temple, one hallway displayed the names of past kings. When Pacal died, he was buried deep inside this temple. Archaeologists discovered his tomb in 1952.

**People**
**In History**

## Lesson 1 Review

Choose words from the list that best complete the paragraphs. One word will not be used.

In Mayan history, the period from around 300 to 900 is called the __1__ Maya. The Maya created a form of writing that used pictures and __2__ to make words and sentences. The largest Mayan city was __3__. The Mayan number system was based on 20. The Maya created calendars. The Mayan king Pacal improved the city of Palenque. No one knows why the Maya __4__ their cities.

The Toltec settled in Tula. They began building a large empire in modern-day Mexico. The Toltec Empire lasted until the 1100s.

**Word List**

smelt
Tikal
deserted
Classic
glyphs

## LESSON 2

# South America and North America

**New Words**

ceramics
lagoons
lost wax method
fibers

**People and Places**

Nazca
Moche
Chimu
Moche River
Chan Chan
Anasazi
Mogollon
Hohokam
Inuit

## Before You Read

- How do scientists learn about cultures that did not have a written language?
- How did climate affect what early people ate and how they lived?

Civilizations in South America continued to develop and grow. The story of the Nazca began around 200 B.C., the Moche appeared around A.D. 100, and the Chimu rule began around A.D. 1000. In North America, more groups settled and developed their own ways of life.

The Nazca made this huge spider. The full spider can only be seen from the sky.

## The Nazca

The Nazca lived on the coast of modern-day Peru, near the ancient city of Caral. Little is known about these early South Americans. Archaeologists do know that the Nazca were experts at making pots. They used many colors to decorate their pots with birds and other animals.

The Nazca are best known for the huge shapes they carved into the ground. They did this by cutting away the dark soil on the top. The lighter soil below then showed the shapes. But the figures were so huge that the whole shape could not be seen from the ground. These shapes could only be seen from the sky. It is still a mystery why the Nazca made these figures. The Nazca lived in Peru until around A.D. 800.

## The Moche

Around A.D. 100, the Moche also settled on the coast of Peru, north of the Nazca. They settled in the Moche River valley, which was rich with clay and metals. With these materials, the Moche crafted works of art. They were most famous for their **ceramics**. The Moche made ceramics by heating clay. They shaped the heated clay into pots, bottles, and other kinds of pottery. The Moche often shaped their pottery to look like people or animals. Moche artists also worked with gold, copper, and silver.

Like other South American groups, the Moche had no written language. But the decorations on their pots tell us how they lived. The decorations show scenes from daily life. Some decorations show religious ceremonies. Others show that the Moche had a class system. Priests and warriors were at the top. Artists came next. Farmers and fishermen followed. Servants and slaves were at the lowest level.

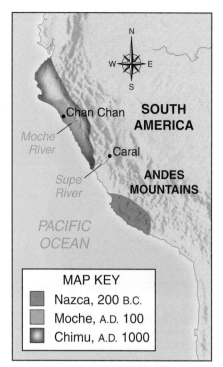

Early Civilizations in South America

MAP KEY
- Nazca, 200 B.C.
- Moche, A.D. 100
- Chimu, A.D. 1000

Moche ceramic bottle in the shape of a deer-man

## The Chimu

The Chimu built their capital at Chan Chan in the Moche River valley about 300 years after the Moche civilization ended. Chan Chan was one of the largest cities in the Americas at the time. Chan Chan had pyramids made from bricks. It had parks and **lagoons**.

The Chimu used the **lost wax method** to make gold objects. First, they carved wax into a certain shape. Then, they covered the wax shape with clay. Once the clay was hard, they heated it so that the wax inside would melt. Then, they drained the wax and poured in liquid gold. When the gold hardened, they broke the clay. What was left was a solid gold object.

Chimu gold vase

## North American Cultures

In what is now the United States, several different cultures developed during this time. By 500, these people lived in small villages. Those in warmer climates grew corn, squash, beans, and other crops. The North American groups also learned how to store food and to make pottery.

The Anasazi lived in caves and rock cliffs of the southwestern United States.

Each group did something special. The Anasazi used the **fibers**, or long threads, of plants to weave beautiful baskets. Around 750, they began to live in caves and rock structures of the desert.

The Mogollon produced new forms of ceramics. They made black and white bowls. They also painted designs and pictures that told a story on their pottery.

The Hohokam lived in a very dry area, so they built a series of canals. The Hohokam used these canals to bring water to their fields. Some of the canals were 10 feet deep and more than 10 miles long.

In the far north, the Inuit began to move into the Arctic region around 1050. They lived in small villages. They survived by hunting large animals and by fishing.

Mogollon bowl

# Lesson 2 Review

Choose words from the list that best complete the paragraph. One word will not be used.

Several civilizations developed in the Americas. The Nazca from South America carved mysterious figures into the ground that can be seen only from the sky. The Moche made __1__ by heating clay and shaping it into pots. They decorated these pots with scenes from daily life. The Moche had a __2__ system. The Chimu built their capital at Chan Chan. It had parks and __3__. The Chimu used the lost wax method to make gold objects. The Anasazi from North America used plant __4__ to make baskets. The Mogollon made ceramics, and the Hohokam built canals. The Inuit lived in the far north.

**Word List**

fibers

lagoons

ceremonies

class

ceramics

# Chapter 15: Using What You've Learned

## Summary

- The Classic Maya period in Central America lasted from A.D. 300 to A.D. 900. The Maya created a complex writing system and were excellent mathematicians.

- The Toltec were master builders. They spread their influence throughout Central America.

- Three ancient civilizations formed in Peru. The Nazca carved huge shapes into the ground. The Moche made fine pottery. The Chimu made objects out of gold.

- Four civilizations also developed in North America. The Anasazi were known for their baskets. The Mogollon made black and white ceramics. The Hohokam built canals. The Inuit lived in the Arctic region.

**Find Out More!**

After reading Chapter 15, you're ready to go online. **Explore Zone**, **Quiz Time**, and **Amazing Facts** bring this chapter of world history alive.

Visit www.exploreSV.com and type in the chapter code **1-Ch15**.

## Vocabulary

Number your paper from 1 to 6. Finish the sentences from Group A with words from Group B. Write the letter of the correct answer.

### Group A

1. Mayan writing used characters called _____ to stand for ideas or sounds.

2. Mayan _____ used a number system based on 20.

3. The Toltec knew how to _____, or melt, metals.

4. The Moche heated clay to make _____.

5. The Chimu capital of Chan Chan had parks and _____.

6. The Anasazi wove baskets using the _____ of plants.

### Group B

a. fibers

b. glyphs

c. ceramics

d. lagoons

e. mathematicians

f. smelt

## Comprehension

Number your paper from 1 to 4. Write the letter of the correct answer.

1. Where did the Maya live?
   a. South America
   b. Africa
   c. Europe
   d. Central America

2. Which group built an empire after A.D. 700 in what is now Mexico?
   a. Moche
   b. Anasazi
   c. Toltec
   d. Hohokam

3. What are the Nazca best known for?
   a. their calendars
   b. their stories
   c. their number system
   d. their huge carvings in the ground

4. What did the Mogollon people produce?
   a. black and white bowls
   b. a series of canals
   c. pyramids made from bricks
   d. beautiful baskets

## Critical Thinking

**Cause and Effect**  Number your paper from 1 to 4. Read the causes in the left column. Then choose the correct effect from the right column. Write the letter of the correct effect.

| Cause | Effect |
|-------|--------|
| 1. The Maya built terraces on hillsides, so | a. he created Earth. |
| 2. According to the Maya, the god Heart-of-Sky was lonely, so | b. they built a series of canals. |
| 3. The Toltec wanted their gods to stay alive and happy, so | c. they would have more area for planting. |
| 4. The Hohokam lived in a very dry area, so | d. they sacrificed humans. |

## Writing

Write a paragraph telling why the Maya might have left their cities.

# UNIT 4

# Change and Growth Around the World

## 1000–1500

The world faced great changes between the years 1000 and 1500. For some, this was a time of suffering. Religious wars killed thousands of people. A mysterious disease destroyed whole villages. For others, this was a time of learning and wealth. The first universities developed. Increased trading brought great riches.

This unit tells how the world changed during these 500 years. Some groups brought about changes by spreading their religion and conquering new lands. Other groups fought change by protecting their lands from invaders.

A.D.       1000       1100       1200

**A.D. 1113**
**The Khmer Empire in Southeast Asia begins building Angkor Wat.**

**A.D. 1230**
**The Kingdom of Mali rises to power in West Africa.**

A.D. 1347
**Rats spread a deadly disease, killing one third of the people in Europe.**

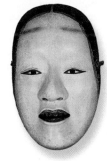

A.D. 1400
**The Japanese enjoy a new type of drama.**

A.D. 1500
**The Aztec Empire in Central America is at its height.**

211

## LESSON 1

# The Crusades

**New Words**

Holy Land
crusade
truce
Moors
Reconquista

**People and Places**

Seljuk Turks
Alexius
Urban II
Saladin
Frederick I
Philip II
Richard I
Cordoba
Spain
Granada

**Before You Read**

- Why might two religious groups go to war?
- What might Christians and Muslims learn from one another?

Europe's late Middle Ages, from around 1000 to 1500, were a time of change. For nearly 200 years, European Christians and Arab Muslims fought one another in a series of wars. The wars were hurtful to both groups. But the two groups learned from each other. Europeans, for example, were surprised by the Muslim advances in science and medicine. The contact with the Muslim world helped bring Europe out of the Dark Ages.

Muslim doctors used advances in science and medicine to help patients.

## A Call for Help

Christians and Muslims fought for control of Palestine, the land where Jesus lived and died. Christians called Palestine the **Holy Land**. After the Roman Empire fell, Palestine was ruled by the Byzantines and then by the Arabs. For hundreds of years, Christians went to Palestine to pray. The Arabs welcomed the Christians. They let Christians visit holy places in Jerusalem.

Then a new Muslim group rose to power, the Seljuk Turks. In 1071, the Turks defeated a Byzantine army. Later, the Turks captured Jerusalem. It looked as though they might conquer Constantinople, so the Byzantine Emperor Alexius asked Pope Urban II for help.

Urban II agreed to help Alexius. He was looking for a way to unite Europeans and thought a common cause would help. In 1095, Urban II asked knights to launch a **crusade**, or holy war, against the Turks. He said it was their Christian duty to free the Holy Land from Muslim rule.

In return, Urban II promised to forgive the knights' sins. He also promised them lands in Palestine. The Christian knights were eager to fight and win lands.

Pope Urban II asks knights to launch a crusade to free the Holy Land.

Crusaders set sail for Jerusalem.

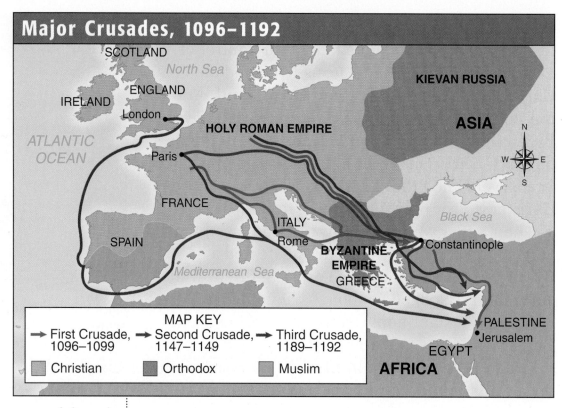

## Major Crusades, 1096–1192

SCOTLAND

North Sea

IRELAND

ENGLAND

KIEVAN RUSSIA

London

ATLANTIC OCEAN

HOLY ROMAN EMPIRE

ASIA

Paris

FRANCE

ITALY

Black Sea

SPAIN

Rome

Constantinople

BYZANTINE EMPIRE

Mediterranean Sea

GREECE

PALESTINE

Jerusalem

EGYPT

AFRICA

**MAP KEY**
→ First Crusade, 1096–1099
→ Second Crusade, 1147–1149
→ Third Crusade, 1189–1192

Christian      Orthodox      Muslim

The Crusaders crossed through Christian, Orthodox, and Muslim lands. Were Muslim lands north or south of Christian lands?

Leaders of the First Crusade

## The First Crusade

The First Crusade lasted from 1096 to 1099. The Crusaders traveled a difficult journey from France to Jerusalem. Many died from hunger and disease along the way. But the Crusaders reached Jerusalem in 1099. There, the Crusaders fought a long battle with the Turks and drove them from the city. The Crusaders killed many Muslims as well as Christians and Jews living in Jerusalem.

## More Crusades

Many Crusaders decided to go home. Others stayed behind and divided the Holy Land into small states. The Christians ruled the Holy Land for almost 100 years. But the Christians began to fight among themselves, while the Muslim armies grew stronger. In 1144, Muslims defeated one of the Christian states.

European rulers and the pope launched the Second Crusade in 1147. Two European armies joined forces and tried to defeat the Turks. The

Turks won the battle, and the Crusaders returned home in 1149.

A new Muslim leader, Saladin, gained control of Jerusalem in 1187. Emperor Frederick I of the Holy Roman Empire, King Philip II of France, and King Richard I of England led the Third Crusade in 1189. Frederick died on the way to Jerusalem. Philip returned home before reaching the Holy Land. Richard and his army continued on and fought Saladin.

Richard became known as Richard the Lion-Hearted for his bravery. But the Crusaders could not capture Jerusalem. In the end, Richard and Saladin reached a **truce** and agreed to stop fighting. Saladin allowed Christians to visit Jerusalem. He also allowed them to keep some of their states.

After Saladin died, the truce ended. Europeans tried again to win back Jerusalem and failed. They launched more crusades. One was the Children's Crusade. In 1212, an army of about 50,000 European children began their march to the Holy Land. Along the way, most got sick, died, or were sold into slavery. In 1291, Muslims captured the last Christian state in the Holy Land, ending the deadly Crusades.

Saladin

## Results of the Crusades

Many thousands of Muslims and Christians died in the Crusades. Thousands of Jews, caught in the middle, also died. After all the fighting, the Holy Land remained under Muslim control. The Crusades left both Muslims and Christians angry. Neither group trusted the other.

On the other hand, the Crusades brought some good changes to Europe, too. Europeans admired parts of Muslim culture. The Europeans learned about advances in science and medicine. They also began to trade for new products, such as sugar, silk, lemons, and spices.

A Christian and Muslim playing chess

The Crusades also sparked European interest in the rest of the world. This curiosity led to more exploration.

## Muslims in Spain

The Christians were able to defeat one Muslim group, the **Moors**. The Moors had set up the Caliphate of Cordoba. In 1000, they controlled most of Spain. When the Moors fought among themselves, the Christians attacked, winning back most of the Spanish lands.

By 1450, the Moors held only Granada in southern Spain. Then the Spanish Christians began the **Reconquista** to win back Granada. In 1492, they drove the Moors out of Spain completely.

The Moors built beautiful mosques in Spain.

# Lesson 1 Review

Choose words from the list that best complete the paragraphs. One word will not be used.

**Word List**

truce

crusade

Reconquista

Alexius

Saladin

Christians and Muslims fought for control of Palestine. In 1095, Pope Urban II urged European knights to launch a __1__ to free the Holy Land. The First Crusade captured Jerusalem in 1099. The Muslims fought back. In 1187, __2__ gained control of Jerusalem. During the Third Crusade, Saladin and Richard I of England reached a __3__. In time, the Muslims defeated the Christians.

Thousands of Muslims, Christians, and Jews were killed during the Crusades. The Christians had one victory against the Muslims. The Spanish Christians began the __4__, which successfully pushed the Moors out of Spain in 1492.

**LESSON 2**

# Life in the Late Middle Ages

## Before You Read

- Why might people move from the country into a town?

- How might a deadly disease be spread?

During the late Middle Ages, Europeans became better farmers. There was often a **surplus**, or extra amount, of food. Fewer people needed to be farmers, so more people moved into towns. In towns, workers began to **specialize**. One worker might make shoes, while another worker might make candles or bread.

### New Words

surplus
specialize
bartered
guilds
apprentice
journeyman
masterpiece
cathedrals
plague
Black Death

### People and Places

Bologna
Oxford
Cambridge
Salerno
Salamanca
Paris
Thomas Aquinas
Henry of Knighton
Norwich

This worker specialized in making leather.

Towns were crowded during the late Middle Ages.

## Town Life

Town life in the Middle Ages was rather grim. The streets were narrow and often muddy. People tossed their garbage into the streets. Wooden houses were packed tightly together inside the town walls. Fire was always a danger. There were no fire departments or police departments.

Still, most people liked town life better than country life. Town life was more free than life on a manor, especially for serfs. Sometimes a serf would run away. If the serf didn't get caught for a year and a day, he was legally free.

Merchants earned money in towns.

Also, people could make money in towns. On a manor, no one had any money. Instead, they **bartered**, or traded one good for another. For example, a person might trade firewood for a pair of shoes. In towns, merchants and traders could grow rich.

## Crafters Join Together

Workers who specialized began forming **guilds**. There was a guild for almost every craft. Only the best workers could join. The guild set the price for its goods. It also limited the number of goods that could be made. In this way, guilds kept control over their products.

A young man wanting to join a guild first worked as an **apprentice**. He learned the trade from a skilled worker. He did not get paid. He did, however, get a room, clothing, and food. After a few years, he became a **journeyman**, who was paid. Finally, he became a master by showing he had mastered the skill. He did this by producing what was called a "**masterpiece**."

## Universities

Life in towns was very different from life on the feudal manor. The towns needed people with more education. Governments, for example, needed educated people to help keep records. Universities began developing from around 1100 to 1300.

Unlike schools of the early Middle Ages, the universities taught more than religion. Students learned a variety of subjects. One of the first universities was in Bologna, Italy. In England, universities began at Oxford and Cambridge. Spain had a medical school in Salerno and a university in Salamanca. The French city of Paris developed a university, too.

Perhaps the most famous teacher from the Middle Ages was Thomas Aquinas. Aquinas wrote about philosophy and religion. Some beliefs, he wrote, could be understood by reason. Others could only be understood by faith. Aquinas developed many of his ideas from studying the ancient Greek philosophers.

These workers are making clothes.

A university in the Middle Ages

This cathedral in France was completed in the 13th century.

Stained glass window

## Cathedrals

Another change in the late Middle Ages was the increased building of **cathedrals**. Some of these magnificent churches took more than 100 years to build. The cathedral was always the highest building in a town, showing how important religion was in people's lives.

Many cathedrals had stained glass windows. The windows were made with small pieces of colored glass held together with metal. Many of the windows showed stories from the Bible.

## The Black Death

In 1347, a **plague** struck Europe. It killed one person out of every three. Known as the **Black Death**, it was carried by fleas that lived in the fur of rats. The plague began in China. It spread to Southwest Asia, Russia, and Europe along the trade routes.

People at the time had no idea what caused the plague. They were afraid and began blaming people they did not understand. Some people thought Jews were causing the plague. Many Jews were killed as a result.

Henry of Knighton, an English writer, described what the Black Death was like.

> **"**Many villages . . . have now become quite [empty]. No one is left in the houses, for the people are dead. . . . And truly, many of these [villages] will now forever be empty.**"**

**Voices**
**In History**

The Black Death lasted in Europe from 1347 to 1351. It killed the rich and the poor, the young and the old. Norwich, a town in England, had a population of about 70,000 people before the plague. After the Black Death, it had fewer than 13,000 people. Some people stopped plowing their fields. They stopped caring for their animals. One man even wrote, "This is the end of the world."

But it was not the end of the world. In time, Europe recovered. It suffered other plagues. But none were as deadly as the Black Death.

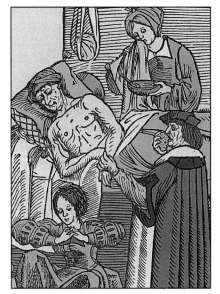

A man dying from the Black Death

# Lesson 2 Review

Choose words from the list that best complete the paragraphs. One word will not be used.

Better farming in the late Middle Ages allowed more people to move into towns. Workers began to __1__, or do only one craft. They formed __2__ to control their craft. Universities opened to improve education. Stained glass windows in __3__ often showed stories from the Bible.

In 1347, a plague struck Europe. The __4__ killed one third of Europe's population. The plague ended in 1351.

**Word List**

cathedrals

specialize

masterpiece

**Black Death**

guilds

## Summary

- For almost 200 years, Christian crusaders and Muslims fought for control of the Holy Land. This period was called the Crusades.

- Surplus food allowed people to move into villages and towns in Europe's late Middle Ages. Town life offered people freedom and a chance to make money.

- Workers began to specialize by making just one product. They also started guilds to keep control over their products and to train new workers.

- A plague called the Black Death began in China and spread along trade routes to Europe. Between 1347 and 1351, the plague killed one third of the population of Europe.

## Find Out More!

After reading Chapter 16, you're ready to go online. **Explore Zone**, **Quiz Time**, and **Amazing Facts** bring this chapter of world history alive.

Visit www.exploreSV.com and type in the chapter code **1-Ch16**.

## Vocabulary

Number your paper from 1 to 5. Write the word or words from the list that best complete each sentence. One word will not be used.

1. The Third Crusade ended in a _____ when Richard I and Saladin agreed to stop fighting.

2. In the _____, the Spanish Christians fought to win back Granada from the Moors.

3. As Europeans became better farmers, there was often a _____ of food.

4. The people on manors _____, or traded one good for another.

5. The _____ was carried by fleas that lived in the fur of rats.

### Word List

**Holy Land**

**surplus**

**Reconquista**

**Black Death**

**bartered**

**truce**

## Comprehension

Number your paper from 1 to 5. Write **True** for each sentence that is true. Write **False** for each sentence that is false.

1. In 1095, Urban II asked knights to start a crusade against the Turks.

2. Saladin is called the Lion-Hearted for his bravery in the Crusades.

3. The Moors set up the Caliphate of Cordoba.

4. Thomas Aquinas's writings about philosophy and religion were based on the ideas of ancient Greek philosophers.

5. Henry of Knighton wrote a book describing the great cathedrals of Europe.

## Critical Thinking

**Points of View**   Number your paper from 1 to 5. Read each sentence below. Write **Christian** if the point of view is from a Christian in the late Middle Ages. If the point of view is from a Muslim in the late Middle Ages, write **Muslim**.

1. We call Palestine our Holy Land.

2. After the First Crusade, we ruled Palestine for almost 100 years.

3. Saladin is the best leader that my people have ever had.

4. I do not trust the pope and his followers.

5. We have traveled far to fight in the Crusades.

## Writing

Write a paragraph explaining the three steps a young man would have to take to become a member of a guild during the Middle Ages.

## Skill Builder: Reading a Line Graph

A **line graph** shows how something has changed over time. The line graph below shows how the population of England changed from 1348 to 1375. During this time, crop failures, wars, and plagues caused the population of England to fall.

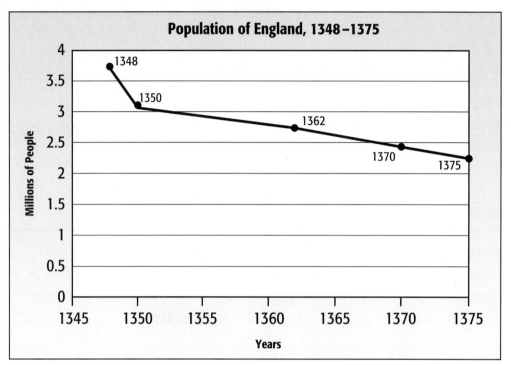

Number your paper from 1 to 5. Write the letter of the correct answer.

1. In 1348, England's population was just below _____ people.
   **a.** 3 million        **b.** 3.5 million        **c.** 4 million

2. Between 1348 and 1350, the population of England _____.
   **a.** fell        **b.** stayed the same        **c.** rose

3. In _____, the population was almost 2.5 million people.
   **a.** 1350        **b.** 1362        **c.** 1370

4. The line graph shows that many people _____ in England during this time.
   **a.** were born        **b.** died        **c.** moved into towns

5. By 1375, the population was just more than _____ people.
   **a.** 1.5 million        **b.** 2 million        **c.** 2.5 million

## LESSON 1

# The Mongol Empire

## Before You Read

- What makes a group of people skilled warriors?

- How could a traveling writer change the way one culture thinks of another?

By the 1100s, the Song Dynasty of China was one of the most advanced civilizations in the world. But it constantly faced pressure from the **Mongols**. The Mongols were nomads to the north and west of China. They raised sheep, cattle, and horses on open plains called the **steppe**. The steppe was a rough land with little rain and few trees. The Mongols lived in wool tents called **yurts**. They became skilled horse riders as they moved from place to place.

The people of the Song Dynasty enjoyed festivals before the Mongols invaded.

## New Words

Mongols
steppe
yurts
siege warfare
surrender
catapults
mercy
conquest
bathhouses

## People and Places

Genghis Khan
Kublai Khan
Yuan
Beijing
Marco Polo

Mongol warrior

## The Conquering Mongols

The Chinese built the Great Wall of China to keep out invaders such as the Mongols. But the Mongols found weak spots in the wall. In the early 13th century, they began attacking China. A Chinese soldier on foot had little chance against a Mongol warrior on a horse. Under the leadership of Genghis Khan, the Mongols quickly captured the countryside. They had trouble, however, taking over cities. The walls around the cities forced the Mongols to find new ways to fight.

The Mongols began using **siege warfare**. They surrounded a city and waited. They would not allow people to go in or out of the city. After a while, the city ran out of food and water. Finally, the people had to **surrender**.

The Mongols also developed **catapults**. These huge slings tossed bombs over high city walls. The Mongols also built special ladders to help them climb over the walls.

When Genghis Khan took over a city, he showed little **mercy**. His army sometimes killed everyone inside the city.

Genghis Khan died in 1227, but the Mongols continued to conquer new lands. In 1279, Genghis Khan's grandson, Kublai Khan, completed the **conquest** of China by defeating the Song forces in the south. He began a new dynasty in a united China. He called the dynasty the Yuan, which meant "original."

The Yuan Dynasty ruled China for more than 100 years. Kublai Khan built his capital in the modern-day city of Beijing. He built a huge palace there. The walls were covered with gold and silver. One hall was large enough to hold 6,000 people.

The Mongols also defeated the Abbasid Caliphate and conquered lands in Central Asia,

Mongols attacking a Chinese city

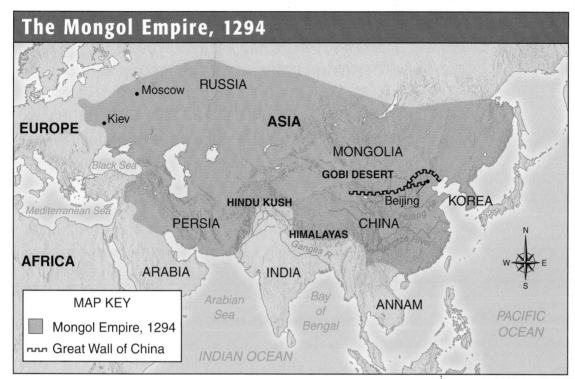

## The Mongol Empire, 1294

MAP KEY
■ Mongol Empire, 1294
ᴖᴖ Great Wall of China

Russia, and Persia. Stretching from eastern Europe all the way to the Pacific Ocean, the Mongols ruled the biggest empire in history.

The Mongols ruled the biggest empire in history. What desert was a part of the Mongol Empire?

## The Mongol Government

Kublai Khan was kinder and more educated than earlier Mongol rulers. Kublai Khan knew he needed to keep peace within his empire if it was to stay together. He tried to govern well and improve life in the empire. Under his rule, the Mongols built new roads. They dug new canals and improved the Grand Canal. They also built **bathhouses** that were heated by coal.

Problems remained, however, between the Mongols and the Chinese. Kublai Khan did not treat the Chinese fairly. Only Mongols and a few select outsiders were allowed to take important positions in government. The Chinese were forced to pay taxes and to do the difficult work on building projects.

Kublai Khan

## A Visitor from Europe

During Kublai Khan's rule, a young Italian traveler named Marco Polo arrived in China. Marco Polo lived in China for 17 years. He was impressed by all that he saw. He called the palace in Beijing "the greatest palace that ever was." Marco Polo wrote a book about his journeys. It was called *The Travels of Marco Polo*.

His book was very popular in Europe. Still, many Europeans didn't believe Marco Polo. They couldn't believe China had so many beautiful cities with good roads and working canals. To them, Marco Polo's stories seemed like fairy tales. Some even called his book "The Million Lies." Marco Polo died in 1324 at the age of 70. As he was dying, he said, "I have only told the half of what I saw!" Later travelers proved that Marco Polo had told the truth about China's greatness.

Kublai Khan died in 1294. During the following years, several weak leaders ruled the vast Mongol Empire. In 1368, Chinese peasants led a successful revolt and brought an end to the Yuan Dynasty.

Marco Polo

This statue of a Chinese goddess was made during the Yuan Dynasty.

## Genghis Khan (c. 1162–1227)

The Mongol leader Genghis Khan is one of the most well-known rulers in history. Genghis Khan was actually his title, not his name. The term *Genghis Khan* means "top ruler." He was born with the name Temujin around 1162. An enemy killed his father when Temujin was just 12 years old. The tribe leaders thought Temujin was too young to take his father's place. They left him and his mother to die.

Somehow the boy and his mother lived. Then, one by one, Temujin defeated his enemies. By 1206, he was the leader of all the Mongol tribes. That was when he earned the title Genghis Khan. He then raised a great army and began a massive conquest. He is remembered for his cruel treatment of those he captured. But he is also remembered for his skill in war.

## Lesson 1 Review

Choose words from the list that best complete the paragraphs. One word will not be used.

The Mongols moved from place to place across the Asian __1__ . The Mongols easily defeated Chinese armies in the countryside. But they had to find new ways to conquer cities. They became experts at __2__ .

Genghis Khan was a cruel leader. His grandson, Kublai Khan, began the __3__ Dynasty. He made improvements in China, but he did not treat the Chinese fairly. Mongol rule in China lasted more than 100 years. Europeans learned about Mongol China from __4__ . He wrote stories about his travels in China.

**Word List**

Yuan

steppe

siege warfare

Marco Polo

Beijing

## LESSON 2

# Islam Comes to India

## New Words

devout
infidels
plunder
dominion
sultanates
sultans
sack

## People and Places

Mahmud of Ghazni
Muhammad Ghuri
Delhi
Amir Khusro
Jalalud-Din
Timur

## Before You Read

- How might the spread of Islam have changed India?

- What are some differences between Hindu and Muslim beliefs?

In Chapter 10, you read that the Huns brought an end to the Golden Age of the Gupta by 550. Then in 711, Arab Muslims reached India. For 300 years, the Indians stopped the Muslims from spreading beyond the Indus River. Then, around 1000, a Muslim Turk named Mahmud of Ghazni

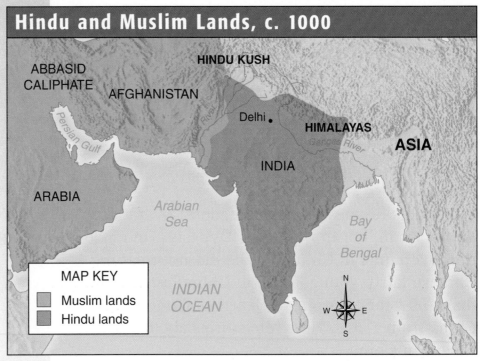

**Hindu and Muslim Lands, c. 1000**

HINDU KUSH

ABBASID
CALIPHATE

AFGHANISTAN

Delhi

HIMALAYAS

ASIA

INDIA

ARABIA

Persian Gulf

Arabian
Sea

Bay
of
Bengal

MAP KEY

INDIAN
OCEAN

Muslim lands

Hindu lands

N
W  E
S

began new attacks on India. His efforts were successful, and Islam spread into the Indian subcontinent.

Mahmud was a **devout** Muslim. He saw the Hindus as **infidels**. Mahmud did not like the way Indians divided people into castes. He believed all people were equal in the eyes of Allah. He also disliked the way Hindus prayed to idols. Mahmud felt he had a duty to conquer India and spread the Muslim religion.

## Muslims Conquer India

In 1000, India was divided into small Hindu states that often argued with one another. The Muslim Turks easily conquered northern India. The Hindus only allowed members of the warrior class to fight, but the Turks accepted anyone as a soldier.

At first, the Turks wanted to **plunder** India. They stole gold and jewelry from Indian cities. They took riches from Hindu temples before destroying them. When the hot monsoon season arrived, Mahmud went into the cooler mountains and waited to attack again the next year. In all, Mahmud launched 17 raids into India.

Hindu woman

| Muslim and Hindu Beliefs | |
|---|---|
| **Islam** | **Hinduism** |
| ■ The Qur'an is the holy book of Islam. | ■ The Vedas are the holy books of Hinduism. |
| ■ Muslims believe there is only one God, Allah. Muhammad is a prophet of Allah. | ■ Hindus believe in many gods. Two gods are Shiva and Vishnu. |
| ■ Islam teaches that all people are equal. | ■ Hindus follow a caste system and believe in reincarnation. |

Muslim children

A Delhi sultan

## Muslims Stay in India

The raids continued after Mahmud's death. Muslim Turks struck deeper and deeper into India. Another leader, Muhammad Ghuri, led his army south to the Ganges River valley. His soldiers carried away what they could and destroyed the rest.

In time, the Turks learned the value of India. They discovered its rich spices and its importance to trade. The Muslim Turks stopped raiding India and began to stay there. By 1206, much of India was under Muslim **dominion**.

## The Delhi Sultanate

The Turks divided India into independent Muslim kingdoms. These kingdoms were called **sultanates**. The most powerful was the Delhi Sultanate, centered in the city of Delhi. The Delhi Sultanate lasted from 1210 to 1526.

The Delhi **sultans** were harsh conquerers. They often were cruel to the Hindus. The Muslims of the Delhi Sultanate were even cruel

This picture is from a book of Amir Khusro's poems.

to one another. Often a sultan was murdered by someone wanting to become the next sultan.

Amir Khusro was a court poet born in 1253. He served under six Delhi sultans. Khusro wrote poems for the sultans. He described how a sultan named Jalalud-Din ruined Hindu temples.

**Voices**
**In History**

"Jalalud-Din went again to the temples and ordered their destruction. There were two [large] bronze idols of the Brahma. These were broken into pieces and the fragments were [scattered]."

In time, the Muslims of the Delhi Sultanate became less cruel. They improved prisons and built hospitals, bridges, and dams. Many sultans welcomed Muslim artists and teachers into their courts. Delhi became a center of Islamic culture. Beautiful buildings were made that combined both Islamic and Indian styles.

These carved columns show the style of building under the Delhi Sultanate.

## Timur Invades India

The Delhi Sultanate was the largest kingdom in India. Even the powerful Mongols did not defeat it. But the sultanate could never conquer all of India. By the 1350s, the sultanate began to break into smaller states. In 1398, a Muslim warrior named Timur, or Tamerlane, invaded India.

Timur claimed to be a relative of Genghis Khan. Timur led his army from central Asia into India. He killed tens of thousands of people.

His four-month invasion ended with the **sack** of Delhi. The city was completely destroyed. The people either fled or were killed. One man wrote that "not even a bird was left to fly" over the city.

The sack of Delhi greatly weakened the sultanate. Delhi regained some control, but it was never the same. Muslim and Hindu rulers took over parts of India. In 1526, the Delhi Sultanate was destroyed by yet another invasion.

Timur

# Lesson 2 Review

Choose words from the list that best complete the paragraphs. One word will not be used.

**Word List**

Timur

devout

Delhi

infidels

dominion

Around 1000, Muslim Turks invaded India. Their leader was Mahmud of Ghazni. He saw the Hindus as __1__ and wanted to conquer them. The Turks defeated the Hindus and developed several Muslim states. The biggest state was the __2__ Sultanate.

By 1206, much of India was under Muslim __3__. In time, Muslim and Hindu cultures influenced one another. Buildings combined the Islamic and Indian styles. The Delhi Sultanate began to weaken. In 1398, __4__ sacked the city of Delhi. The sultanate ended in 1526.

## LESSON 3

# New Ideas in Japan

### Before You Read

- How did the geography of Japan help protect it from invaders?

- Why might a country have a feudal system?

The Taika reforms of the seventh century gave Japan a central government. But they never gave Japan the full control shown by governments in China. By the 1100s, the power of the Japanese emperor was weak. Nobles fought one another. Robbers attacked people traveling through forests. Pirates attacked ships at sea. Many people ignored the laws and refused to pay taxes.

Then in 1192, a new leader named Minamoto Yoritomo came to power. He forced the emperor to make him **shogun**, or top general.

Minamoto Yoritomo was the first shogun of Japan.

### New Words
shogun
shogunate
daimyo
samurai
Bushido
seppuku
defend
kamikaze
haiku
Noh drama

### People and Places
Minamoto Yoritomo
Kamakura
Kyushu
Ashikaga
Kyoto

Samurai armor

The emperor was still the head ruler, but Yoritomo controlled the army, money, and laws of Japan. Yoritomo could punish criminals and spend tax money. He could appoint government officials and make laws. Yoritomo's rule, and later the rule of his family, became known as the Kamakura **Shogunate**.

## The Feudal System in Japan

Japan developed a feudal system similar to the one in Europe. The emperor was at the top of the system but had little real power. Next came the shogun. The **daimyo**, or powerful landowners, were below the shogun. The **samurai**, or warriors, were next. The peasants were below the samurai. The samurai received land from a daimyo. In return, the samurai were loyal to the daimyo and promised to fight for them.

The samurai lived by a strict code of honor called **Bushido**. Samurai had to be brave and loyal. For samurai, nothing was worse than losing

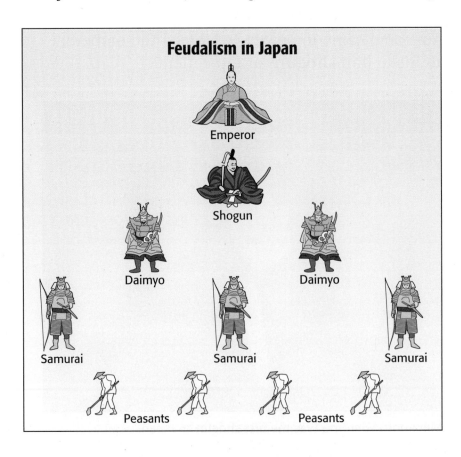

**Feudalism in Japan**

Emperor

Shogun

Daimyo

Daimyo

Samurai

Samurai

Samurai

Peasants

Peasants

honor. If they lost their honor, samurai might kill themselves in a practice called **seppuku**. By doing so, they believed they regained their honor.

## The Mongols Attack Japan

The sea had long protected Japan from attack. But the Mongols did not fear the sea. In 1266, Kublai Khan sent a message to the Japanese. He said he wanted to add Japan to his empire. The Japanese joined together to **defend** their country.

In 1274, a Mongol army landed on the Japanese island of Kyushu. The samurai fought off the Mongols. Then a strong storm came and sank many of the Mongol ships. The Japanese believed that their gods had sent the winds that defeated the Mongols. In Japanese, holy winds are called **kamikaze**.

In 1291, the Mongols attacked again. Kublai Khan sent an even bigger army to Japan. The Mongols brought their best weapons. But the Japanese built a wall to keep the Mongols from landing. Once again, a storm came. Strong winds sank many of the Mongol ships, along with most of the Mongol army.

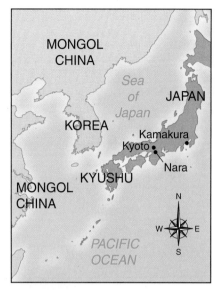

Feudal Japan

This painting shows the winds that defeated the Mongols.

The victory over the Mongols was costly. The Japanese spent a lot of money defending their country. The Kamakura Shogunate weakened, and by 1333, it had ended.

## Art Under the Ashikaga Shogunate

After several years of civil war, the Ashikaga Shogunate took control in 1394. They made Kyoto their capital city. The new shoguns controlled the city. During the Ashikaga Shogunate, the Japanese developed several new forms of art.

The Japanese created their own form of poetry called **haiku**. The haiku poems had just three lines. The first line had five syllables. The second line had seven syllables. The third line had five syllables. Haiku poets tried to capture one thought or idea. Often it was about nature or a person's role in the world.

The **Noh drama** was a type of theater. The actors wore masks and costumes and made slow and graceful movements. A chorus sang poetry to music.

Haiku poem with illustration

This modern actor is performing Noh drama.

The Japanese also made flower arranging into an art form. Priests, nobles, samurai, and young women all studied the art. They learned how to cut and place flowers to best appreciate the flower's beauty.

The Japanese made an art out of serving tea. It became a special event called a tea ceremony. The tea was served in a peaceful surrounding. There were no loud noises. People sipped their tea and spoke in soft voices.

Another Japanese art was landscape gardening. Some landscape gardens were made with plants, bridges, waterfalls, and ponds. Others simply had small and large rocks placed on sand. The sand was raked into certain patterns. With either type of garden, everything had to be in its proper place.

Modern Japanese rock garden

# Lesson 3 Review

Choose words from the list that best complete the paragraphs. One word will not be used.

In 1192, Minamoto Yoritomo forced the emperor to make him shogun of Japan. Japan developed a feudal system. Powerful landowners were called __1__. Japanese warriors were called __2__. The warriors lived by a strict code of honor.

The Mongols attacked Japan twice. Both times the Japanese defeated the Mongols. The Japanese believed their gods sent the __3__, or holy winds, to defeat the Mongols.

The Ashikaga Shogunate took control of Japan in 1394. The Japanese developed new forms of art, such as __4__ poetry and the Noh drama.

**Word List**

seppuku

haiku

kamikaze

samurai

daimyo

**LESSON 4**

# Kingdoms of Southeast Asia

## New Words
Sanskrit
evacuated
declined

## People and Places
Ly Thai
Champa
Khmer Empire
Angkor Wat
Bach Dang River
Le Loi
Nguyen Trai
Majapahit

## Before You Read
- How might a country's culture influence nearby countries?
- Why might one group fight for freedom from another group?

The Vietnamese won their freedom from China in 938. In 1010, Ly Thai started the Ly Dynasty in northern Vietnam, known as Annam. Ly kings developed a strong central government. They collected taxes. They built dikes and canals to bring water to farmlands. The Ly kings were heavily influenced by China. They accepted

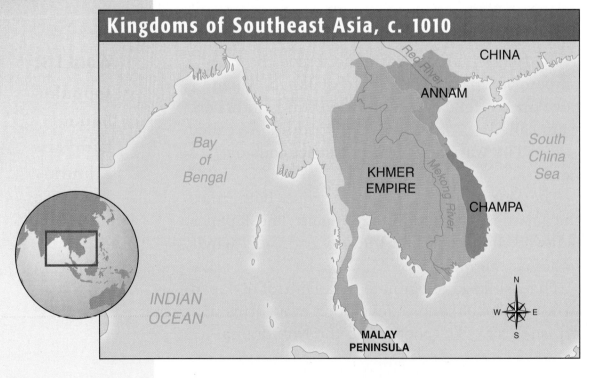

### Kingdoms of Southeast Asia, c. 1010

CHINA

ANNAM

Red River

Bay of Bengal

KHMER EMPIRE

Mekong River

South China Sea

CHAMPA

INDIAN OCEAN

MALAY PENINSULA

N
W E
S

Angkor Wat was built as a Hindu temple. Buddhist temples were later added to the religious center.

Buddhism, the religion of China. Buddhist leaders helped the Ly kings rule Annam.

## Wars with Neighbors

During their rule, Ly kings often had to fight China to keep Annam's freedom. They also fought the Kingdom of Champa to their south and the Khmer Empire to the west. Both Champa and the Khmer Empire were influenced by India. Their people practiced Hinduism and spoke an Indian language called **Sanskrit**.

The Khmer Empire controlled a large piece of land west of Annam and Champa. Around 1113, the Khmer king ordered the building of a massive Hindu temple, known as Angkor Wat. It took thousands of people about 30 years to build Angkor Wat. When they finished, it was the largest religious center in the world.

In time, the culture of Annam began to influence the Khmer Empire. The people of the Khmer Empire even added Buddhist temples to the religious center at Angkor Wat.

Bas-relief from Angkor Wat

## The Tran Dynasty

In 1225, the Tran Dynasty replaced the Ly Dynasty. The Tran remained in power for 175 years. Tran rulers improved education and helped farmers. But the Tran are most known for defeating the Mongols. Three times, armies of Kublai Khan invaded Annam. Each time, the Vietnamese **evacuated** the capital city. When the Mongols arrived, they found an empty city. Then the Vietnamese attacked. They used guerrilla tactics to drive the Mongols away.

On the third attack, the Mongols sent a huge fleet of ships up the Bach Dang River. The Vietnamese drove iron stakes in the bottom of the river. They waited until the tide went out and the river dropped. Then the Vietnamese attacked. The Mongols tried to flee. But the iron stakes trapped their ships. The Vietnamese then shot fire arrows into the ships and burned much of the Mongol fleet.

## Le Loi

The Tran Dynasty fell in 1400. In 1407, China gained control over Annam once more. The

The Vietnamese defeated the Mongols at a battle on the Bach Dang River.

Chinese ruled harshly. A Vietnamese man named Le Loi refused to work for the Chinese. He wanted the Chinese to leave Annam. He raised an army and fought the Chinese. In 1427, after ten years of fighting, the Vietnamese drove the Chinese out. The following year, Le Loi began the Le Dynasty.

Le Loi was a hero to the Vietnamese people. Legends developed about him. One legend says that a turtle gave Le Loi a huge sword. Le Loi used the sword to defeat the Chinese. After the war, Le Loi was sailing in a lake when the same turtle appeared. Le Loi thought that the gods must have given him the sword to win freedom. Now that Annam was free, it was time to give the sword back. So Le Loi returned the sword to the turtle. Then Le Loi gave the lake a new name— Lake of the Returned Sword. That is still the name of the lake today.

## Nguyen Trai

Le Loi did not defeat China alone. One of his partners, Nguyen Trai, was given a high position in the Le Dynasty government. Nguyen Trai was a brave soldier and also a poet. Although he held a high office under Le Loi, he did not want fame or power. His poems tell how he longed for a more simple life.

> **Voices In History**
>
> "[Now] with half my life gone by,
> Why should I bother with fame and gain?
> Do I really need wealth and position?
> Since rice with vegetable and plain water are more than enough."

In 1471, the Vietnamese conquered Champa. The Khmer Empire **declined**, and in time, the Vietnamese gained control of some Khmer lands, too. Rulers of the Le Dynasty stayed in power over the next 300 years.

# Did You Know?

## Cut Out the Knives

Today, many Asian people eat with chopsticks. This custom began in China long ago when there was a low supply of cooking fuel. To use less fuel, the Chinese people cut food into little pieces. The food cooked faster that way. Food was then served in bite-sized amounts, so knives were not needed at meals anymore. Chopsticks took their place. Today, chopsticks are mostly made of wood, but they can also be made of ivory, jade, silver, or even gold.

## Islam Comes to Indonesia

You have read that the Buddhist kingdom of Sriwijaya was centered on the Indonesian island of Sumatra. Sriwijaya lasted until the 1200s. In the 1300s, the Hindu kingdom of Majapahit controlled much of Indonesia. It was centered on the island of Java.

A mosque in Indonesia

Then, in the late 1300s, Arab traders began arriving in Indonesia. They brought the teachings of Islam to the Indonesians. The Arab traders told the people about Muhammad and the Qur'an. Indonesians along the coast began to convert to Islam. Islam spread throughout the islands of Indonesia. In time, Islam became the most popular religion in Indonesia.

# Lesson 4 Review

Choose words from the list that best complete the paragraphs. One word will not be used.

**Word List**

evacuated

Angkor Wat

Le Loi

Champa

Sanskrit

The Ly Dynasty continued fighting wars with China. It also fought against __1__ and the Khmer Empire. The Khmer Empire built a massive religious center known as __2__.

When the Mongols attacked Annam, Tran leaders __3__ the capital city. When the Mongols arrived, the city was empty.

China took over Vietnam in 1407. __4__ and Nguyen Trai worked together to defeat China. Le Loi began the Le Dynasty.

In Indonesia, Islam replaced Buddhism and Hinduism. Islam became the most popular religion in Indonesia.

### Summary

- The Mongols were fierce warriors who conquered much of Asia. In 1279, they started the Yuan Dynasty in China.

- Muslim Turks led by Mahmud entered India around 1000. By 1206, much of India was under Muslim control.

- In 1192, Yoritomo became the first shogun of Japan. Like western Europe, Japan had a feudal system.

- The Vietnamese fought to keep their freedom from China. They extended their empire by defeating Champa and the Khmer Empire.

- In the late 1300s, Arab traders brought Islam to Indonesia. In time, Islam became more popular than Hinduism and Buddhism in Indonesia.

## Find Out More!

After reading Chapter 17, you're ready to go online. **Explore Zone**, **Quiz Time**, and **Amazing Facts** bring this chapter of world history alive.

Visit www.exploreSV.com and type in the chapter code **1-Ch17**.

### Vocabulary

Number your paper from 1 to 6. Write the word from the list that best completes each analogy. One word will not be used.

1. Bedouins were to Arabia as _____ were to the area north and west of China.

2. Short is to tall as _____ is to attack.

3. A defeat is to a loss as a _____ is to a win.

4. Emperors are to empires as sultans are to _____.

5. A lord was to western Europe's feudal system as a _____ was to Japan's feudal system.

6. Less is to more as _____ is to increased.

**Word List**

declined

Mongols

sultanates

conquest

daimyo

seppuku

surrender

## Comprehension

Number your paper from 1 to 5. Write the word or words from the list that best complete each sentence. One word will not be used.

1. Kublai Khan started the _____ in China.

2. The most powerful Muslim kingdom in India was the _____.

3. Mahmud did not like the way Indians divided people into _____.

4. The _____ was at the top of the feudal system in Japan.

5. Le Loi was a hero to the _____ people.

**Word List**

infidels

Yuan Dynasty

castes

Vietnamese

Delhi Sultanate

emperor

## Critical Thinking

**Main Idea**   Number your paper from 1 to 4. Write the sentence that is the main idea in each group.

1. The Turks destroyed Hindu temples in India.
   The Turks plundered India.
   The Turks stole gold from Indian cities.

2. Many Delhi sultans welcomed Muslim artists and teachers into their courts.
   Many buildings in Delhi combined Islamic and Indian styles.
   Delhi became a center of Islamic culture.

3. Samurai lived by a strict code.
   Samurai had to be brave and loyal.
   For samurai, nothing was worse than losing honor.

4. Arab traders taught Indonesians about Islam.
   Islam spread throughout Indonesia.
   Indonesians along the coast began to convert to Islam.

## Writing

Write a haiku poem about something that is important to you.

## LESSON 1

# West African Kingdoms

### Before You Read

- What changes might traders bring to an area?
- How might a king show other countries that his kingdom is rich and powerful?

There were three ancient West African kingdoms. The first was Ghana. After it fell, the West African kingdom of Mali rose to power. Mali began as a province of Ghana. The last king of Ghana tried to weaken Mali by killing its leaders.

One leader named Sundiata survived and raised an army in Mali. First, he took over other provinces of Ghana. Then, he conquered neighboring lands. By about 1230, he had created the Kingdom of Mali. It was twice the size of the Kingdom of Ghana. Sundiata accepted Islam and made Mali a Muslim kingdom. Sundiata ruled from 1230 to 1255 as **mansa**, or emperor, of Mali.

There are many mosques in modern-day West Africa.

### New Words
mansa
madrasas
resisted

### People and Places
Mali
Sundiata
Mansa Musa
Ibn Battuta
Timbuktu
Leo Africanus
Songhai
Sonni Ali
Gao
Askia Mohammad
Morocco

## The Kingdom of Mali

The decline of Ghana led to a slow down in trade. When Mali rose to power, the old caravan routes opened again. Arab traders came to the Sahel once more. Mali had taken over the gold fields of Ghana. It began trading slaves again as well. But Sundiata did not want to depend on trade alone. The land of Mali was rich. He urged people to farm. They grew crops such as grains, peanuts, and cotton.

The Kingdom of Mali was at its height in the early 1300s under Mansa Musa. Mali had a strong Islamic government. The laws of Islam gave the people a sense of justice. Anyone who broke the law was quickly punished. Mali was a kingdom of law and order. A famous Arab traveler, Ibn Battuta, wrote about the Kingdom of Mali in 1352.

Ibn Battuta

"There is complete [safety] in their country. Neither traveler nor [citizen] in it has anything to fear from robbers or men of violence."

From 700–1600, West Africa was ruled by three different kingdoms. Along what river was the Kingdom of Songhai located?

### Kingdoms of West Africa, 700–1600

ATLANTIC OCEAN

SAHARA DESERT

Cairo

Nile River

N W E S

Timbuktu

Kumbi

Gao

Senegal River

Niger River

**MAP KEY**
- Ghana, 700–1075
- Mali, 1230–1400
- Songhai, 1400–1591
- — Trade routes

Timbuktu was a center of trade and learning.

## The City of Timbuktu

The Mali city of Timbuktu became a center of trade and learning. The city began as a camp along the Niger River. Nomads founded the camp around 1100. Traders crossing the Sahara Desert began arriving at Timbuktu. Other people came to the city by canoe. They sailed up the Niger River. By the 14th century, Timbuktu had grown into a major trade city. At its peak, Timbuktu might have had as many as 100,000 people. It was the center of the Kingdom of Mali.

Timbuktu also became a major place for Islamic learning. It was a meeting place for the great thinkers of the time. It had huge libraries and beautiful mosques. The city also had **madrasas**, or Islamic universities. A writer named Leo Africanus praised Timbuktu for its many "doctors, judges, priests, and other learned" people.

Statue from Mali

A mosque in Timbuktu

## The Kingdom of Songhai

Mali was so large that it was difficult to rule. After Mansa Musa's death, the kingdom began to weaken. Local leaders **resisted** the emperor. In the 1400s, civil war broke out. Then the Kingdom of Songhai took control. It was the third and last of the ancient West African kingdoms.

Sonni Ali was the first Songhai ruler. His capital city was Gao on the Niger River. In 1468, Sonni Ali took over Timbuktu and other Mali cities. Sonni Ali ruled for 35 years. He built a strong army with soldiers both on foot and on horses. He also used a navy on the Niger River.

After Sonni Ali died in 1492, Askia Mohammad became the second Songhai leader. He expanded the empire and trade. He passed fair tax laws. He treated enemies with justice and tolerance. He also encouraged his people to accept Islam.

The Kingdom of Songhai ended in 1591. Morocco, a North African country, sent an army across the Sahara Desert and defeated the Songhai army. But the Moroccans could not hold the empire together. The age of ancient West African kingdoms was over.

This painting shows a busy day at a market in Timbuktu during the Kindgom of Songhai.

## Mansa Musa (unknown–1332)

The most famous emperor of the West African kingdoms was Mansa Musa of Mali. He was a strong leader who encouraged education and the arts. He was also a devout Muslim.

Mansa Musa began his hajj, or journey to Mecca, in 1324. It was perhaps the most famous hajj in history. Some people think Mansa Musa took as many as 80,000 people with him. He took soldiers, government officials, his wives, and 500 slaves. He also took an incredible amount of gold. One hundred camels each carried 300 pounds of gold. Every slave carried a golden rod.

As he traveled, Mansa Musa began giving the gold away. He gave so much away that the value of gold dropped in the areas he traveled. Mansa Musa's incredible hajj made him famous as far away as Europe. People learned of the great wealth and power of Mali.

## Lesson 1 Review

Choose words from the list that best complete the paragraph. One word will not be used.

Mali began as a province of Ghana. __1__ led an army that captured other provinces. He then set up the Kingdom of Mali. The city of __2__ was a major center for trade and learning on the Niger River. The most famous leader of Mali was __3__. He became known for giving away gold during his hajj to Mecca. The last ancient West African kingdom was __4__. It continued to rule West Africa until 1591.

**Word List**

**Sonni Ali**

**Sundiata**

**Songhai**

**Mansa Musa**

**Timbuktu**

## LESSON 2

# Eastern and Southern Africa

**New Words**

commodity

oral

mortar

**People and Places**

Mogadishu

Kilwa

Malindi

Mombasa

Zanzibar

Zambezi River

Great Zimbabwe

**Before You Read**

- What trade goods might bring riches to a region?

- What can be learned about a people by studying the ruins of their cities?

Between 700 and 1591, West Africa was ruled by three great kingdoms. In East Africa, however, there were no large kingdoms. Instead, East Africa had smaller city-states.

Around 1000, Bantu-speaking people settled along the coast of the Indian Ocean. Merchants from India, Arabia, and Persia also settled there. Arab culture changed East Africa. The Swahili language developed. It was a mixture of Bantu and Arabic. The Swahili culture was also a mixture of Bantu and Arab cultures.

This modern hunter lives in eastern Africa.

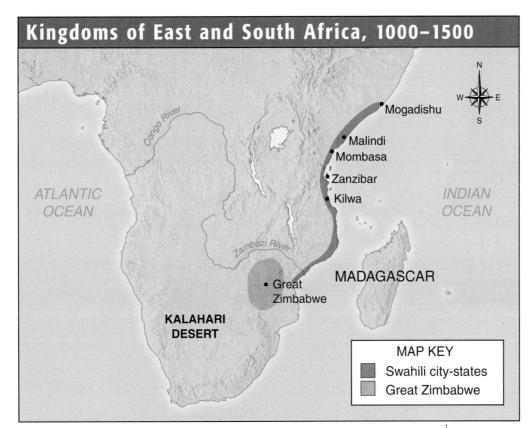

## Kingdoms of East and South Africa, 1000–1500

MAP KEY
- Swahili city-states
- Great Zimbabwe

*Several city-states developed along the east coast of Africa. Which city-state was the farthest south?*

## East African Trade

The Swahili city-states were port cities. They stretched from Mogadishu in the north to Kilwa in the south. Malindi, Mombasa, and Zanzibar were three other important city-states. Each one had its own laws, government, tax system, and rulers. The city-states often competed fiercely against one another. Each city-state wanted to control as much trade as possible.

One valuable **commodity** was ivory. Ivory was made from the tusks of African elephants. It was soft, so it could be carved easily. But it was also strong, so it could last a long time.

Gold was another valuable commodity. Like West Africa, East Africa had rich gold fields.

Another African commodity was iron. Traders from as far away as China bought African iron. In return, the East Africans bought cotton cloth, jewelry, spices, and Chinese porcelain.

African ivory spoon

Ruins of a mosque in Kilwa

## The City of Kilwa

Kilwa was perhaps the most powerful city in East Africa. It was closer to the gold fields than other cities, so it controlled most of the gold trade. It also collected taxes on the sale of gold. Kilwa leaders built grand palaces, mosques, and parks.

The Arab traveler Ibn Battuta visited Kilwa in 1331. He had already been to the great cities of China and India. Still, he thought Kilwa was one of the most amazing cities he had ever seen.

**Voices**
**In History**

"[Kilwa was] one of the most beautiful and best constructed towns in the world."

Kilwa remained powerful until Europeans arrived in 1497. They were amazed by the wealth of the East African cities. They wanted to control East African trade. In 1505, they burned Kilwa. They also captured Mombasa. This ended the great trading days of the East African city-states. Swahili culture, however, survived.

Kilwa was once an active trading city. Today, there are only ruins.

## Great Zimbabwe

Far to the south of the city-states, a kingdom developed near the Zambezi River. It was called Great Zimbabwe. The people of Great Zimbabwe lived near gold fields.

Little is known about Great Zimbabwe culture. The people left no written record. Also, they left no **oral** traditions. They did, however, leave behind ruins in the form of stone walls. The stone ruins of Great Zimbabwe show that the stones were cut perfectly. The stones fit together without the use of any **mortar**, or cement. The skill of the stonework gave the city its name. The word *Zimbabwe* means "house of rock."

At one point, Great Zimbabwe might have had as many as 20,000 people. Then, about 1600, the culture disappeared. Without a written record, the full story of Great Zimbabwe remains a mystery.

Stones without mortar

Stone ruins of Great Zimbabwe

# Lesson 2 Review

Choose words from the list that best complete the paragraphs. One word will not be used.

Swahili city-states developed along the coast of East Africa. The Swahili language was a mixture of Bantu and __1__. The East African city-states competed with one another for trade. One East African trade good was __2__. One of the most powerful Swahili city-states was __3__. It controlled much of the gold trade.

Less is known about the history of southern Africa during this time. There are stone ruins of a city called __4__. The stones of that city fit together without the use of mortar.

**Word List**

ivory

**Great Zimbabwe**

**Kilwa**

**porcelain**

**Arabic**

## Chapter 18: Using What You've Learned

### Summary

- Sundiata created the Kingdom of Mali in 1230. The Mali city of Timbuktu was once a great center for trade and Islamic learning.

- The last of the ancient West African kingdoms was Songhai. In 1591, Songhai was defeated by Morocco.

- Mansa Musa led a hajj to Mecca in 1324. The amount of gold he gave away on the journey made him famous.

- City-states developed on the east coast of Africa. Kilwa was perhaps the most powerful city in East Africa.

- The rise and fall of Great Zimbabwe, a kingdom in southern Africa, remains a mystery.

## Find Out More!

After reading Chapter 18, you're ready to go online. **Explore Zone**, **Quiz Time**, and **Amazing Facts** bring this chapter of world history alive.

Visit www.exploreSV.com and type in the chapter code **1-Ch18**.

### Vocabulary

Number your paper from 1 to 4. Write the letter of the correct answer.

1. In the African kingdom of Mali, a **mansa** was _____.
   - **a.** a trade center
   - **b.** an emperor
   - **c.** a journey
   - **d.** an infidel

2. **Madrasas** are Islamic _____.
   - **a.** beliefs
   - **b.** universities
   - **c.** mosques
   - **d.** villages

3. A valuable **commodity** in East African trade was _____.
   - **a.** language
   - **b.** wood
   - **c.** government
   - **d.** ivory

4. The walls of Great Zimbabwe were built without **mortar**, or _____.
   - **a.** dirt
   - **b.** sand
   - **c.** cement
   - **d.** glue

## Comprehension

Number your paper from 1 to 6. Write one or more sentences to answer each question below.

1. Why did Mali's leader, Sundiata, urge his people to farm?

2. Why did Mali weaken after Mansa Musa's death?

3. What did Askia Mohammad do as leader of Songhai?

4. What two cultures was the Swahili culture a mixture of?

5. How did Europeans end the great trading days of the East African city-states?

6. Why is so little known about the people of Great Zimbabwe?

## Critical Thinking

**Fact or Opinion**   Number your paper from 1 to 5. For each fact, write **Fact**. Write **Opinion** for each opinion. You should find two sentences that are opinions.

1. The Kingdom of Mali was more important than the Kingdom of Ghana.

2. The people of Mali followed the laws of Islam.

3. Each Swahili city-state had its own laws, government, tax system, and rulers.

4. Kilwa controlled most of the gold trade in East Africa.

5. The people of Great Zimbabwe were the most skilled stoneworkers in Africa.

## Writing

Write a short paragraph explaining why Timbuktu became a major center of learning in Mali.

# Skill Builder: Reading a Bar Graph

A **bar graph** uses bars of different lengths to show facts. The bar graph below shows the greatest population of African kingdoms at the peak of their civilizations.

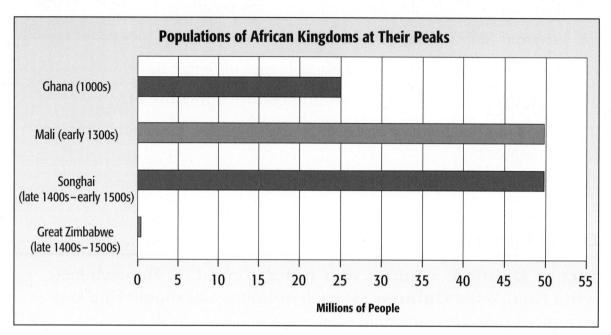

Number your paper from 1 to 4. Write the letter of the correct answer.

1. How many people might have lived in Ghana in the 1000s?
   **a.** 20,000       **b.** 25 million       **c.** 50 million

2. About how many people lived in Mali when it was at its peak?
   **a.** 20,000       **b.** 25 million       **c.** 50 million

3. When did Songhai have around 50 million people?
   **a.** 1000s       **b.** early 1300s       **c.** late 1400s to early 1500s

4. Which of these kingdoms had the smallest population at its peak?
   **a.** Ghana       **b.** Mali       **c.** Great Zimbabwe

## LESSON 1

# The Aztec and the Inca

## Before You Read

- How do most civilizations choose where to build their cities?
- How might people communicate without using language?

The Toltec built a huge empire in Central America from around 700 to 1100. Then around 1200, their empire fell to the Aztec. These warlike people had wandered in northern Mexico for centuries. Then the Aztec moved into central Mexico and conquered the Toltec, as well as many other groups. The Aztec then created the most powerful empire in North America.

## New Words
causeways
chinampas
quipu

## People and Places
Aztec
Lake Texcoco
Tenochtitlán
Inca
Andes Mountains
Cuzco
Machu Picchu

This shield shows the colorful decorations of the Aztec.

Mexican flag

## Looking for a Sign

The Aztec searched for a place to build their capital city. Legend says that one of their gods told them to look for a sign. They were to look for an eagle sitting on a cactus, holding a snake in its mouth. Where they saw that sign, they were to build their capital city. The Aztec found this spot on an island in Lake Texcoco. The Aztec built their capital on that island in 1325. They named the city Tenochtitlán. Today, the flag of Mexico shows an eagle sitting on a cactus, holding a snake in its mouth.

The Aztec had another reason for building Tenochtitlán on an island. The water protected them from their enemies. The island also gave them a safe place from which to launch their own attacks.

## The Island City

The Aztec turned the island into a great city. It had a large main square. Tenochtitlán also had parks, a zoo, temples, gardens, canals, a library,

The Aztec capital city, Tenochtitlán, was built on an island in Lake Texcoco.

and thousands of houses. Aztec rulers lived in a huge palace with enough room for the royal family and 3,000 servants. To get in and out of the city, the Aztec built **causeways**, or roads over water. They also built canals.

Up to 250,000 people might have lived in Tenochtitlán. To help feed them all, the Aztec built **chinampas**. These were floating gardens in the shallow parts of the lake. On the chinampas, Aztec farmers planted corn and many other crops.

## The Aztec Way of Life

War was a way of life for the Aztec. Boys were taught to fight at an early age. The Aztec conquered many neighboring groups. At its height, the empire covered most of modern-day Mexico. In total, about 15 million people lived under Aztec rule.

Human sacrifice was also a part of their lives. The Aztec believed that the sun god demanded such sacrifices. Without the sacrifices, the world would come to an end. For the Aztec, the sun god controlled life and death. One Aztec poet wrote about the power of the sun god.

**Voices**
**In History**

"He [laughs at] us.
As he wishes, so he wills.
He places us in the palm of his hand,
He rolls us about;
Like pebbles we roll, we spin . . .
We make him laugh."

## The Inca

In South America, the Inca lived on the western slopes of the Andes Mountains. They began around 1100 as one small group among many. For about 300 years, they fought a series of wars with neighbors. By the 1400s, the Inca had set up a vast empire.

## Did You Know?

### Chocolate Money

The next time you eat chocolate, think of the Maya and the Aztec. The Maya first learned how to roast cacao beans. They then ground up the beans and made a chocolate drink. There was no sugar, so they added hot peppers for spice. The Aztec kings valued chocolate so much that they drank it from a golden cup. The Aztec even used the cacao beans as money. An Aztec could buy nearly anything with enough cacao beans.

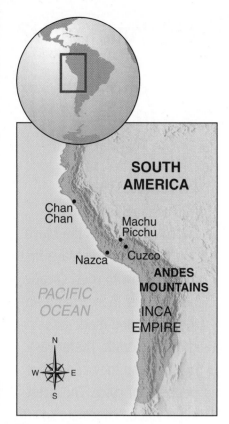

The Inca Empire

Today, visitors are impressed by the ancient ruins of Machu Picchu.

The Inca Empire stretched 2,500 miles north to south and 500 miles east to west. The Inca built their capital in the mountains of modern-day Peru. They named it Cuzco. Another famous Inca city was Machu Picchu. Because Machu Picchu was located high in the mountains, Europeans did not discover it until 1911.

An emperor ruled the Inca people. The people believed the emperor came from the sun god. He was treated as if he were a god. The Inca emperor set strict laws. Almost everything in the empire belonged to the emperor. The Inca people had little freedom. But the Inca did take good care of people who became ill or were too old to work.

## Roads and Knotted Strings

The Inca built a system of roads to unite their empire. They had no horses and no wheeled carts, so the roads did not have to be very wide. Still, building them wasn't easy. Their land had high mountains and deep canyons. The Inca built rope bridges over the canyons. They carved steps up steep mountain passes. Where they could, the

Inca made roads with stone. The longest road went the full length of the empire.

The Inca used the roads to send messages from one end of the empire to the other. One runner would run for a few miles. Then a new runner would take over. Using this system, a message could travel more than 100 miles in a day.

The Inca had no written language. The runners had to memorize messages. They used a system of knotted strings called a **quipu**. A quipu was a group of colored strings. The color of the string and the way it was knotted stood for a particular word or number. For example, a certain colored knot could mean danger.

Both the Aztec and the Inca civilizations were at their height around 1500. They continued to grow until Spanish explorers arrived.

Inca quipu

## Lesson 1 Review

Choose words from the list that best complete the paragraphs. One word will not be used.

In 1325, the Aztec built Tenochtitlán on an island in Lake Texcoco. They built __1__, which made it easy to get in and out of the capital. To grow more food, the Aztec built __2__, or floating gardens. The Aztec practiced human sacrifice to please the sun god.

The Inca made __3__ their capital city. They built a system of roads to unite the empire. Runners carried messages along the roads. The Inca used a system of knotted strings called a __4__ to communicate because they had no written language.

**Word List**

quipu

causeways

Peru

Cuzco

chinampas

## LESSON 2

# North American Civilizations

### New Words

ancestors
pueblos
mesas
burial grounds

### People and Places

Navajo
Pueblo Indians
Colorado
Hopi
Zuni
Mound Builders
Hopewell
Ohio River
Mississippians
Mississippi River
Cahokia Mound
Illinois

### Before You Read

- Why might people build their villages into the side of a cliff?
- Why might a group of people be called the Mound Builders?

The Anasazi lived in the southwestern part of what is now the United States. Once nomads, the Anasazi began to settle and farm around 750. The word *Anasazi* is a Navajo word that means "ancient ones." Most people believe the Anasazi were the **ancestors** of the modern Pueblo Indians.

This pueblo in Mesa Verde, Colorado, was built in the 12th century.

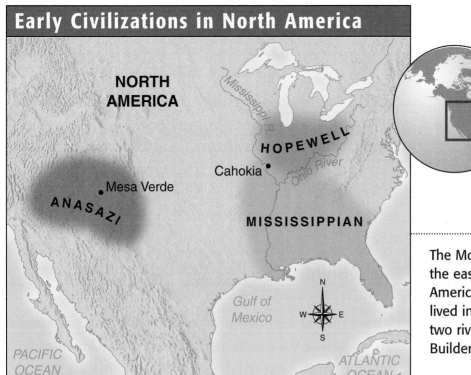

## Early Civilizations in North America

NORTH AMERICA

Mississippi R.

HOPEWELL

Cahokia

Ohio River

Mesa Verde

ANASAZI

MISSISSIPPIAN

Gulf of Mexico

PACIFIC OCEAN

ATLANTIC OCEAN

The Mound Builders lived in the eastern part of North America, while the Anasazi lived in the western part. What two rivers did the Mound Builders live near?

## The Anasazi

The Anasazi built villages called **pueblos**. They often built them on the top of **mesas**, or flat-topped mountains with steep sides. They also lived in caves that they dug into the sides of cliffs. These homes protected them from the weather and from enemies. Some pueblos were quite large. One pueblo was built in the modern-day state of Colorado. It had 1,800 rooms that held about 3,000 people.

The Anasazi continued their tradition of making beautiful baskets. They began to grow new crops, such as beans. They also made beautiful pottery for cooking and storing food.

The Anasazi civilization declined after 1300. The people began leaving their pueblos. By around 1400, the Anasazi pueblos were empty.

Many scientists believe that the Anasazi people ran out of water. There was a drought from about 1275 to 1300. Overpopulation might have been another cause of the Anasazi decline.

Anasazi frog pin

Modern Hopi woman weaving a basket

Another reason for the Anasazi decline might have been poor health. The Anasazi left their garbage near their homes. This could have brought diseases to the people. Still another cause might have been a neighboring group that drove the Anasazi from their homes.

After leaving their homes, the Anasazi joined other groups such as the Hopi and Zuni. Many Native Americans today still farm land, weave baskets, and make pottery in the same way as the Anasazi.

## Mound Builders

Another group of North Americans are known as the Mound Builders. They lived mostly in the eastern half of what is now the United States. They were known for the huge mounds they formed on the ground.

The mounds were built in different shapes and sizes. Some were built in the shape of pyramids. Others were built to look like snakes or birds. Many of these mounds are so large that they can only be seen from the sky.

Several groups built mounds. The Hopewell built mounds in the Ohio River valley. Many

This mound in the Ohio River valley is shaped like a snake.

archaeologists believe that the Hopewells' mounds were **burial grounds**. Another group, the Mississippians, lived along the Mississippi River. Their mounds were foundations for their temples. Other groups might have built mounds as symbols for religious ceremonies or defense.

The Cahokia Mound in the modern-day state of Illinois is one of the largest mounds. Shaped like a pyramid, it is 1,000 feet long, 300 feet wide, and 100 feet high. Scientists believe that 30,000 people might have lived at or near this mound.

The Mound Builders carried dirt in baskets to the place of the mound. The larger mounds must have taken years to build. Scientists have found shark teeth from the Gulf of Mexico in mounds far away from the coast. This could mean that the Mound Builders had contact and traded with other North American groups.

Cahokia Mound

# Lesson 2 Review

Choose words from the list that best complete the paragraphs. One word will not be used.

The Anasazi built villages called __1__. They often settled on the top of __2__ to protect themselves from enemies. The Anasazi began to leave their pueblos around 1300. The Anasazi way of life continued in the cultures of many modern Native Americans.

The __3__ lived mostly in the eastern half of the United States. Archaeologists believe that the __4__ used their mounds as burial grounds. Other groups built temples on their mounds.

**Word List**

Hopewell

Zuni

mesas

Mound Builders

pueblos

## Chapter 19: Using What You've Learned

### Summary

- The Aztec took control of central Mexico from the Toltec. They built their capital, Tenochtitlán, on an island in Lake Texcoco.

- The Inca built a vast empire in South America. Their capital city, Cuzco, was located in the mountains of modern-day Peru.

- Historians believe the Anasazi were ancestors of the modern-day Pueblo Indians. Around 1300, the Anasazi began to leave their villages and join other groups, such as the Hopi and Zuni.

- Mound Builders lived in the eastern United States. They built huge mounds in the shapes of pyramids, snakes, and birds. These mounds served many purposes.

### Find Out More!

After reading Chapter 19, you're ready to go online. **Explore Zone**, **Quiz Time**, and **Amazing Facts** bring this chapter of world history alive.

Visit www.exploreSV.com and type in the chapter code **1-Ch19**.

### Vocabulary

Number your paper from 1 to 6. Finish the sentences from Group A with words from Group B. Write the letter of the correct answer.

| Group A | Group B |
|---|---|
| **1.** The Aztec built _____ so they could get in and out of Tenochtitlán. | **a.** mesas |
| **2.** To grow crops, the Aztec built _____ in the shallow parts of the lake. | **b.** burial grounds |
| **3.** The Inca kept records by using knotted strings called a _____. | **c.** quipu |
| **4.** The Anasazi built villages called _____. | **d.** causeways |
| **5.** The Anasazi often built their villages on the top of _____. | **e.** chinampas |
| **6.** Archaeologists believe that the Hopewell used their mounds as _____. | **f.** pueblos |

## Comprehension

Number your paper from 1 to 5. Write the word or words from the list that best complete the paragraph. One word will not be used.

The Aztec moved into central Mexico around 1200 and conquered the __1__ . The Aztec built their capital on an island in __2__ . The Inca lived in South America in the __3__ Mountains. The Inca built a system of __4__ to unite their empire. The Aztec and the Inca civilizations grew until __5__ explorers arrived.

### Word List

**Lake Texcoco**

**mesas**

**Toltec**

**Spanish**

**roads**

**Andes**

## Critical Thinking

**Conclusions**  Number your paper from 1 to 3. Read each pair of sentences below. Then look for a conclusion that follows from these sentences. Write the letter of the correct conclusion.

1. The Anasazi built pueblos on steep, flat-topped mountains. They also lived in caves dug into the sides of cliffs.

2. The Anasazi left their garbage near their homes. This may have given the people diseases.

3. Scientists have found shark teeth in Mound Builder mounds. These mounds are far away from the Gulf of Mexico.

### Conclusions

a. Poor health might be one reason for the Anasazi decline.

b. Mound Builders might have traded with other North American groups.

c. Anasazi homes were built to protect the people from enemies and weather.

## Writing

Write a paragraph comparing the ways the Inca sent messages within their empire with the ways messages are sent today.

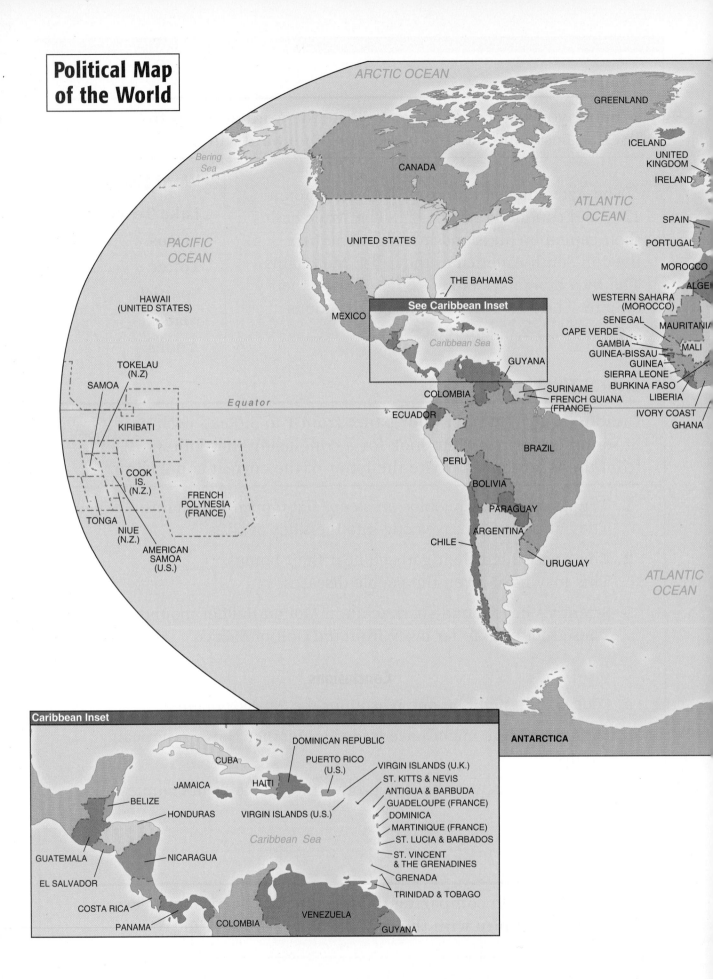

# Political Map of the World

ARCTIC OCEAN

GREENLAND

ICELAND

UNITED KINGDOM

IRELAND

CANADA

ATLANTIC OCEAN

SPAIN

PORTUGAL

MOROCCO

PACIFIC OCEAN

UNITED STATES

THE BAHAMAS

See Caribbean Inset

WESTERN SAHARA (MOROCCO)

ALGE

HAWAII (UNITED STATES)

MEXICO

Caribbean Sea

SENEGAL

CAPE VERDE

MAURITANIA

GAMBIA

GUINEA-BISSAU

MALI

GUINEA

GUYANA

SIERRA LEONE

BURKINA FASO

TOKELAU (N.Z)

SURINAME

FRENCH GUIANA (FRANCE)

LIBERIA

SAMOA

COLOMBIA

IVORY COAST

Equator

ECUADOR

GHANA

KIRIBATI

BRAZIL

PERU

COOK IS. (N.Z.)

BOLIVIA

FRENCH POLYNESIA (FRANCE)

PARAGUAY

TONGA

ARGENTINA

NIUE (N.Z.)

CHILE

URUGUAY

AMERICAN SAMOA (U.S.)

ATLANTIC OCEAN

Bering Sea

ANTARCTICA

## Caribbean Inset

DOMINICAN REPUBLIC

CUBA

PUERTO RICO (U.S.)

VIRGIN ISLANDS (U.K.)

JAMAICA

HAITI

ST. KITTS & NEVIS

BELIZE

ANTIGUA & BARBUDA

HONDURAS

GUADELOUPE (FRANCE)

VIRGIN ISLANDS (U.S.)

DOMINICA

MARTINIQUE (FRANCE)

Caribbean Sea

ST. LUCIA & BARBADOS

GUATEMALA

NICARAGUA

ST. VINCENT & THE GRENADINES

EL SALVADOR

GRENADA

TRINIDAD & TOBAGO

COSTA RICA

PANAMA

COLOMBIA

VENEZUELA

GUYANA

270

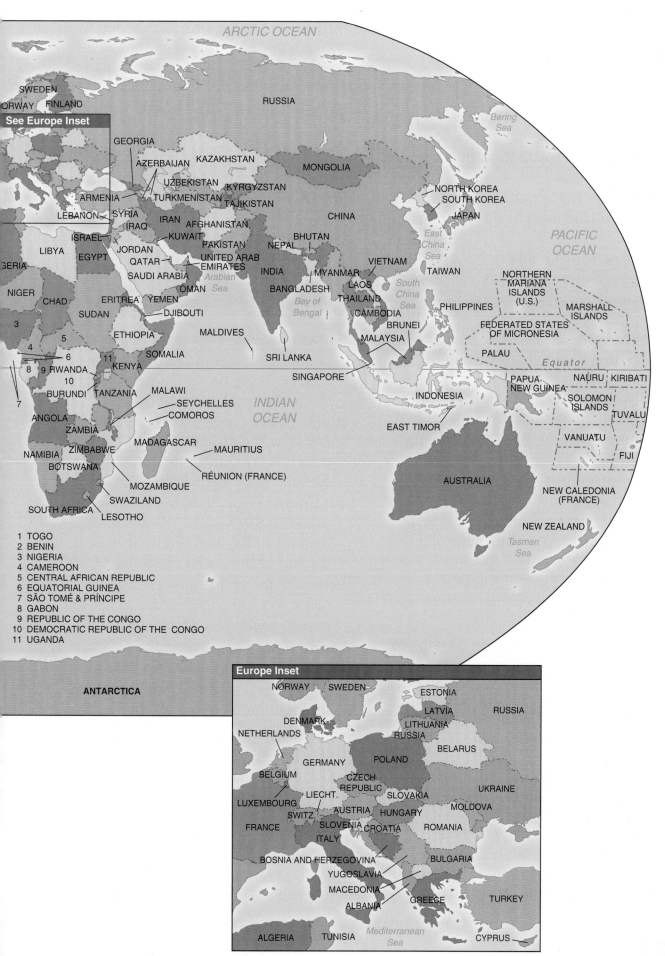

ARCTIC OCEAN

SWEDEN
NORWAY FINLAND
**See Europe Inset**

RUSSIA

*Bering Sea*

GEORGIA
AZERBAIJAN
KAZAKHSTAN
MONGOLIA
NORTH KOREA
SOUTH KOREA
UZBEKISTAN KYRGYZSTAN
ARMENIA TURKMENISTAN TAJIKISTAN
JAPAN
LEBANON SYRIA
IRAQ IRAN AFGHANISTAN
CHINA
*East China Sea*
PACIFIC OCEAN
ISRAEL KUWAIT PAKISTAN NEPAL
BHUTAN
LIBYA JORDAN QATAR UNITED ARAB EMIRATES
EGYPT
SAUDI ARABIA
*Arabian Sea*
INDIA MYANMAR
VIETNAM
TAIWAN
NORTHERN MARIANA ISLANDS (U.S.)
GERIA
NIGER CHAD
OMAN YEMEN
BANGLADESH
LAOS
THAILAND
*South China Sea*
PHILIPPINES
MARSHALL ISLANDS
ERITREA
SUDAN DJIBOUTI
CAMBODIA
BRUNEI
FEDERATED STATES OF MICRONESIA
3
ETHIOPIA
MALDIVES
MALAYSIA
PALAU
5
4
6 11
SOMALIA
KENYA
SRI LANKA
SINGAPORE
*Equator*
8 9 RWANDA
10
BURUNDI TANZANIA MALAWI
SEYCHELLES
*INDIAN OCEAN*
INDONESIA
PAPUA NEW GUINEA
NAURU KIRIBATI
SOLOMON ISLANDS
7
COMOROS
EAST TIMOR
TUVALU
ANGOLA
ZAMBIA
MADAGASCAR
MAURITIUS
VANUATU
FIJI
NAMIBIA ZIMBABWE
BOTSWANA
RÉUNION (FRANCE)
AUSTRALIA
NEW CALEDONIA (FRANCE)
MOZAMBIQUE
SWAZILAND
SOUTH AFRICA LESOTHO
NEW ZEALAND
*Tasman Sea*

1 TOGO
2 BENIN
3 NIGERIA
4 CAMEROON
5 CENTRAL AFRICAN REPUBLIC
6 EQUATORIAL GUINEA
7 SÃO TOMÉ & PRÍNCIPE
8 GABON
9 REPUBLIC OF THE CONGO
10 DEMOCRATIC REPUBLIC OF THE CONGO
11 UGANDA

**ANTARCTICA**

**Europe Inset**

NORWAY SWEDEN
ESTONIA
LATVIA
RUSSIA
DENMARK
LITHUANIA
NETHERLANDS
RUSSIA
BELARUS
GERMANY
POLAND
BELGIUM
CZECH REPUBLIC
LUXEMBOURG
LIECHT.
SLOVAKIA
UKRAINE
SWITZ.
AUSTRIA
HUNGARY
MOLDOVA
FRANCE
SLOVENIA
CROATIA
ROMANIA
ITALY
BOSNIA AND HERZEGOVINA
YUGOSLAVIA
BULGARIA
MACEDONIA
ALBANIA
GREECE
TURKEY
ALGERIA TUNISIA
*Mediterranean Sea*
CYPRUS

**271**

# Glossary

## A

**afterlife** (page 18) An afterlife is a life after one's death.

**ahimsa** (page 120) Ahimsa means never hurting others.

**Allah** (page 157) Allah is the Arabic word for God used in the religion Islam.

**ally** (page 175) An ally is a country that helps another country during a war.

**ancestors** (page 264) Ancestors are people of one's family who lived long ago.

**apprentice** (page 219) An apprentice is a person who learns a trade from a skilled worker.

**aqueducts** (page 104) Aqueducts are channels that are used for carrying water.

**Arabic numerals** (page 165) Arabic numerals are the numbers 1 through 9.

**archaeologists** (page 8) Archaeologists are people who study old bones and objects to learn about the past.

**archipelago** (page 176) An archipelago is a chain of islands.

**artifacts** (page 68) Artifacts are objects made by people.

**assassinate** (page 117) To assassinate someone is to kill that person. The person killed is usually a leader or someone else important.

## B

**Bantu migrations** (page 191) The Bantu migrations were a mass movement of people from West Africa to the eastern and southern areas of Africa from around 100 B.C. to A.D. 1000.

**barbarians** (page 140) Barbarians were Germans and other people who entered the lands of the ancient Western Roman Empire by force.

**bartered** (page 218) Bartered means traded one good for another.

**basalt** (page 57) Basalt is a kind of rock formed from cooled lava.

**bas-reliefs** (page 70) Bas-reliefs are carvings made on a flat surface.

**bathhouses** (page 227) Bathhouses are public places where people can take baths.

**bazaar** (page 163) A bazaar is a market of shops.

**bedouins** (page 156) Bedouins are people who live in the deserts of Arabia, Syria, or North Africa. They do not have permanent homes.

**Black Death** (page 220) The Black Death was a disease that killed many people during the 14th century. It was carried by fleas that lived on rats.

**Brahman** (page 49) A Brahman was a priest in the Aryan civilization of ancient India. The Brahman was at the top of the social classes.

**bribes** (page 111) Bribes are money given to someone in order to get that person to do something wrong.

**bronze** (page 42) Bronze is a hard metal that is a mixture of copper and tin.

**Buddhism** (page 118) Buddhism is a religion that is based on the teachings of a man called the Buddha.

**bureaucracy** (page 129) A bureaucracy is a group of government officials.

**burial grounds** (page 267) Burial grounds are places in which dead people are buried.

**Bushido** (page 236) Bushido was the code of honor followed by Japanese warriors.

## C

**calendar** (page 57) A calendar is a system that divides a year into months, weeks, and days.

**caliph** (page 162) A caliph is the head of the Islamic communities.

**caliphate** (page 163) A caliphate is the land ruled by the head of the Islamic communities.

**calligraphy** (page 164) Calligraphy is a kind of beautiful writing.

**caravans** (page 66) Caravans are groups of people traveling through the desert.

**castes** (page 49) Castes are classes of people. Hindus believe that people are born into castes.

**catapults** (page 226) Catapults are huge slings used to toss bombs or rocks over high walls during wars.

**cathedrals** (page 220) Cathedrals are large, magnificent churches.

**Catholic Church** (page 152) The Catholic Church is the Christian church based in western Europe. It is headed by the pope.

**causeways** (page 261) Causeways are roads over water.

**ceramics** (page 205) Ceramics are pottery and other objects made by heating clay.

**chariots** (page 22) Chariots are two-wheeled carts that are pulled by horses. Long ago people used chariots in battles or in races.

**chinampas** (page 261) Chinampas were floating gardens made by the Aztec in order to grow crops.

**Christianity** (page 106) Christianity is a religion based on the teachings of Jesus.

**citadel** (page 48) A citadel is a strong fort built to protect a city.

**city-states** (page 30) City-states are towns or cities that rule themselves and the land around them.

**civil war** (page 127) A civil war is a war in which people of the same country fight against one another.

**civilizations** (page 13) Civilizations are large communities that have a written language and a government.

**clans** (page 10) Clans are groups of people that live and hunt together in order to have a better chance of surviving.

**Classic Maya** (page 199) Classic Maya refers to a time period during which the Mayan civilization was at its height, between A.D. 300 and A.D. 900.

**climate** (page 7) The climate is the average weather of a place over several years.

**Code of Hammurabi** (page 31) The Code of Hammurabi is a set of about 282 laws put together by Hammurabi, a king of ancient Babylon.

**commodity** (page 253) A commodity is a good that is bought and sold.

**Confucianism** (page 132) Confucianism is a philosophy based on the teachings of a man named Confucius, who was born in China around 550 B.C.

**conquered** (page 77) Conquered means used force to take control of a place or group of people.

**conquest** (page 226) A conquest is the act of taking control of a land by force.

**consuls** (page 90) Consuls were leaders of the ancient Roman republic. Two consuls led the government at a time.

**contact** (page 37) To have contact with a group of people is to have communication with them.

**continents** (page 5) Continents are very large masses of land. There are seven continents on Earth.

**convents** (page 149) Convents are places where nuns live, work, and follow their religion.

**converted** (page 163) Converted means changed one's religion.

**covenant** (page 35) A covenant is a strong agreement.

**crucified** (page 107) To have crucified someone is to have nailed that person to a cross in order to kill him or her.

**crusade** (page 213) A crusade is a holy war.

**culture** (page 65) Culture is the ideas, customs, skills, arts, and way of life of a group of people.

**cuneiform** (page 31) Cuneiform is a form of writing used by Sumerians and other people of ancient Mesopotamia. The writing used different symbols that were carved on a clay tablet.

## D

**daimyo** (page 236) Daimyo were powerful Japanese landowners in feudal Japan.

**Daoism** (page 133) Daoism is a Chinese religion that teaches people to look to nature to see how to live.

**daric** (page 78) A daric was a gold coin of the Persian Empire. The Persians used it to create a money system.

**Dark Ages** (page 145) The Dark Ages is another name for the early Middle Ages in western Europe.

**declined** (page 243) Declined means weakened.

**defend** (page 237) To defend is to protect.

**delta** (page 180) A delta is an area of land where a river leaves soil and sand as it enters a sea.

**democracy** (page 83) A democracy is a kind of government that is run by the people.

**devout** (page 231) Devout means very religious.

**dictator** (page 90) A dictator is a leader with absolute power.

**dikes** (page 30) Dikes are mounds of dirt that are used to stop flooding.

**disciples** (page 107) Disciples are people who follow the teachings of another.

**domesticate** (page 12) To domesticate wild animals is to tame them for human use.

**dominion** (page 232) Dominion means rule.

**dynasty** (page 42) A dynasty is a series of rulers from the same family.

## E

**edict** (page 108) An edict is an order.

**Edict of Milan** (page 108) The Edict of Milan was an order by the Roman emperor Constantine in A.D. 313, making it legal to be a Christian.

**Eightfold Path** (page 124) The Eightfold Path is a series of steps a person must follow in order to find true peace, according to the Buddha.

**elders** (page 195) Elders are older people who are leaders in a community.

**emperor** (page 96) An emperor is a ruler of an empire.

**empire** (page 23) An empire exists when one group of people rules over another.

**enlightenment** (page 124) Enlightenment is the understanding of the truth and nature of life.

**epic** (page 82) Epic means having to do with a long poem or story.

**evacuated** (page 242) Evacuated means removed all the people from an area.

**evaporate** (page 189) To evaporate is to dry up.

**examination system** (page 128) The examination system in ancient China was a system in which people had to pass a test in order to become a government official.

**Exodus** (page 35) Exodus is one of the books of the Torah. This book tells how Moses led the Hebrews out of Egypt.

## F

**fast** (page 159) To fast is to not eat food for a period of time.

**Fertile Crescent** (page 29) The Fertile Crescent is a region in Southwest Asia that has good land for growing crops. It extends from the Mediterranean Sea to the Persian Gulf.

**feudalism** (page 148) Feudalism was a system of loyalty among lords and knights in western Europe and among daimyo and samurai in Japan during the Middle Ages.

**fibers** (page 207) Fibers are the long threads of a plant.

**fief** (page 148) A fief was an area of land that a noble gave to a knight in exchange for protection and loyalty during the Middle Ages in western Europe.

**Five Pillars of Islam** (page 158) The Five Pillars of Islam are the duties that all followers of the religion Islam must perform.

**Four Noble Truths** (page 124) The Four Noble Truths are teachings of the Buddha about life and the way things are.

## G

**glaciers** (page 7) Glaciers are vast sheets of ice.

**gladiators** (page 104) Gladiators were slaves or prisoners of war in ancient Rome who fought other men or animals to entertain the public.

**glyphs** (page 200) Glyphs are pictures and characters used to stand for sounds or ideas. They are a form of writing.

**Gospels** (page 107) The Gospels are four books of the Bible that describe the life and teachings of Jesus.

**granary** (page 48) A granary is a building used for storing grain.

**Grand Canal** (page 169) The Grand Canal is a human-made waterway that connects the Huang He with the Yangtze River in China.

**gravity** (page 119) Gravity is the force which pulls objects and people toward Earth.

**guerrilla tactics** (page 181) Guerrilla tactics are methods of war, including surprise nighttime attacks.

**guilds** (page 218) Guilds are groups of people who do the same kind of work. Guilds in western Europe's Middle Ages kept control over their products and trained new workers.

**gunpowder** (page 173) Gunpowder is a powder that can explode. It is used to make fireworks and weapons.

## H

**haiku** (page 238) Haiku is a form of Japanese poetry. A haiku poem has just three lines. The first and third lines have five syllables. The second line has seven syllables.

**hajj** (page 159) A hajj is a journey to Mecca, located in Saudi Arabia. It is a journey that followers of the religion Islam are expected to make during their life if they are able.

**hieroglyphics** (page 18) Hieroglyphics are pictures and symbols used as a form of writing.

**highlands** (page 191) Highlands are lands high above sea level.

**hijrah** (page 158) The hijrah was the journey of Muhammad from Mecca to Medina, two Arabian cities, in A.D. 622.

**Hinduism** (page 119) Hinduism is a religion that is based on the ancient religion of the Aryans. It is the main religion of India.

**historians** (page 41) Historians are people who study and write about history.

**Holy Land** (page 213) The Holy Land is what Christians called the region of Palestine.

## I

**Ice Age** (page 11) An Ice Age is a very cold period of time that can last many thousands of years. During an Ice Age, ice covers much of the earth.

**icons** (page 152) Icons are images important to a religion. People sometimes pray to icons.

**idols** (page 157) Idols are statues of gods.

**infidels** (page 231) Infidels are people who do not believe in a certain religion.

**influence** (page 176) Influence is the effect or power someone has over another.

**invaded** (page 22) Invaded means attacked a country or other place in order to gain control of it.

**invasions** (page 113) Invasions are attacks into a country or other place in order to gain control of it.

**iron ore** (page 66) Iron ore is a material from which iron can be removed and used to make things.

**Islam** (page 141) Islam is a religion based on the teachings of Muhammad.

## J

**jaguar** (page 58) A jaguar is a large cat that can be found in South America, Central America, and the southern parts of North America.

**jihad** (page 190) A jihad is a struggle to protect the Islamic faith against an enemy.

**journeyman** (page 219) A journeyman is a person who is skilled enough in a craft to be paid but is not yet a master.

**Judaism** (page 36) Judaism is the Jewish religion.

**Justinian Code** (page 151) The Justinian Code was a set of laws issued by the Byzantine emperor Justinian. The laws were based on Roman laws.

## K

**Kaaba** (page 158) The Kaaba is an important Muslim temple in the city of Mecca, located in Saudi Arabia.

**kamikaze** (page 237) Kamikaze were winds that the Japanese believed were holy.

## L

**lagoons** (page 206) Lagoons are shallow ponds connected to lakes or seas.

**land bridge** (page 54) A land bridge is an area of land that connects two larger areas of land that are otherwise separated by water.

**legends** (page 41) Legends are stories that have been told since earlier times. Legends might be based on history, but they cannot be proven.

**location** (page 182) A location is the place where someone or something is.

**looted** (page 111) Looted means robbed.

**lord** (page 148) A lord was a noble who ruled over land in western Europe during the Middle Ages.

**lost wax method** (page 206) The lost wax method was a method used to make gold objects.

## M

**madrasas** (page 249) Madrasas are Islamic universities.

**mainland** (page 175) A mainland is the largest part of a continent.

**maize** (page 55) Maize is corn.

**Mandate of Heaven** (page 43) The Mandate of Heaven was the right to rule ancient China.

**manor** (page 148) A manor was land ruled over by a noble during the Middle Ages.

**mansa** (page 247) A mansa was a ruler of ancient Mali in West Africa.

**maritime** (page 81) Maritime means living near the sea.

**masterpiece** (page 219) A masterpiece is a work done with great skill.

**mathematicians** (page 201) Mathematicians are people who study numbers and math.

**mayor of the palace** (page 141) The mayor of the palace was an official who held much power in the Merovingian Dynasty of western Europe.

**mercy** (page 226) Mercy is kindness, especially to enemies.

**mesas** (page 265) Mesas are flat-topped mountains with steep sides.

**Messiah** (page 107) A Messiah, or chosen one, is a person whom others believe will bring peace and freedom.

**Middle Ages** (page 140) The Middle Ages was the period of European history between the fall of Rome and the modern world (A.D. 476 to A.D. 1500).

**migration** (page 54) A migration is an act of people moving across a large area.

**millet** (page 42) Millet is a kind of grass with small seeds that are used to make cereal.

**monasteries** (page 149) Monasteries are places where monks live, work, and follow their religion.

**Mongols** (page 225) Mongols are people who live in a region north and west of China.

**monopoly** (page 189) To have a monopoly is to have total control over a good or service.

**monsoon** (page 46) A monsoon is a very strong wind that blows across the Indian Ocean and southern Asia. During the winter, the wind brings dry weather. During the summer, it brings heavy rains.

**Moors** (page 216) The Moors were a group of Muslims who had taken control of most of Spain in A.D. 1000.

**mortar** (page 255) Mortar is a kind of cement.

**mosaics** (page 151) Mosaics are pictures made from small pieces of colored stone or glass.

**mosques** (page 160) Mosques are places where followers of the religion Islam pray.

**movable type** (page 172) Movable type is a method of printing using blocks of wood to make words and sentences on a page.

**mummies** (page 18) Mummies are dead bodies that have been preserved with salts and chemicals so that they will last.

**Muslims** (page 141) Muslims are people who believe in the religion Islam.

**myth** (page 82) A myth is a type of legend or story.

## N

**nirvana** (page 125) Nirvana is a state of mind in which there is no desire or greed, only true peace.

**Noh drama** (page 238) A Noh drama is a type of Japanese theater in which actors wear masks and costumes and a chorus sings.

**nomads** (page 10) Nomads are people who do not have a permanent home. They move when necessary to find food.

## O

**obelisks** (page 23) Obelisks were tall stone columns that were built to honor gods.

**opera** (page 171) Opera is a kind of art in which a play's words are sung instead of spoken.

**oracle bones** (page 43) Oracle bones are animal bones or turtle shells that people in ancient China used to tell about the future or to answer questions. A person would determine the answer from the way the bones cracked or broke after being heated.

**oral** (page 255) Oral means spoken.

**Orthodox Church** (page 152) The Orthodox Church is the Christian church based in eastern Europe.

**overpopulation** (page 193) Overpopulation is too many people living on a land that cannot support them.

## P

**Papal States** (page 142) The Papal States were lands belonging to the pope.

**papyrus** (page 18) Papyrus is a tall water plant found in northern Africa and southern Europe.

**patricians** (page 90) Patricians were wealthy people who owned land in ancient Rome.

**Pax Romana** (page 102) Pax Romana means "peace of Rome." It was a period of time in which ancient Romans enjoyed much peace, good government, and open trade. It lasted from 27 B.C. to A.D. 180.

**peasants** (page 127) Peasants are farmers and workers.

**peninsula** (page 72) A peninsula is a large piece of land that is mostly surrounded by water.

**pharaohs** (page 18) Pharaohs were rulers of ancient Egypt.

**philosophy** (page 83) Philosophy is the study of life, ideas, values, and knowledge.

**plague** (page 220) A plague is a disease that kills many people very quickly.

**plazas** (page 69) Plazas are big open areas in a city.

**plebeians** (page 90) Plebeians were farmers and other common people in ancient Rome.

**plunder** (page 231) To plunder is to rob by force.

**pope** (page 113) In ancient Rome, the pope was the head of the western Christian church. Today, the pope is the head of the Catholic Church.

**population** (page 55) An area's population is all of its people.

**porcelain** (page 129) Porcelain is a kind of delicate pottery first made by the ancient Chinese.

**prehistoric** (page 9) Prehistoric means before people began recording written history.

**Promised Land** (page 35) The Promised Land was an area called Canaan. Jews believe that God promised this land to the Hebrews.

**prophet** (page 159) A prophet is an inspired teacher of a religion.

**provinces** (page 77) Provinces are regions of a nation or empire.

**public works** (page 169) Public works are roads, dams, bridges, and other structures that a government builds for people to use.

**pueblos** (page 265) Pueblos are Native American villages in the southwestern United States.

**pyramids** (page 17) Pyramids are buildings that have four sides shaped like triangles. The sides come together to form a point at the top.

## Q

**quipu** (page 263) A quipu was a system of knotted, colored strings used by the Inca to keep records.

**Qur'an** (page 158) The Qur'an is the holy book of the religion Islam.

## R

**rebirth** (page 123) Rebirth is the act of being born again.

**reborn** (page 122) Reborn means born again.

**Reconquista** (page 216) In the Reconquista, Spanish Christians fought to drive a group of Muslims called the Moors out of Spain.

**reforms** (page 177) Reforms are changes made in order to improve something.

**reincarnation** (page 122) Reincarnation is the act of a soul being born again in a new body.

**relic** (page 162) A relic is a holy object.

**religion** (page 19) A religion is a belief in a god or gods.

**religious** (page 19) Religious means having to do with religion.

**representatives** (page 89) Representatives are leaders who represent the people of a nation or group.

**republic** (page 89) A republic is a government in which the leaders are elected by the people.

**resisted** (page 250) Resisted means stood against or fought.

**resources** (page 66) Resources are materials that can be used to fill a need.

**resurrection** (page 107) A resurrection is an act of a dead person coming back to life.

**revolt** (page 79) A revolt is a fight or struggle against a ruler or government.

## S

**sack** (page 234) A sack of a city is the act of capturing and robbing a city by force.

**sacrifice** (page 71) A sacrifice is an act of killing a person or an animal in order to honor a god.

**sagas** (page 144) Sagas are stories of Viking adventures.

**sage** (page 132) A sage is a very wise person.

**Sahel** (page 187) The Sahel is a hot region of dry grasslands south of the Sahara Desert in Africa.

**samurai** (page 236) The samurai were Japanese warriors.

**sanctuary** (page 113) Sanctuary is protection by a church.

**Sanskrit** (page 241) Sanskrit was a language spoken by Hindus in ancient India.

**senate** (page 90) The Roman senate was a group of 300 men who advised the leaders of the ancient republic.

**senators** (page 94) Senators are members of a senate.

**seppuku** (page 237) Seppuku was a practice in which Japanese warriors killed themselves if they lost their honor.

**serfs** (page 148) Serfs were people who farmed the land owned by a noble or a knight during the Middle Ages.

**shamans** (page 58) Shamans were Olmec priests.

**Shinto** (page 176) Shinto is an important religion in Japan. Followers of Shinto honor nature.

**shogun** (page 235) A shogun was a top general in feudal Japan.

**shogunate** (page 236) A shogunate was the rule by the family of a top general in Japan.

**shrines** (page 177) Shrines are buildings and other places that are used for worship.

**siege warfare** (page 226) Siege warfare is a method used to capture a city or fort, such as blocking any routes of escape or delivery of new supplies.

**Silk Road** (page 129) The Silk Road was a trade route that stretched from China to the Mediterranean Sea.

**silt** (page 16) Silt is rich soil and other materials that have been brought to an area by moving water.

**slash-and-burn** (page 72) Slash-and-burn refers to a method in which farmers cut down plants and then burn the fields in order to clear the land.

**smelt** (page 202) To smelt is to melt metals.

**specialize** (page 217) To specialize is to focus on one area of work.

**steppe** (page 225) A steppe is an open plain.

**Stone Age** (page 9) The Stone Age was a period of time when early humans made tools and weapons out of stone. The Stone Age ended around 3500 B.C.

**strait** (page 53) A strait is a thin body of water that connects two larger bodies of water.

**stylus** (page 31) A stylus is a pointed tool used for making marks in clay or another material.

**subcontinent** (page 46) A subcontinent is a very large area of land that is part of a continent.

**sultanates** (page 232) Sultanates are Muslim kingdoms.

**sultans** (page 232) Sultans are Muslim rulers.

**surplus** (page 217) A surplus is an extra amount.

**surrender** (page 226) To surrender is to admit defeat.

**Swahili** (page 192) Swahili is a Bantu language that is mixed with Arabic.

# T

**Taika reforms** (page 177) The Taika reforms were changes made to the government of Japan in 645. One change was to make the emperor the true ruler of Japan.

**Ten Commandments** (page 36) The Ten Commandments are laws that tell how people should behave. Jews and Christians believe God gave Moses the Ten Commandments.

**terraces** (page 71) Terraces are levels on a hill or pyramid.

**terracotta** (page 68) Terracotta is a baked, brown-red clay used to make statues and pottery.

**tolerance** (page 77) Tolerance is an act of allowing others to follow their beliefs or customs.

**tomb** (page 24) A tomb is a room or grave where a dead person is placed.

**tones** (page 192) Tones are vocal sounds or pitches used to change the meaning of a word.

**Torah** (page 34) The Torah is a set of five books that contains the Hebrew laws. The Torah forms the first part of the Bible.

**treason** (page 162) Treason is a crime against one's state or country.

**tribunes** (page 91) Tribunes were leaders that represented the common people in ancient Rome.

**tribute** (page 77) Tribute is a kind of tax paid to a ruler or ruling nation.

**triumvirate** (page 95) A triumvirate is a group of three rulers.

**truce** (page 215) A truce is an agreement to stop fighting.

## U

**untouchables** (page 49) Untouchables are people in ancient India that were below the caste system. Another word for "untouchables" is "outcastes."

## V

**vassal** (page 148) A vassal was a knight who was given land by a noble in exchange for protection and loyalty during the Middle Ages.

**Vedas** (page 48) The Vedas are a set of books containing stories and poems of the Aryan religion in ancient India. Today, the Vedas are an important part of the Hindu religion.

**Vikings** (page 142) Vikings traveled from northern Europe to attack other European lands. They were skilled sailors.

## Y

**yin and yang** (page 131) Yin and yang is the Chinese philosophy that there are two forces that must be balanced in order for there to be peace. Yin is darkness and weakness. Yang is brightness and strength.

**yurts** (page 225) Yurts are Mongol tents made of wool.

## Z

**ziggurats** (page 30) Ziggurats were temples built by Sumerians in ancient Mesopotamia.

**Zoroastrianism** (page 79) Zoroastrianism is a religion based on the teachings of a man named Zoroaster, who lived in Persia around 600 B.C.

# Index